D0849055

To Offer Compassion

TO OFFER COMPASSION

A HISTORY OF THE CLERGY CONSULTATION SERVICE ON ABORTION

DORIS ANDREA DIRKS

and

PATRICIA A. RELF

The University of Wisconsin Press

The University of Wisconsin Press
1930 Monroe Street, 3rd Floor
Madison, Wisconsin 53711-2059
uwpress.wisc.edu

3 Henrietta Street, Covent Garden
London WC2E 8LU, United Kingdom
eurospanbookstore.com

Printed in the United States of America

This book may be available in a digital edition.

Library of Congress Cataloging-in-Publication Data
Names: Dirks, Doris A. (Doris Andrea), 1969– author. | Relf, Patricia, author.
Title: To offer compassion: a history of the Clergy Consultation Service on Abortion /
Doris Andrea Dirks and Patricia A. Relf.
Description: Madison, Wisconsin: The University of Wisconsin Press, [2017]
| Includes bibliographical references and index.
Identifiers: LCCN 2016041572 | ISBN 9780299311308 (cloth: alk. paper)
Subjects: LCSH: Clergy Consultation Service—History.
| Abortion counseling—United States—History.
| Pastoral counseling—United States—History.
Classification: LCC HQ767.5.U5 D57 2017 | DDC 261.8/3219888—dc23
LC record available at https://lccn.loc.gov/2016041572

Contents

Acknowledgments

The story of the Clergy Consultation Service on Abortion (CCS) is the story of its members, and we owe our greatest debt to the participants who talked with us—sometimes at great length and in multiple sessions. The clarity and immediacy of their recollections astounded us. For many, the memory of particular women they had counseled brought tears to their eyes decades after the fact. We thank them for the caring support they gave as CCS counselors, and we thank them for sharing their stories. We also spoke with a number of people who worked with, used, or otherwise had memories of the CCS, and we are grateful for the light they shed on the group. We interviewed more than seventy people for this book, and although we didn't cite all of them, we did learn a great deal from each one.

We were lucky enough to get to know Howard Moody best. We had several lengthy interviews in person, spoke by telephone, chatted when we visited Judson Memorial Church, and we were treated to a beautiful brunch when we visited him and Lorry in Santa Barbara. We both wished to adopt ourselves into their family, and we felt Howard's death deeply. He was a truly prophetic voice, decades ahead of his time, and one of the most genuinely compassionate people we had ever met. He was confident and far from reticent in speaking about the causes that mattered to him, yet he was also genuinely humble, always praising the contributions of others and never claiming direct credit for the ideas and work for which he had, at the very least, been a driving force. He made it possible for us to study the otherwise closed CCS archive at New York University, and his trust in us to use it carefully was one of the best gifts we could have received. To Howard and Lorry, we offer our heartfelt thanks and love.

We also spent many days poring over archival materials, and we thank the librarians, archivists, and assistants—often students—who were unfailingly helpful and gracious. Thanks to the staff of the archives we've cited, not only for their help at the time but for so carefully preserving these valuable materials and making them available to researchers. We owe particular thanks to Marvin

J. Taylor, now director of Special Collections at New York University's Fales Library. The CCS archive there was the first we visited, and although the archive was embargoed at the time, he told us that there were many nonsensitive items—newspaper clippings, for instance—in the collection and encouraged us to ask Howard Moody for access to those, which he and his staff were willing to extract.

One of the archives we consulted consisted of the private research papers of Joshua D. Wolff, who grew up at Judson and wrote his undergraduate thesis on the CCS at Amherst in 1998. Josh went on to earn a doctorate and become a published historian. He had also helped prepare Moody's files for donation to the Judson archive at NYU and so had access to material that we did not at first. We were fortunate to meet Josh as we were just beginning this project, and he could not have been more encouraging and helpful. We owe him tremendous thanks for his ongoing support and generosity in sharing files.

Similarly, Abigail Hastings, a longtime Judson member who helped Howard Moody with his memoir, *A Voice in the Village*, was an early encourager and had something—perhaps a great deal—to do with persuading Moody to make the CCS archive at NYU available to us.

One of our very earliest encouragers was Rev. Mark Pawlowski, then the chief executive of Planned Parenthood of South Central Michigan (which is now part of Planned Parenthood of Mid and South Michigan). Mark offered introductions to many of our first interviewees and other contacts. Friends at the Kalamazoo affiliate of Planned Parenthood were all early and enthusiastic cheerleaders for this project, and we thank them.

We have many other friends who have shown their interest and support over the course of this extended undertaking. In all of these fifteen years, not one has revealed to us the slightest—and justifiable—doubt that we would finish the project. Instead, they have offered patient ears, kind suggestions, and fortifying words. Thanks to them all. Special thanks to Louise Hanavan and other friends and family who inspired and taught us through their own activism; and Bridget Carol, who helped us transcribe some of the interviews. Most of all, we thank Scott Murray for his encouragement and his historian's eye on our work; Emily Hanavan Leslie for her research assistance and for being a mighty advocate for women, putting her work where her conscience is; and Bill Hanavan for supporting the project in every way, including subsidizing our travel.

Finally, we thank Gwen Walker, our editor at University of Wisconsin Press, for championing this book, and to all at the press who have helped make it into a real thing. We are glad the story and lessons of the CCS will be shared with a new generation.

Preface

In January 2002, the Kalamazoo, Michigan, affiliate of Planned Parenthood organized an interfaith service honoring the anniversary of the 1973 *Roe v. Wade* Supreme Court decision, which legalized abortion in the United States. A Planned Parenthood board member at the time, Pat Relf attended the event at First Presbyterian Church and, paging through the program, came across an interesting story: the Planned Parenthood Federation of America had recently honored Rev. Robert Hare for his participation in the Clergy Consultation Service on Abortion, a network of ministers and rabbis who had referred women to physicians for safe abortions during the years before *Roe v. Wade*. Hare was receiving special recognition because, as a Presbyterian minister in Cleveland in 1969, he had been indicted in Massachusetts for referring a young woman to a doctor who happened to be under investigation. The charges against Hare evaporated after *Roe*.

Pat had never heard of the Clergy Consultation Service on Abortion (CCS), and asked First Presbyterian's minister, Rev. David Van Arsdale, if he knew anything about it. Yes, Van Arsdale said; in fact, his own father, a Baptist minister in upstate New York, had been a member of the group. Pat was astonished: the CCS must have had a substantial number of members doing radical—and borderline illegal—work on behalf of women, yet she had never heard of the group, either as a Planned Parenthood volunteer or as a Presbyterian—or even as a college student before and after the *Roe* decision.

D. A. Dirks, who in 2002 was working on a history Ph.D. at Western Michigan University, taught gender studies courses and had been a longtime social justice activist but hadn't heard of the CCS either. D. A. asked the question that set this book in motion: Had anyone written about the group?

We found a slim paperback about the CCS written by one of the founding clergy members, American Baptist minister Rev. Howard Moody, and Arlene Carmen, who administered the national group from the office of Judson Memorial Church in New York. That book had come out in 1973, immediately after the *Roe* decision. It turned out that the group wasn't secretive at the time. The

CCS had started in 1967 in New York City with an announcement—on the front page of the *New York Times*, no less—by twenty-one rabbis and ministers, including Moody, all from major denominations and congregations, that they would counsel women seeking abortions and, when appropriate, refer them to safe physicians. Finding an overwhelming demand from women around the country, the group quickly expanded to other states. Newspapers and a few popular magazines carried articles about the CCS in the late 1960s and early 1970s. We later learned that Joshua D. Wolff, who had grown up at Judson, had written his undergraduate thesis at Amherst College about the CCS in 1998. There had been mentions in several books. But no one had published a comprehensive history.

It was not surprising that not many people knew the story of the CCS in 2002. At that time—and since then—some of the loudest speakers in the political debate about abortion were conservative religious voices, leading the general public to believe that people of faith, especially the clergy, were necessarily opposed to abortion. That wasn't true, of course: the Planned Parenthood Federation of America and many of its affiliates had clergy advisory boards, and many—including the Kalamazoo chapter—had clergy volunteers who counseled women before and after their abortions and sometimes stayed with them throughout the procedure. The chief executive of the Kalamazoo affiliate in 2002 was Rev. Mark Pawlowski, another Presbyterian minister. Yet in the media, the work and testimony of pro-choice people of faith were overpowered by the more conservative voices against abortion, and most young people assumed that religion generally condemned abortion and always had.

The story of the CCS seemed important to tell, partly because it refuted this prevailing assumption. The service also seemed historically unique as a feminist group whose members were almost all men. We wanted to try to tell the story—or at least record the recollections of participants for future historians. Members of the group, having been ordained clergy in the late 1960s, would be getting on in years, so time was limited. We determined to find as many participants as we could and interview them, recording it if possible. If a book came out of the project, we assumed it would be in the form of an oral history, since we imagined that the clergy counselors would not have kept written records that could have increased their legal risk.

We began to track down clergy who had been a part of this radical group. We had a few names from Carmen and Moody's book, and Moody was still at Judson Memorial Church. In Kalamazoo, Van Arsdale and Pawlowski, who had not been CCS members themselves, nonetheless could provide the names of some clergy who were members or who might know someone who had participated. As we found and interviewed CCS members, they passed along names of others. Nearly everyone we contacted was happy to talk with us; they spoke movingly of their experiences counseling women—and sometimes very young girls and their families—many of whom were desperate in their search for an abortion. There was a pattern among these clergy: most had been involved in other areas of social justice, usually the civil rights movement or antiwar activism. They were fascinating and articulate speakers, so we frequently found ourselves spending much longer talking with them than we had planned and on many more topics than our list of questions covered.

When we were able to interview together, D. A. tended to ask about the big-picture things—theology and the historical context of the work of the CCS—and Pat tried to make sure we had dates, names, and numbers. Out of necessity, some interviews were conducted by just one of us, and many were done not in person but by telephone or Internet. We interviewed more than seventy people for this book; a list of the interviews we've cited follows the bibliography. We are proud of the number of women CCS members we were able to talk with; we regret that we were not able to contact any of the few known black participants. Not all of our interviewees were CCS members; by chance, we encountered women who used the service, and we sought out a few people—a doctor and two lawyers, for instance—who advised the group in various ways. We made the decision early on to focus on the members of the CCS and their experience, not on the women they counseled nor on the physicians to whom they referred, though either group could be the subject of a separate book. (Some of the doctors' stories have been told in Carole Joffe's *Doctors of Conscience*.) Here the women who used the CCS are represented mainly in the stories told by the clergy who counseled them and by the letters—mostly of gratitude—that they wrote to the clergy.

As we spoke with CCS participants, we learned that some of them had, in fact, kept written records pertaining to their CCS work. Moody and Carmen, as administrators of the national group, had kept files, which Moody had recently deposited at New York University, but under an embargo for many years to come. Every time we saw Moody we asked him whether he might lift the embargo, at least for such nonsensitive items as newspaper clippings, and his answer was some variation on "I'll see what I can do." Meanwhile, we learned from Rev. Spencer Parsons, who had headed the Chicago CCS, that his papers were available at Northwestern University; we found more Chicago CCS archives at the University of Illinois at Chicago. Letters, meeting records, and lists from these archives provided us with many more names of participants. Several shared smaller personal files with us, as did Wolff, the author of the thesis on the subject. Our oral history project thus changed to a general history that would include what we were learning from the documentary evidence, one that we hope would still interest nonspecialist readers.

We worked on the project as we could—as a labor of love, because we had other occupations. We made several special research and interview trips at our own expense. When we traveled for almost any other reason, we tried to fit in-person interviews into the trips. During the time we were working on this book, D. A. earned a doctorate, had demanding jobs at four different universities, and moved several times, while Pat completed other writing projects, was active with a community organizing group, and saw two daughters finish college and graduate school. We had long fallow periods, but our enthusiasm for this project never waned.

In 2012, Howard Moody passed away. We felt his loss personally, as we had grown very fond of Howard and his wife, Lorry. We wished we had been able to complete our CCS history before he died. As a practical matter, we lamented that we had not secured his permission to research the CCS files at NYU. Miraculously, after his death, the files were opened to us, and they proved to be a treasure trove for this book. It took three trips to New York to go through all those files. At the end of the last day of research, Pat caught the eye of Marvin J. Taylor, the Special Collections librarian who had helped us the first time we tried to access the CCS collection back in 2003. She thanked him for his help and told him how glad we were that the CCS archive was now open. It wasn't, he said; special permission had been granted only to us. We were moved and tremendously grateful for that gift from Moody and Judson Memorial Church, and it has proven invaluable to this book.

While most CCS members worked publicly—or at least not clandestinely, even if they weren't named in newspapers—at the time that Moody and Carmen wrote their book in 1973, privacy was still a concern for some of the CCS partici-pants. That concern continues today, with abortion an even more polarizing issue than it was in the 1960s, and with the intervening history of violence against clinics and people associated with abortion. With that in mind, we have made every effort to seek permission to name living participants if their participation had not already been made public elsewhere.

Since the *Roe v. Wade* decision and up to this writing, the political climate and state laws have steadily eroded women's access to abortion. From our first inter-views to now, many participants told us that they feared that referral networks like the CCS might need to be revived, and some said—only half-jokingly—that they would participate all over again if necessary. Such statements were testimony to their experience of how important access to abortion can be to women and testimony to their dedication. We hope that telling the story of the Clergy Consultation Service on Abortion will contribute to the conversation about reproductive justice and abortion access.

If you have your own CCS story to share, please visit offercompassion.com.

To Offer Compassion

Introduction

At a time when abortion was illegal in the United States, an article on the front page of the *New York Times* on May 22, 1967, announced that twenty-one New York City clergy would counsel and refer women to licensed doctors for safe abortions.[1] The group called itself the Clergy Consultation Service on Abortion (CCS).

The group's spokesperson, Reverend Howard Moody, an American Baptist minister and pastor of Judson Memorial Church in Greenwich Village, had approached the *Times* religion editor, Edward B. Fiske, and given him the names and affiliations of nineteen ministers and two rabbis and the telephone number of the group's new answering machine. Women seeking abortions were invited to call the number, hear the contact information of the two or three ordained clergy who were on call that week, choose one, and call the person directly to make an appointment. They would meet in person and discuss all options; if requested, the clergy would provide contact information for licensed physicians, vetted by the clergy group, who were willing to perform abortions. Because abortion was either illegal or for practical purposes unavailable in all fifty states, the women would be sent abroad if they could afford it or to a nearby state for a clandestine procedure. The counseling service was free.[2]

The group was the first organization in the United States to publicly offer abortion referrals.[3] The members had no idea whether police would knock on their doors as soon as the article appeared, but they were determined to make safe abortion accessible to New York women. They had seen the desperation of women burdened with unwanted pregnancies, had worked to reform state abortion law, and had been frustrated with the lack of legislative progress. It was time to take action, and they hoped that their positions as clergy would make a strong moral statement and offer some legal protection. Their lawyers urged caution, warning them that they shouldn't make their point by getting arrested, because they would not be useful to women if they landed in jail. They took some precautions, such as referring women to doctors in neighboring states to confuse jurisdictions. But they did not fear arrest. All were activists, and some had already been arrested during the civil rights movement or as protesters against the Vietnam War.[4]

The *Times* article began:

> Twenty-one Protestant ministers and rabbis in New York City have announced the establishment of a Clergymen's Consultation Service on Abortion to assist women seeking abortions. The Rev. Howard R. Moody, spokesman for the group, said that its services, which begin today, would include assistance in obtaining legal therapeutic abortions and advice on such alternatives as keeping the child or having him put up for adoption. "If legal therapeutic abortion is not possible, but an abortion is indicated, we will try to get the woman the best possible medical advice to take care of her problem pregnancy," he said. "In some instances it is possible we would attempt to facilitate her getting an abortion in a country where it is legal." . . . Mr. Moody acknowledged that the project involves "some legal risk," but he added: "We are not willing to admit that it is illegal." Jacques Nevard, deputy commissioner of the Police Department for press relations, said the department "cannot comment on a program that has not yet begun."

Fiske quoted Moody as saying that the group's purpose was "not to encourage abortions, but to offer compassion and to increase the freedom of women with problem pregnancies."[5]

Immediately, the CCS was deluged with calls. That week, the answering machine's message gave the names and phone numbers for Rabbi Lewis E. "Buz" Bogage, then an assistant rabbi at Central Synagogue, and Rev. Richard Johnson of Emmanuel Baptist Church in Brooklyn. Bogage reported receiving thirty-five calls on the first day alone.[6] In addition to the outpouring of calls from women wanting referrals, including many from across the country, the group received supportive letters and calls from clergy, lawyers, and health professionals and small donations from individuals. Several clergy from other states wanted to know how to set up their own networks. New York City newspapers gave neutral to positive editorial responses. A very small number of negative letters came in, but there was no outcry, and no police knocked on the clergy's doors.[7]

The CCS began as a small group of ministers and rabbis who saw the need—the desperation—of women seeking abortions under restrictive laws. Frustrated by unsuccessful efforts to change the law, they determined to use their own privilege—as clergy, and as a group mostly of white men—to support women in circumventing the law while continuing their efforts to change it. The group has been called a kind of "underground abortion railroad."[8] By the time the U.S. Supreme Court's *Roe v. Wade* decision made abortion legal nationwide in 1973, the CCS was working from coast to coast. They had referred hundreds of thousands of women for abortions without a fatality and established the safety of abortion as an outpatient procedure.[9] The CCS had become a medical consumer advocacy group, vetting doctors for their credentials and the quality and dignity of their treatment and negotiating consistent prices and low-cost care for poor women. The group had even opened its own nonprofit, outpatient abortion and women's health clinic in New York City, which served as a model for clinics around the country. The work of the CCS inspired other faith-based organizations that continue to advocate for reproductive justice today.

In the years since *Roe v. Wade*, abortion has met with new obstacles: harassment and violence at clinics and against providers have added to patients' and providers' anxiety, state laws and regulations have decreased the number of clinics, forcing many women to travel greater distances and sometimes to stay overnight or longer at the expense of work and family obligations, and antiabortion rhetoric couched in religion has fostered the impression that people of faith necessarily condemn abortion. From today's vantage point, the work of the CCS was not just a compassionate pastoral answer to an immediate need— it was also prophetic.

1

How Can It Not Be Legal?

In the 1950s, Judson Memorial was an unusual church, situated on Washington Square in the heart of Greenwich Village, in the midst of New York University. Its small congregation was an eclectic mix of people, and most members had not grown up in the Baptist church. Social justice—including work with neighborhood youth, mostly Italian American kids from the tenements south of Washington Square—had long been a part of what drew people to Judson. The longtime minister, Rev. Howard Moody, later wrote that "Judson's take on being 'a church for the world' simply meant to be present out there wherever pain, suffering, injustice, and inequality enveloped people's lives." His predecessor said in his farewell, "My deepest prayer is that Judson Church will never *play it safe*."[1] Moody had kept those words before him and taken up the work with enthusiasm.

Howard Moody

In 1967, Moody did not fit any hippie stereotype of the liberal—or even radical—Greenwich Village activist that he was. A tall, rugged Texan with a gravelly drawl, Moody in his mid-forties wore the same crew cut he'd had as a marine during his service in World War II. He had started life as a Southern Baptist from Dallas and entered Baylor University in 1939 intending to become a minister. Even then, his job in a café where non-Baptists danced to a jukebox and his attendance at prayer meetings in the homes of black people signaled that he and the Southern Baptist denomination of the time might not be a match made in heaven.[2]

He quit school to join the marines just six months before the United States entered World War II, and he served in the South Pacific, flying on B-17 bombing raids to do aerial mapping of Japanese island bases and document the accuracy of bombs dropped from 10,000 feet. Moody recalled that he sometimes had a camera in one hand and a machine gun in the other as Japanese Zero fighters pursued them. As Jerry Tallmer reported in the *New York Post* at the time Moody and the others founded the CCS, "Once you've fallen out of a bomb bay over the Japanese fleet, you'[r]e not apt to worry for the rest of your life about being shot down. It was as a Marine attached to the Air Corps in the early days after Pearl Harbor that Howard Moody, a heavy K-2 camera in one hand, fell out of the underside of a B-17. With his other hand he snatched at a strut and hung on. When he pulled himself back into the airplane with one hand, the other was still holding the camera." Moody's commander remarked: "It's a damn good thing you brought back the camera. Don't let it happen again."[3] Moody said he also served in combat at Guadalcanal before a serious case of malaria sent him back to the United States to recover. Stationed in Santa Barbara, California, he joined a Northern Baptist church, married Lorraine (Lorry) McNeill, and once the war was over, finished college there. As he read the writings and sermons of Walter Rauschenbusch (*A Theology for the Social Gospel*) and Harry Emerson Fosdick ("Shall the Fundamentalists Win?"), he became convinced that religion could and needed to be relevant to modern society. He returned to his seminary studies, first at Colgate-Rochester and then at Yale Divinity School to study ministry in higher education. Howard and Lorry spent a summer at Judson Memorial Church, running its urban service project for visiting students, and in fall 1950 Howard joined the church and was ordained there as a Baptist minister. He took a job as a pastor at Ohio State University and continued his relationship with Judson, bringing students there for an urban life tour each spring. Five years later, he was asked to come to Judson to stay, as senior minister.[4]

Moody certainly didn't play it safe. He added a special ministry to the arts and culture that became a hallmark of Judson Memorial, starting with a 1957 concert by the great gospel singer Mahalia Jackson. He became involved in Greenwich Village politics and eventually in the civil rights movement and protests against the Vietnam War. He later recalled that his straight-arrow looks were sometimes an asset: "During the whole Vietnam War thing, because I had a crewcut and I wear my [suit], people thought I was FBI or CIA or something, every time I went to a demonstration. So I was down the other side of these barricades and nobody would bother me. And I'd listen to what they were doing, and then I'd go back on the other side and tell 'em, listen, cool it, here, this is going to happen."[5] Under Moody, Judson was both sanctuary and cauldron for avant-garde arts of every kind—theater, music, modern dance, and visual art. In his long history of activism, Moody said, he faced legal charges only twice: his arrest in a 1963 civil rights demonstration in Brooklyn and the summons charging him and Judson's assistant minister, Al Carmines, with "desecration of the flag" for the church's hosting a 1970 art exhibit called "The People's Flag Show." (The case was dismissed when the person who filed the complaint failed to appear in court.)[6]

Abortion Access

Not long after he started his ministry at Judson, Moody learned of the challenges women faced if they wanted an abortion. He recalled that in 1957 a former Judson minister, then in Florida, sent a woman to him for help. The woman was divorced and had two teenage children. She was pregnant and trying desperately to get an abortion. Moody knew her chances were better in New York than in Florida, but at that time, even in New York, abortions were only available at hospitals if one had connections. Young and inexperienced, Moody had no such connections, but a congregation member had heard of a doctor in West New York, New Jersey, who might be able to help. Worried about breaking the law but determined to help, Moody accompanied the woman to an ordinary house. When the woman who answered the door heard what they wanted and saw a man there, she slammed the door in their faces. It was a nerve-racking experience. Moody then turned to another parishioner, a woman in the entertainment industry, who arranged for the Florida woman to receive an abortion in New York. "But after that, I knew that there would be other occasions. And, sure enough, there were. I found a doctor in Puerto Rico, and I referred several of our women who lived in [Judson's] student house and got pregnant. So then I knew the field. I'm not saying I was experienced, but I knew something more than most ministers knew."[7]

Moody had had a glimpse of the frightening situation that women faced in the 1950s and '60s. Those with unwanted pregnancies had few choices. In most states, the only justification for a legal abortion was a threat to the woman's life. Officially, these legal, therapeutic abortions were available only in hospitals, generally only after a committee of physicians—usually all men—ruled on whether to allow the procedure. These committees were instituted by hospitals in the 1940s in response to a study by two Catholic physicians showing widely varying rates of abortions at different hospitals and concluding that some were performing abortions that were not strictly needed to save women's lives.[8] The hospital committees were nearly universal by the 1950s and required at least an appearance by the physician making the request. Some required the woman to appear before the full committee for questioning, a demeaning experience that discouraged applicants. The process could involve repeated physical examinations. Women who applied for abortion on psychiatric grounds sometimes studied psychology texts to feign symptoms and answer the boards' questions "correctly."[9] Many abortions were approved contingent on the woman undergoing sterilization at the same time; this requirement was particularly applied to black women.[10] Of course this process was time-consuming, even as a pregnancy progressed. Additionally, it presumed the patient was well-off enough to pay doctor and laboratory fees for the procedure and hospital bills for an overnight or longer stay.

Hospitals were reluctant to provide the service at all, and some limited the number of abortions they would permit. Journalist and abortion activist Larry Lader estimated that by the 1960s, U.S. hospitals provided only 8,000 abortions a year—8,000 out of more than 1 million abortions being performed annually in the United States, according to Planned Parenthood's estimate.[11] Safe abortions were not easy to arrange, but wealthy, well-connected women could usually secure sympathetic doctors, find psychiatrists to approve abortions for mental health reasons, or speak convincingly to the hospital committees.

Most women who sought abortions were at the mercy of a shadowy underground system that was frightening and demeaning and could be very dangerous. Most practitioners were not licensed physicians, much less gynecologists. An early 1960s analysis of 111 convictions for practicing abortion in New York City found that less than a third of those convicted were physicians or former physicians; the occupations of the convicted abortionists included clerk, barber, and salesman.[12] Many procedures involved dangerous methods, unhygienic practices, or crude instruments. Contacting the abortionist and eventually meeting in person usually required some furtive maneuvers—the use of a password, meeting a third person in a parking lot or on a corner, and sometimes being driven (blindfolded in some cases) to the location in seedy neighborhoods or in hotel or motel rooms. Women often had to go alone to their appointments. Many recalled being treated roughly or sexually harassed, even raped. Some practitioners demanded more money than had been agreed on.[13]

The alternative to this underground system was for women to attempt their own abortions, often with tragic results. Desperate women used improvised tools, such as knitting needles, pens, or straightened coat hangers that could cause perforations; some injected liquids into the uterus—from brine or soap to bleach solution, lye, or kerosene; others drank large quantities of alcohol or took herbal "remedies" in an effort to cause a miscarriage.[14]

Deaths from botched abortions, including self-induced ones, were estimated at 5,000 a year in the United States in the early 1960s—although it is likely that many such deaths were not recorded as such. They accounted for half of all childbearing deaths in New York City. Those who died were disproportionately women of color: 80 percent of women who died from bad abortions in New York City in the 1960s were black or Puerto Rican.[15] An untold number of women committed suicide rather than carry an unwanted pregnancy to term.

Motivation

For many of the clergy, as for Moody, it was a personal experience with illegal abortion that opened their eyes to the problem and motivated them to join the CCS. Rev. Huw Anwyl, a United Church of Christ (UCC) minister and later the director of the Los Angeles Clergy Consultation Service for Problem Pregnancies, recalled a 1965 visit to a parishioner, who told Anwyl that his fourteen-year-old daughter was pregnant. At the time, this meant to Anwyl that either the family would bring up the baby or the girl would go out of state on the pretext of visiting an aunt and give the baby up for adoption.[16] But the father told Anwyl that his daughter would have an abortion—a word that Anwyl had never heard. The father, a physician, explained. Anwyl recalled, "I said, 'Will it be done in your hospital?' How green can you be?" He was baffled to learn that the procedure was illegal. "I said, how can it not be legal? If somebody has their leg amputated, it's not a legal issue. Brain surgery, you don't— why this? What's the difference?" The physician had not been able to find anyone in Los Angeles willing to perform the abortion, but through his medical connections heard of a provider—reportedly a physician—in Tijuana. Anwyl insisted on accompanying them. In Tijuana, someone met them on a street corner, checked their identities, and drove them to a house in the suburbs. After they were scrutinized again, furniture was moved out of the front room, an examining table brought in, and the procedure was done right there. Anwyl said, "Well, my eyes were like saucers. The girl came out of it fine, but what was going through my mind through all of that was that my little girl Jane, she was the same age. I couldn't get it out of my head: This could be Jane. This should not be."[17]

In 1966 Rev. Tom Davis, then a thirty-two-year-old UCC campus chaplain at Skidmore College, had a similarly eye-opening experience in his very first month on the job. Six sophomore and junior women met with him to say that they were concerned about a first-year student who was pregnant. She didn't want to tell her family, so she planned to fly to Puerto Rico alone and ask a cab driver where she could get an abortion. They recognized that this was a bad idea but didn't know what to do, so they left the dilemma with Davis. He recalled, "I was floored. I had not the slightest idea what to do." If he went to the dean, he worried not about the dean's reaction but that students would never again come to him with a problem. He went instead to the campus infirmary doctor, a woman, and she showed him how to handle such situations. She called the terrified young woman in and reassured her that the college was sympathetic and that even if the dean knew of her situation she would not be expelled. "But we are a little concerned about your plan," Davis recalled the doctor saying. "Tell us about your family." Davis and the doctor were soon convinced that the family would be supportive. After an hour of conversation, the young woman agreed to call her family, who took her home to New England and arranged an abortion. "She was back in five days," Davis said. "I learned that was the way it was done. And I also learned: nobody cared. There was no big outcry about what was happening here."[18]

These stories all involved privileged white women who had the support of family and friends, had access to information and contacts, could afford to travel long distances if necessary, and could pay the fees of illegal practitioners. Even for these women, in the best of circumstances, obtaining an abortion was traumatic and potentially dangerous. Seeing their experiences, the clergy realized that most women—the poor, those with unsympathetic families, the uneducated, those with responsibilities to jobs or other children—faced a much worse situation. As Moody later wrote about many of the projects he undertook at Judson Church, "We were presented with opportunities to alleviate suffering, and that was motive enough."[19]

Closing in on half a century after *Roe v. Wade* legalized abortion, the number of abortion providers has declined substantially, and as a result abortion for many women is inaccessible: too far away, too expensive, and too legally restricted. Both judicial and legislative actions have steadily chipped away at *Roe v. Wade*. At the state and local level, laws and regulations have imposed requirements on abortion providers that are far more onerous than those placed on other medical practices, forcing some clinics to close. Abortion opponents have waged a political battle to defund Planned Parenthood at the state and federal levels. The GOP included in its 2012 platform an endorsement of the medically unsupported claim that fetuses can feel pain before they are viable. More than that, it said, "the unborn child has a fundamental individual right to life which cannot be infringed."[20] During the 2016 election cycle, calls to overturn *Roe v. Wade* continued. As a candidate in the Republican primaries, Donald J. Trump went so far as to say that if abortion were recriminalized, "there has to be some form of punishment" for women who have abortions, a position so extreme that even antiabortion groups such as Right to Life disavowed it. He quickly modified his stance to call only for punishment for the person performing the abortion, saying, "Women punish themselves."[21] Many of the same battles that played out in the 1960s were repeated almost fifty years later, with the voices of clergy defending a woman's right to access a safe and legal abortion becoming lost in the polarized media atmosphere.

2

The Push for Change

Historical Ideas about Abortion

Historically, Catholicism, Judaism, and Protestant sects all struggled with the topic of abortion. There is no discussion of abortion in the Hebrew or Christian Bibles, although Exodus (21:22–23) discussed punishment for one who harms a pregnant woman and causes a miscarriage; it prescribed not one of the punishments for killing a person (Exodus 21:12–14) but a fine set by the woman's husband—that is, the fetus did not have the same legal status as a person.[1] A common belief in the ancient world (often attributed to Aristotle) was that of "ensoulment," that is, when a fetus became "formed," which came at forty days for a male fetus and ninety days for a female. Augustine of Hippo (354–430) and Thomas Aquinas (1225–1274) adhered to this ancient concept. It was only during the nineteenth century, with more knowledge about biology and its processes that Pope Pius IX (1792–1878) did away with the notion of ensoulment and extended a prohibition on abortion to any time during pregnancy from the moment of conception.[2] Historically, the position of Protestant churches has tended to be less official and less absolute than that of the Catholic Church. Abortion was not a topic of particular concern at the time of the Protestant Reformation during the sixteenth century. Morality, in the Protestant view, was considered more a matter of "rational discernment than of revealed truth"; Protestants tended to see pregnancy as a "sign of God's blessing and its deliberate denial as at least impious."[3] Historically, the Jewish faith was generally not in favor of abortion, but was tolerant of the practice where it was viewed as necessary.

Abortion law in the earliest decades of the U.S. republic (1780–1830) imitated British common law, which failed to recognize abortion before "quickening" (when the woman feels the movement of the fetus) as a crime.[4] Abortions became illegal by statute in Britain in 1803 and various antiabortion statutes began to appear in the United States from the 1820s codifying or expanding the common law rules.[5] In 1821, a Connecticut law targeted apothecaries who sold "poisons" to women for purposes of inducing an abortion, and New York made post-quickening abortions a felony and prequickening abortions a misdemeanor eight years later.[6] In spite of these laws, there was a rapid decline in the birth rate of whites from 1820 (average of 7 children) to 1890 (average of 3.6 children). Paralleling the decline of fertility was an increase in literature that discussed the use of abortion. Madame Restell became America's best-known abortionist, plying her trade in New York City from the late 1830s until her death in 1878.[7] During the 1860s and 1870s, there was a flurry of popular writing about abortion—the *New York Times* reported that there were abortion providers at work in every part of the city. An 1881 report from Michigan that surveyed 100 physicians estimated that nearly a third of Protestant pregnancies ended in abortion.[8] There were acute concerns during the nineteenth century that Anglo-Saxon women would no longer produce enough children to outpace or even keep up with the number of children produced by recent immigrants from Germany, Ireland, France, and other countries. In particular during the nineteenth century, ideas about "races" differentiated Anglo-Saxon from other "lesser" peoples, including Celtic and Teutonic. Physicians weighed in on the topic of abortion, arguing that the practice of abortions spawned social disorder and threatened demographic disaster. When physicians addressed the public on this topic, arguments about the "racial" dangers of abortion were frequently invoked.[9] This strain of thinking about racial superiority and inferiority gave rise to the eugenics movement of the late nineteenth and early twentieth centuries.

Since the beginning of the scientific revolution in the sixteenth century, some form of the Hippocratic Oath was taken by students at medical schools in Europe. When formal medical education in the United States began at the University of Pennsylvania in 1765 (based on the University of Edinburgh model) the oath was retained.[10] Between 1810 and 1840, twenty-six medical schools were founded in the United States.[11]

The American Medical Association (AMA) was founded in 1847, and one of the group's early campaigns was a push for laws against abortion. The AMA's motivation to advocate for anti-abortion legislation was threefold. First, the Hippocratic Oath specifically prohibited giving women an "abortive remedy."[12] Second, the medical profession attempted to assert control over the issue by "defending the claim that life begins at conception and highlighting the medical risks of abortion as reasons for prohibiting the practice."[13] Lastly, doctors—nearly all men at the time—also had an interest in setting standards that would give physicians higher professional status than other practitioners, particularly midwives—nearly all women—and it was midwives who traditionally performed many abortions. Most feminists of the time supported the antiabortion campaign because they considered abortion degrading to women and believed there would be little need for the procedure if men stopped sexually exploiting women within and outside marriage. However, none of the churches that opposed abortion at the time—the Catholic Church and some Protestants—allied themselves with the AMA's drive to criminalize abortion, nor was there organized opposition to the AMA's campaign. By 1900 abortion at any stage of pregnancy had been made illegal in every state, except to save a woman's life. Women continued to seek abortions, but now had to find sympathetic doctors who were willing to interpret the law liberally or go to midwives or backstreet practitioners. Prosecutions of abortion providers were common, and gruesome cases were sensationalized in the press. For some time after about 1880, the number of abortions in the United States decreased.[14]

In the 1930s, during the Depression, illegal abortions increased to an estimated 800,000 a year, and thousands of women were dying as a result.[15] There were a few calls to liberalize laws to make safe, legal abortions more accessible, but many physicians and hospitals wanted as little to do with it as possible and began to tighten restrictions at the hospital level. Starting in the 1940s, hospital committees took over the official approval process for therapeutic abortions.[16] The National Association of Colored Women's Clubs, founded in 1896, worked on civil rights causes, including the abolition of Jim Crow laws and women's suffrage. The club movement also supported the establishment of family planning clinics and opposed the coerced or forced sterilization of black women. Black newspapers of the 1930s and 1940s reported the mortality rates of women who had septic abortions.[17] Historical statistics on abortions among black women are scarce, but Loretta J. Ross cites a survey of black women by a doctor in Nashville in 1940 who found 28 percent had obtained at least one abortion.[18] At the same time, abortion providers became more stigmatized within the medical profession. Safe abortions performed by licensed physicians became less and less available, especially to poor women.

Assertions of fetal personhood were also a deterrent. From 1939 to 1958, court rulings in five states and the District of Columbia recognized the fetus as a person. In 1948, the World Medical Association urged doctors to respect life starting at the time of conception. And the United Nations Declaration of the

Rights of the Child in 1959 included a call for legal protection for children "before as well as after birth."[19]

Abortion Law in the 1950s and Early 1960s

In the late 1950s and early 1960s, concern about women's access to abortion began to be expressed in public forums. In 1955 Planned Parenthood held a conference on abortion, focusing mainly on how good, available contraception could help prevent illegal abortions. However, Dr. Mary S. Calderone's 1958 publication that came out of the conference included a piece by retired physician G. Lotrell Timanus of Baltimore, accounting for more than 5,000 abortions he had performed during his career without a single fatality, and the book attracted some general notice.[20] In 1959, the well-respected American Law Institute (ALI) developed wording for a model statute that would permit a licensed physician to terminate a pregnancy for reasons that included the risk of serious harm to the physical or mental health of the mother, risk of a serious birth defect, or if the pregnancy was the result of rape or incest. The proposal would liberalize the circumstances under which women could seek abortion, while leaving physicians in control of the procedure and protecting them from prosecution. The ALI model was a concrete recommendation that could be discussed, promoted, and introduced in state legislatures.[21]

Calls for abortion law reform began to be heard in other professions. A psychiatrist and a lawyer coauthored a paper for the 1960 meeting of the American Medical Association, urging physicians to take the lead in liberalizing abortion laws.[22] The next year, the liberal Protestant magazine *Christian Century* ran an editorial favoring limited reform, and the National Council of Churches (NCC) issued a statement favoring birth control and condemning abortion, but admitting an exception for the health as well as the life of the mother, placing the NCC in a position of endorsing more liberal laws.[23] Efforts began to reform the law in some states. In California, Patricia Maginnis formed the Citizens' Committee for Humane Abortion Laws in January 1962. The following year, one of the first bills modeled on the ALI recommendation made it to hearings in the California legislature but was quickly shot down by protest letters from Roman Catholics.[24]

Other events put abortion in the popular headlines. In 1962, Sherri Finkbine, a host of the local Phoenix, Arizona, edition of the children's television show *Romper Room*, was pregnant with her fifth child when she took antinausea pills her husband brought back from England. The pills contained the drug thalidomide. When Finkbine read that the drug could cause serious fetal deformities, she arranged an abortion at a Phoenix hospital. She then called the local newspaper editor to thank him for their article on thalidomide and suggest that the paper run another article to warn women of the dangers of the drug. The paper did so immediately, describing Finkbine's case without identifying her. Following this publicity, the Phoenix hospital where she had planned to have the abortion canceled her procedure. Finkbine later recalled, "I said how can they cancel it? They don't even know who I am. And they said the news went out on the Associated Press, and we're getting calls from all over the world. Somebody went into the county attorney's office and said they'd like to make a citizen's arrest on the hospital and on the woman who is going to have that termination."[25] The Finkbines went to court to get an order that would force the hospital to provide the service, but the court dismissed their request. The case became a national controversy, attracting massive press attention. Eventually, the couple traveled to Sweden, where Finkbine was able to have a legal abortion on the basis of mental health needs. Back home, the family endured continuing publicity and received death threats, and Sherri and her husband, Bob, a history teacher, lost their jobs. Nonetheless, the case had people discussing the ethics of abortion, and a Gallup poll showed that 52 percent of Americans thought Finkbine had done the right thing.[26]

Abortion received more public attention in 1964 and 1965, when a rubella epidemic broke out in the United States. Rubella (German measles), if contracted during pregnancy, can cause miscarriage or serious problems such as blindness, deafness, heart defects, and developmental disabilities in an infant. As a result of the epidemic, 20,000 babies were born with congenital rubella syndrome, and there were an estimated 11,000 miscarriages, stillbirths, and therapeutic abortions.[27] There was general support for abortion in these cases, and physicians widely accepted that rubella was an indication for abortion. In fact, in 1966 when the California Board of Medical Examiners charged nine physicians with providing abortions to women who had been exposed to rubella, physicians across the country protested and offered their support.[28]

Meanwhile, social changes had helped bring abortion into public discourse. Well into the 1960s, social norms had kept women from speaking openly about sex and reproductive choices. In her 1963 book, *The Feminine Mystique*, Betty Friedan made public the unspoken desires and disappointments of a generation of women (mostly privileged, well-educated white women) who felt pressure to become mothers at a relatively young age and were compelled to present a happy housewife facade.[29] Friedan's book was the beginning of a second-wave feminist movement in which women gathered in formal and less formal groups, told their own stories, raised their consciousness of the limits and burdens that society had placed on them, openly expressed their sexual and reproductive concerns (topics which had been taboo), and organized to demand equal education, employment, and legal treatment. As Jo Freeman, a founder of one such group in Chicago, put it in 1970, "From this public sharing of experiences comes the realization that what was thought to be individual is in fact common; that what was thought to be a personal problem has a social cause and probably a political solution."[30] As feminist organizations formed in the mid-1960s, many addressed abortion law as the critical issue that kept women from achieving full reproductive rights. Friedan and others founded the National Organization for Women (NOW) in 1966, and repeal of abortion laws was adopted as part of its platform at its national convention in 1967.[31] Since that time, of course, there has been a robust critique of second-wave feminism (roughly the early 1960s through the early 1980s) for its institutionalized racism, exclusion of lesbians, and hostility to trans women. In the 1980s, writer and activist bell hooks criticized Friedan's book for ignoring the existence of poor and nonwhite women in her book, many of whom were working both outside and inside of their homes. Since about 1994, many women of color have been reframing pro-choice rhetoric as *reproductive justice* to address intersections of race, class, gender, and sexual identity and their involvement in reproductive oppression. Reproductive justice links sexuality, health care, and human rights to social justice movements by placing reproductive health in a larger context of the well-being and health of women and their communities.[32]

The development of effective oral contraception, approved for use in the United States in 1960, almost overnight had given women greater control over their sexual and reproductive lives and therefore over their education and careers. "The Pill" was a topic that was openly discussed and even sensationalized, leading to more public debate and a demand to repeal the last of the state laws that banned or limited the distribution or even discussion of contraceptives. As a state, Connecticut was the longest holdout. It was 1965 before the Supreme Court ruled in *Griswold v. Connecticut* that married persons had a right to privacy that included obtaining and using contraceptives. (The same right was not extended to unmarried persons until 1972, in *Eisenstadt v. Baird.*) Many who favored reform or repeal of abortion laws immediately saw in the *Griswold* decision the basis for a similar argument for a right to abortion; indeed, *Griswold* served as a precedent in later cases, including *Roe v. Wade.*[33]

Abortion Law Reform

In October 1964, the Committee for a Humane Abortion Law—later the Association for Humane Abortion and then the Association for the Study of Abortion—was formed in New York state to advocate for reform. It brought together a prestigious, mainstream group of doctors, lawyers, academics, and clergy in an effort to educate the public through talks, films, brochures, and newsletters. Its status as a nonprofit educational organization prevented it from doing really effective political advocacy, although members of the group testified before a commission on revising state law.[34] Of greater influence was a study by Dr. Robert E. Hall, a gynecologist at Columbia Presbyterian and president of the Association for Humane Abortion, reporting that 87 percent of 1,200 OB-GYN physicians surveyed supported a change in the abortion law to follow the ALI model. The *New York Times* cited this figure in a February 1965 editorial that called the existing state law "barbarous." The editorial urged legal reform to permit abortion in cases of fetal deformity and to allow a physician's "expert medical judgment" to determine whether an abortion is justified to protect a woman's physical or mental health.[35]

In April 1965, CBS aired a documentary, "Abortion and the Law," and this provoked another *New York Times* editorial in favor of reform. The *New York Times Magazine* ran a long article called "The Scandal of Abortion—Laws" by Lawrence Lader.[36] By the end of 1965, the *Saturday Evening Post, Time, Look, Newsweek*, the *Atlantic*, and other national mass-market publications had covered the abortion issue in depth. With the rubella epidemic ongoing, public opinion favored reform of existing abortion laws. Most activists were pushing for ALI-style reforms; only a few voices went so far as to call for a complete repeal of abortion laws, which would leave the decision entirely to women and their medical practitioners.[37] Garrett Hardin, a biology professor at the University of California, Santa Barbara, gave a campus lecture in the fall of 1963 calling for repeal of the abortion laws. (Hardin later said that after the lecture, he began to receive calls from women asking where they could get abortions; he referred them to doctors in Mexico and later worked with the Los Angeles Clergy Consultation Service.) Hardin's lecture at Berkeley the following year also helped bring California activist Patricia Maginnis around to favor complete repeal.[38]

While the Catholic Church hierarchy was staunchly antiabortion, a 1965 survey by the National Opinion Research Center found that of ordinary U.S. Catholics, 64 percent of men and 58 percent of women believed that legal abortion should be available to women whose health was in danger.[39] Indeed, there was a moment when it seemed the Catholic Church might soften its rigid stance, at least on family planning. The Second Vatican Council, the twenty-first ecumenical council in the history of the Catholic Church (the first was the Council of Nicaea in 325), convened from 1962 to 1965 to address relations between the modern world and the Catholic Church. Out of this council came ten conciliar commissions, including one for the Study of Problems of Population, Family, and Birth.[40] In 1966, the commission's preliminary report included the results of the fifty-eight-member majority vote that recommended lifting the ban on birth control. For a brief period from 1966 to 1968, a change in Church teachings seemed possible. A number of liberal reforms came out of what was known as Vatican II, including the use of vernacular languages instead of Latin for mass and ecumenical connections with other religions. But the recommendation on birth control went no further: a 1968 encyclical from Pope Paul VI titled *Humanae Vitae* reiterated the Church's ban on both abortion and artificial contraception. It was believed that the Church could not change its position on abortion without undermining papal authority.[41] Yet a survey of Catholic priests from the early 1970s showed that about 60 percent of them believed the prohibition of birth control was wrong.[42]

Many of the groups that set out to change state laws on abortion were associated with universities or medical schools, and for most of the 1960s, the issue was mainly argued in medical terms—protecting the rights of medical practitioners.[43] In addition to academics and physicians, these reform groups often drew in campus ministers and rabbis, who served a student population for whom abortion was a common and urgent issue, some of whom had experience in seeking abortion providers for their counselees. The clergy were uniquely able to provide an authoritative moral counterpoint to religious—almost entirely Roman Catholic—voices against abortion.[44]

In Los Angeles in 1966, Ruth Roemer, a professor of public health law, and other eminent physicians and academics, established the California Committee on Therapeutic Abortion (CCTA), based at the University of California, Los Angeles (UCLA). The group was supported financially by Joseph Sunnen, a Missouri inventor and manufacturer of machinery—and, at one time, of Emko contraceptive foam. Rev. Huw Anwyl and Elizabeth Canfield, who later founded the Los Angeles chapter of the Clergy Consultation Service, also were members of the CCTA. (Canfield had also worked for Sunnen; see chapter 4.) The CCTA's first act was to establish a defense fund for two California doctors who were threatened with sanctions for performing abortions on women who had been exposed to rubella during pregnancy. The group was instrumental in changing California law in 1967 to permit abortion in cases of rape, incest, or threat to the woman's life.[45]

In 1967, Dr. Jack Stack, a family physician from Alma, Michigan, formed the Michigan Council for the Study of Abortion. The group worked with Johan Eliot of the University of Michigan School of Public Health, medical students and residents from the university's medical school, members of Michigan Women for the Medical Control of Abortion, representatives from state and county health departments, and clergy to conduct studies of the attitudes of physicians, students, and women toward abortion. Rev. Carl Bielby, a Methodist minister who was then the head of Marriage and Family Life at the Metropolitan

Detroit Council of Churches, was a founding member of Stack's study group. Through Bielby's efforts, the Detroit Methodist Conference provided a grant of $750 toward the cost of the study, and Bielby served as a liaison with Stack's group.[46] Eliot later urged Bielby to start a Michigan CCS; Bielby did so and became its first director. An offshoot of the study group, which Stack also spearheaded, lobbied hard in 1969 for liberalization of Michigan's abortion law.[47]

The 1965 *Griswold* decision, which at last legalized contraceptives in Connecticut, encouraged those who sought change in New York. It was clear, however, that shepherding a test case on abortion through the courts would be difficult and take a long time. With polls showing that a majority of the public—including Roman Catholics and large majorities of obstetricians and psychiatrists—favored liberalizing the abortion laws, advocates decided to push for a change in state law. A public forum on the topic at the Yorkville Democratic Club on the Upper East Side of Manhattan brought positive reactions, and state Assemblyman Percy Sutton and state Senator Manfred Ohrenstein, both Democrats from New York City, introduced a bill to reform the law.[48] The wording was based on the model set out by the ALI, allowing abortion not just to save a woman's life but also in case of "substantial risk" of serious impairment to a woman's physical or mental health, if the child might be born with a grave physical disability or intellectual development disorder, or in the case of incest or rape, including statutory rape of a girl under sixteen. Ten of the eleven witnesses at a March 7, 1966, hearing held by the Assembly's Committee on Health testified in support of the bill. "But," the *New York Times* reported, "legislative leaders made it clear that further study would be needed before an issue of such delicate social and moral implications could be put to a vote"; indeed, the bill died in committee.[49]

The following year, Assemblyman Albert Blumenthal, also a Democrat from Manhattan, sponsored another bill, which followed the ALI model but added that the approval of a committee of physicians would be needed for a hospital abortion. Surely, it was thought, this wording would be restrictive enough to satisfy most legislators. This time, a campaign to support the bill was organized by John V. P. Lassoe Jr., then director of Christian social relations for the Episcopal Diocese of New York. Lassoe brought together a broad coalition of groups to support reform, including medical associations, civic groups, and religious organizations such as the American Lutheran Church, the New York City Protestant Council of Churches, the New York State Council of Churches, and the Episcopal diocese and began a massive petition drive.[50]

The reform drive was going well—until Roman Catholic bishops issued a pastoral letter calling on Catholics to "do all in your power" to oppose liberalizing abortion laws. The bishops directed the letter to be read to congregations at all masses throughout the state on Sunday, February 12, 1967. State legislators were flooded with letters and phone calls opposing the Blumenthal bill. Writer and activist Larry Lader wrote, "The opposition concentrated its wrath on Assemblyman Blumenthal, and consistently linked abortion with godlessness." However, State Senator Basil A. Paterson, a sponsor of the bill and a black Catholic from Harlem, said, "We're not telling other Catholics they have to get abortions. We're only asking them not to dictate to the rest of the population what they can and cannot do."[51] In spite of the support of so many religious and professional organizations and, according to polls, a majority of ordinary citizens, including Catholics, the bill was now toxic. It was killed in committee by a vote of fifteen to three on March 7, 1967.[52]

For Rev. Howard Moody and a group of like-minded clergy, that defeat was the blow that pushed them to act. By then, a small group had already been discussing the idea of doing direct abortion referrals for some months. The exact genesis of the clergy group is not perfectly clear, but its motivating force was certainly author and abortion activist Lawrence Lader.

Larry Lader

Lader was a Manhattan native who graduated from Harvard and served in the army during World War II. He began his writing career during the war with pieces he sent to the *New Yorker* from the South Pacific. After the war he wrote for other magazines, did some political work, and even ran unsuccessfully for New York State Assembly as an American Labor Party candidate in 1948. His first book was a 1955 biography of birth control activist Margaret Sanger (1879–1966), and getting to know Sanger had a profound effect on him.[53] Although Sanger herself was no supporter of abortion, "working with her completely convinced me that a woman's freedom in education, jobs, marriage, her whole life, could only be achieved when she gained control of her childbearing," Lader told the *New York Times*.[54] Lader's 1966 book, *Abortion*, reported in detail on the contemporary practice and legalities of abortion, and it propelled him into public activism. The very mainstream *Reader's Digest* even published excerpts.[55] At his first press conference after the book's publication, reporters asked how women found physicians who were willing to perform illegal abortions as Lader said they did, and, he wrote, "I had to admit that since the publication of my first article the year before [in the *New York Times Magazine*], and now my book, I had received hundreds of appeals from women to learn the names and addresses of such sources. It seemed so inconsequential, the next, obvious question. Did I send them to these doctors? . . . I admitted that I had, and would continue to do so until a district attorney stopped me."[56] After that, pleas for help increased exponentially. His wife, Joan, recalled, "Sometimes I would answer the phone, or he would answer the phone. You could tell by the tone of voice, the tone of desperation. It was just immediately apparent. Before they said anything too much, I would just say, 'Send us a letter.' Because we had no idea when and if our phone would be tapped." Lader answered hundreds of letters, sending the name and telephone number of a safe doctor to each woman who asked.[57]

Lader saw referrals as a form of civil disobedience that could raise awareness and force a change in the abortion laws. Did he fear arrest? Joan Summers Lader said he did not.

> If you had met him, you would know that fear was not a factor in his life. He would get, sometimes, awful mail. If he went down to get the mail first, he would hide it from me; if I got the mail first, I'd hide it from him. He didn't live in fear. He was somebody who got up every morning, and no matter what had happened in his life the day before, whether it was a marital tiff or a tiff within the movement or whatever, he got up every morning, tabula rasa, and said, now, on with the positive things.

He was once called before a grand jury (see chapter 5), but the district attorney never tried to stop his referrals, which eventually numbered about 2,000 by his own count.[58]

Lader was not completely alone in making direct abortion referrals. Patricia Maginnis, who had been lobbying to change California abortion laws since 1961, and Lana Phelan organized the Society for Humane Abortion in San Francisco in 1965 to educate the public and provide abortion training for physicians. At a time when most of the activists for abortion reform were male and arguing for reform on medical and public health grounds, feminists Maginnis and Phelan were among the first to argue for complete repeal of abortion laws on the grounds that abortion was a woman's right.[59] Like Lader, they saw that the practical need for referrals was great, and in 1966 they formed the Association to Repeal Abortion Laws which, despite the lobby group sound of its title, actually referred women to abortion providers in Mexico, Japan, and Puerto Rico; published brochures on where to get abortions and how to perform one's own abortion; and held classes on these topics. Smaller feminist groups and other individuals in communities were making referrals more quietly. Since the early 1960s, an informal network of campus clergy—some through the National Campus Ministers' Association—had shared resources.[60] Lader was the most deliberately public referrer, and unlike Maginnis at the time, he had a national audience. He received pleas for help from women across the country.[61]

For Lader, the referrals were one part of the cause he championed for the rest of his life: making abortion legal and safe. He saw abortion referrals as a form of resistance, in the tradition of the Underground Railroad, which he had written about earlier in a book on Boston abolitionists. Looking back in 1973, Lader wrote that the referrals not only did a humanitarian service for individuals, they also "drew women into the movement, and provided a constant affirmation that the laws were wrong and could only be righted when enough people stepped forward to challenge them."[62] Beyond his own referrals, Lader pushed the clergy to do the same, wrote and lectured tirelessly, and organized to change the laws on abortion. He gave up most other work to spend all his time on the abortion issue, and his family mostly lived on the investments he had made back when he was selling magazine articles regularly. He was a big personality with strong views, and yet, his wife said, "he had differing opinions from some people but never made a mortal enemy out of anyone."[63] In July 1968, Lader and three others—New York activist Ruth P. Smith, Chicago physician Caroline (Lonny) Myers, and Episcopal canon Don Shaw, also from Chicago—met in the Laders' living room to found the National Association for the Repeal of Abortion Laws (NARAL, later the National Abortion Rights Action League and today called NARAL Pro-Choice America), and their work did much to change New York state law in 1970.[64]

In his 1973 book *Abortion II*, Lader wrote that the idea for a clergy abortion referral service first came up on September 6, 1966, during a lunch with Howard Moody and two Episcopal priests, Rev. Lester Kinsolving of San Francisco—who was already part of the California Committee on Therapeutic Abortion—and Rev. Dr. John McGill Krumm, then rector of the Church of the Ascension in New York. "At some point," Lader wrote, "they asked me what they could do to help the campaign. I replied bluntly, 'Start with the women. Organize the clergy to refer women to qualified doctors.'" Lader said he felt that "Moody was the ideal candidate for such a project, combining a commitment to social responsibility with hardheaded realism."[65]

Formation of the CCS

A group of clergy did start discussing the issue of abortion about this time, although the exact sequence of events isn't clear. As Moody remembered it, there was an existing ecumenical group of about a dozen clergy already meeting at Washington Square Methodist Church, just a block from Judson, "talking about theology and social issues and that sort of thing, and one of the social issues was abortion." Moody's lunch with Lader may have set abortion as their exclusive agenda. Reform Rabbi Lewis E. (Buz) Bogage, another member of the

original group, recalled, "That [abortion] was not an agenda item. It was
something way down the list, because abortion was not the big issue. But then it
became a major issue."[66]

In 1966, the new minister at Washington Square Methodist Church was
Rev. Finley Schaef. He attended Yale Divinity School for one year and completed his studies at Union Theological Seminary at the time that theologians
Paul Tillich and Reinhold Neibuhr were on the faculty; he graduated in 1957.
Under Schaef, the church became a Greenwich Village center for resistance to
the Vietnam War, hosting protests and offering counseling and assistance to
draft resisters. As Schaef remembered it, the clergy abortion group formed at
his suggestion specifically to do referrals. In his previous ministry in Queens,
a woman came to him asking for help finding an abortion for her teenage
daughter, who had been raped by the woman's husband. Schaef was unable to
arrange an abortion, but became determined to offer access to them, even
though it was illegal. He later wrote, "In late 1966, I approached Rev. Moody
and proposed starting a clergy counseling service that would refer women for
abortions. He agreed and we co-founded what came to be known as the Clergy
Consultation Service on Abortion." Initial meetings were held at Washington
Square Methodist Church.[67]

Whether the clergy group began as a wide-ranging discussion group or
formed with the original intention of doing abortion referrals, after his lunch
with Moody and Krumm, Lader attended the meetings and pushed the clergy
group beyond talk to take action as soon as possible. A small group—eight or
nine according to Schaef, or perhaps a dozen, as described by Moody—met
regularly to educate themselves about the medical and legal sides of abortion and
discuss how they could establish an abortion referral service. Members of that
original core group also included Krumm and Rev. Jesse Lyons, a Methodist
minister then on staff at Riverside Church on the Upper West Side of Manhattan. Like Judson, Riverside had long been known as a progressive, social
justice church, with a diverse, interdenominational congregation—American
Baptist and Congregational (now United Church of Christ). Lyons, too, had
had a personal experience with abortion: his niece had been refused an abortion
after she contracted rubella during pregnancy, and her child, born with severe
disabilities, was institutionalized.[68]

Lader urged the group on, making it clear that referring women for safe
abortions was something they could and should do, and that doing so publicly
would advance the cause of legal reform. Moody recalled, "He pushed us like
nobody's business to do something. He didn't have to push too hard, but he
was very eager for us to—because he knew how important it would be if church

folks got into this battle."[69] Founding CCS member Rev. Robert Pierce, a
UCC minister, remembered, "He used to *shame* us. That's the only way of saying
it. 'Why aren't you bastards doing something?' He was very vocal, very in your
face."[70] Not long after Lader's September 1966 lunch with Moody, Krumm, and
Kinsolving, the *New Republic* reviewed Lader's book *Abortion*. In the November
26 issue, James Ridgeway wrote that a group of Protestant clergymen were
planning to establish a clinic to refer women for abortions. Historian Joshua
Wolff points out that although the clergy weren't exactly planning a "clinic,"
the fact that the leak appeared so soon after the lunch makes it very likely that
Lader was the source of the information.[71]

Moody, Schaef, and the other core members of the group called on other
clergy members who they thought would be sympathetic — ministers and rabbis
who had been involved in civil rights battles, the school integration fight in
New York, and other civil liberties issues. Moody recalled that they invited
about forty people to the first official meeting, and perhaps twenty or twenty-
five attended.[72] Some, like Schaef, Moody, and Lyons, had personal experiences
with women seeking abortion. One of the early recruits was Rabbi Balfour
Brickner. He was born in Cleveland and grew up in both a Zionist and Reform
Jewish household (Brickner's father was also a rabbi). Brickner was ordained at
Hebrew Union College-Jewish Institute of Religion in 1952. Like many of the
CCS clergy, he was involved with civil rights — and jailed while demonstrating
for voting rights in the South — and with anti–Vietnam War activism. Though
a staunch Zionist, Brickner referred to Israel's occupation of Gaza and the
West Bank as "Israel's Vietnam," and he was committed to reconciliation and
peace in the Middle East. From 1961 to 1980 he was the co-director of the
National Commission on Social Action of the Union of American Hebrew
Congregations (now known as the Union for Reform Judaism).[73] Brickner had
worked with a juvenile court in Washington, DC, in the 1950s, "and in that
capacity I met an awful lot of women who were pregnant who didn't want to
be," he recalled.[74] So he, too, saw the need for safe abortion referrals. A certain
amount of salesmanship must have been required to convince some others.
Many just didn't see a problem. Lader, Schaef, and Moody knew these clergy
would see the need once they offered the service.

Even the clergy who had dealt with abortion in the past felt unprepared to
start counseling larger numbers of women about abortion right away. They
needed to educate themselves. For a start, they wanted to understand what
women would experience during the procedure and what medical information
they should impart beforehand. Moody recalled that a physician in Judson's
congregation put him in touch with women who had had abortions. The

women spoke to the clergy group and described terrible experiences—meeting someone at midnight in a parking lot, for example. "Psychologically for women, it was horrible," Moody said. "And those kind of experiences strengthened us in terms of our resolve." Doctors also educated the clergy about the procedure, bringing in a model of the pelvic area, describing the procedure in detail, and telling them which steps could be painful.[75]

The group brought in legal advisers, too. Aryeh Neier was executive director of the New York Civil Liberties Union (NYCLU) and later became the head of the ACLU and then a founder of Human Rights Watch. NYCLU board member Ephraim London was a great free speech advocate who had defended comedian Lenny Bruce in 1964 and fought against censorship of films.[76] London became the group's ongoing legal consultant. Cyril C. Means Jr. of New York University School of Law, an old college pal of Lader's, later became an attorney for NARAL and filed important friend-of-the-court briefs in the *Roe v. Wade* case. At the clergy meetings, Means outlined the legal risks. The lawyers could not offer the clergy assurance that they would not get arrested for doing what they planned, and the consequences could include up to a year in jail and fines up to $1,000. After hearing the risks, a few of the clergy whose congregations were not supportive resigned.[77]

The lawyers could only offer advice that would make legal problems less likely. To begin with, London advised the clergy to refer women to licensed physicians who were outside New York state. Because laws on abortion varied from state to state, this might be some protection against the charge that New York law had been broken; moreover, they hoped that spanning jurisdictions would make prosecution more difficult. Referring out of state became one of the cardinal rules of the service as it spread nationally.

The clergy also hoped that their counseling would be protected by laws and traditions that respected confidential communications with clergy counselors as privileged (see chapter 6). Moody said, "The only reason for clergy doing it, the *only* reason, was . . . to give the protection of the church, and the backing of the church."[78] London advised them against "anything that gave the CCS the appearance of being clandestine" or underground, so the group decided that when the time came, they would make a public announcement to the press, presenting the assumption that the service was a perfectly legal part of the clergy's confidential pastoral counseling.[79] The lawyers warned the group that money should never pass between women and the clergy counselors, indicating that the counselors considered the work part of their regular professional duties.

Most of these clergy were already veteran activists who had been involved in the civil rights movement and protesting the war in Vietnam. Based on those experiences, some felt that being arrested for making abortion referrals would advance the cause of legal reform more quickly. But the group decided that was not the way to go. Moody said, "Some people wanted [to] be confrontational. We were not interested in committing civil disobedience so we could get arrested; we were interested in helping women. And if we got arrested, we wouldn't be helping women."[80] In the same spirit of civil disobedience, the group decided that if one of their number were arrested, all would turn themselves in. London shot this idea down, advising them that only the district attorney would decide which one person would be charged, so there was no point in sacrificing the whole service.[81]

The group's shared experiences in the civil rights and other social movements had taught them that in getting the word out to the public, messages enunciated by a single spokesperson would be more effective than unfocused comments by all members of the group. The clergy appointed Moody to speak for them and to keep group members informed. Ideally, the clergy had hoped to create a decentralized network of counselors, spreading out the work, responsibility, and potentially any legal liability. Moody recalled, "We didn't want any one church to have to take the brunt."[82] As a practical matter, the group needed a single locus for quick communications and efficient administration. With Moody serving as point man, it was convenient to make his office at Judson Memorial Church the administrative center. The group's finances at this point consisted of a donation of $1,000 from a friend of Moody's, a Pennsylvania dentist, and these funds went through Judson.[83] Judson subsidized the group's costs as needed, although over time donations came close to covering expenses— about $2,000 a year for phones, postage, and incidentals.[84] That figure does not take into account the salary of Judson Church administrator Arlene Carmen, an invaluable donation by the church as she came to spend much of her time on the CCS.

Eventually Judson housed the group's answering machine. The message on the machine would give the names and telephone numbers of several clergy who were on call for the service that week. Rev. Robert Pierce was a member of Judson Memorial Church and worked for the National Council of Churches in upper Manhattan. He had suggested that the NCC offices house the answering machine. Cynthia Clark Wedel, Pierce's supervisor at the NCC's Division of Christian Unity, supported the idea, but when she consulted the NCC's attorney, he ruled the phone line too great a legal risk.[85] So Judson became the home of the machine. Judson's church office served as the national headquarters for the CCS for the rest of its existence.

Finally, what should the group call itself? There was an intense debate at their last meeting before going public. Some members wanted to use the less objectionable phrase *problem pregnancy* in the name of the service, mainly for a bit of legal protection; others, including Lader, Schaef, and Rev. Jesse Lyons, argued for speaking plainly and using the term *abortion*. Lader, whose 1966 book, subsequent speaking engagements, and public offer to refer women for abortions had been an effort to bring the issue out of the shadows and into national debate, argued that "the impact of the service depended on open and total commitment."[86] The clergy also had a practical fear that if they did not use the word *abortion*, the women who most needed them would not find them. The plain speakers won out, and they decided on the name Clergy Consultation Service on Abortion, deliberately choosing to serve women more effectively over making their own public relations task easier. "*Abortion*'s a loaded, fearsome word, but we decided we didn't want to chicken out on it," Moody recalled.[87] In an address at a fortieth anniversary celebration for the CCS, Moody said, "It was important to use the word 'abortion.' At that time it was not used in public discourse. The aim was to normalize that word."[88] Later, in other parts of the country, some regional services (e.g., Los Angeles, Chicago, Wisconsin, and the Albany, New York, area group) made an equally deliberate choice to use the term *problem pregnancy* in their names to emphasize that their counseling included all options. The Centre County, Pennsylvania, CCS chapter used the name CHOICE. In 1973, chapter coordinator Rev. Irmgart Soltau explained to a reporter from Pennsylvania State University's *Daily Collegian*, "We want to help women examine the possibilities of adoption, foster care, marriage and single parenthood as well as terminating pregnancies." She said they avoided the word *abortion* because of its "bad connotations" and preferred the terms *termination of pregnancy* and *problem pregnancy*.[89]

As the last preparation for going public, the newly named group wrote a statement of purpose. It began, "The present abortion laws require over a million women in the United States each year to seek illegal abortions which often cause severe mental anguish, physical suffering, and unnecessary death of women. These laws also compel the birth of unwanted, unloved, and often de-formed children; yet a truly humane society is one in which the birth of a child is an occasion for genuine celebration, not the imposition of a penalty or punishment upon the mother. These laws brand as criminals wives and mothers who are often driven as helpless victims to desperate acts." The clergy pledged to educate the public about the problem and advocate for legal reform in New York state and nationally. "In the meantime," the statement continued, "women are being driven alone and afraid into the underworld of criminality or the dangerous practice of self-induced abortion." The clergy ended by stating their intention: "Therefore believing as clergymen that there are higher laws and moral obligations transcending legal codes, we believe that it is our pastoral responsibility and religious duty to give aid and assistance to all women with problem pregnancies. To that end we are establishing a Clergymen's Consultation Service on Abortion which will include referral to the best available medical advice and aid to women in need."[90] Facing antiquated abortion laws, little hope for reform, and unknown legal repercussions, the service was ready to launch.

3

To Offer Compassion

The Launch

Word of the clergy counseling group hit the news before the CCS was ready to go public. Once again, Larry Lader was the source of the leak—one final prod to the clergy immediately following the failure of the Blumenthal bill to reform abortion law in the New York state legislature on March 7, 1967. The second failure of legal reform in one year was the last straw.[1] The clergy were preparing to launch their referral service. Just in case they thought of wavering or delaying, Lader gave them one last push by providing Martin Tolchin, health care reporter for the *New York Times*, an advance copy of a speech Lader was to give at Cornell University on March 12. On that day the *New York Times* reported, "Mr. Lader said that he had already referred about 300 'women in need' to 'the best medical services.' . . . 'In a few weeks, a group of prominent ministers in New York will publicly announce a similar counseling service in abortion,' he said. 'I confidently expect that dozens of other groups throughout the country will follow suit. Only when such individuals act openly on their moral convictions can the shame and irresponsibility of our legislatures be exposed to the demands of popular will.'" Lader did not name the clergy, but John Lassoe of the Episcopal Diocese of New York confirmed for the *Times* the "existence of a group of 15 Protestant and Jewish ministers" who were planning to do abortion referrals. Dr. Robert Hall, the OB-GYN who headed the Association for the Study of Abortion, immediately "dissociated both himself and the group from Mr. Lader's action."[2]

By this time, the clergy group had been meeting, learning, and making arrangements for some months. They worried that Lader's leak about their plans would make them appear to be a shady, underground operation—exactly the impression they wanted to avoid. They wanted publicity. They wanted women to know of the service and be able to find them, and they wanted to show confidence that their work was entirely legal and above-board. However, they feared that holding an open press conference would expose them to negative and potentially inflammatory questions. In May, when the group was ready to go public, they decided to have Howard Moody take their story directly to Edward B. Fiske, religion editor of the *New York Times*.[3]

On Monday, May 22, 1967, the *Times* ran the front-page article about the Clergy Consultation Service under the headline "Clergymen Offer Abortion Advice: 21 Ministers and Rabbis Form New Group—Will Propose Alternatives." The article included a photograph of Moody with his crew cut and clerical collar. It listed by name nineteen ministers and two rabbis—all men, although one ordained female minister was already meeting with the group—with their congregational or other affiliations and gave the telephone number of the group's answering machine.[4] The group was pleased that the article did not depict the clergy as hot-headed radicals but portrayed their intentions accurately and in unsensational, reasonable terms. Moody and Arlene Carmen wrote, "Long after, we credited that opening announcement as responsible for setting the tone for the CCS."[5]

By the time the article appeared, the group had set up the answering machine at Judson Memorial Church. Each week its outgoing message would name two or more clergy members on call that week, their locations, and their phone numbers. That first week, the clergy on call were Rabbi Buz Bogage of Central Synagogue in midtown Manhattan and Rev. Richard Johnson of Emmanuel Baptist Church in Brooklyn. Callers were not asked to leave a message; they simply listened to the announcement, chose the clergy counselor they preferred—often based on denomination or location—and contacted them for an in-person counseling appointment.[6]

The group's main uncertainty was whether police would come knocking at their doors as soon as the newspaper article was published. The knocks never came. What was much more unexpected was the magnitude of the response from women desperately seeking safe abortions. In the first week following the article, the CCS was deluged with calls, including many from across the country and some from clergy wanting to set up services in their own regions. The *New York Times* reported on May 24 that, according to Rabbi Buz Bogage, the service had received thirty-five calls on its very first day of operation; four or five of the callers were Catholic and 60 percent were Jewish. That number was misleadingly low, because when Bogage spoke to the *Times*, he was reporting only the calls that had come to his own office and did not include the calls to Johnson, the other clergyman identified on the answering machine's message. Nor did the number reflect the callers who reached the machine but did not follow up right away with a call to a counselor.[7]

Public response was mostly positive. In addition to the outpouring of calls from women wanting referrals, Moody received supportive letters from clergy, lawyers, and health professionals, and small donations from a few individuals. A very small number of negative letters came in.[8] There was no public negative reaction from the Roman Catholic Church. Press reaction was mostly neutral or positive. Wire services picked up the *New York Times* article for regional and national distribution. The *New York Post* editorialized in favor of the group as "an important source of both professional and spiritual help." *New York Newsday* ran the least favorable article on May 23, saying, "Members of a newly formed Clergymen's Consultation Service on Abortion appeared uncertain, and perhaps in disagreement, yesterday over whether they would refer women to doctors for illegal abortions." This conclusion was apparently based on reporter Linda Charlton's conversation with Methodist minister and CCS member Rev. Willett R. Porter, in which, she reported, Porter expressed "some reservations about this form of referral"—meaning referral for *illegal* abortions in other states.[9] In fact, there was no dissension within the CCS on this point. The original *Times* article had cited the group's press release: "The statement said the clergymen were 'mindful that there are duly licensed and reputable physicians who in their wisdom perform therapeutic abortions which some may regard as illegal. When a doctor performs such an abortion motivated by compassion and concern for the patient, and not simply for monetary gain,' it continued, 'we do not regard him as a criminal but as living by the highest standards of religion and of the Hippocratic oath.'"[10] Clearly, CCS members knew that as a practical matter, they would sometimes have to refer women for illegal abortions.

The group met on May 25 to review the events of the past four days. They reiterated the need for one designated spokesperson (Moody) to deal with all press inquiries; this would avoid the kinds of confusion caused by the interviews with Porter and Bogage. They also drew up a monthly rotation in which each member would take one week on call followed by three weeks off.[11]

Counseling Guidelines

The group set guidelines for counseling: it would be done in person—never over the phone—at the counselor's regular office; the clergy would not insist that women show identification or even use their real names; and at first women were asked to bring with them some proof of pregnancy, such as the results of a urine test. About six months into their work, they had a close call that showed how important it was to know how far along a pregnancy was. Judson Church administrator Arlene Carmen recalled with emotion the only time she accompanied a patient for an abortion.[12] The sixteen-year-old's family was Catholic and had found it hard to accept that she was going to have an abortion. They had provided the money for her procedure and travel to Puerto Rico but did not have funds to go with her. The clergy counselor who referred her contacted Carmen, who was planning to check on new doctors in Puerto Rico at that time, and she agreed to go with the young woman.

As Carmen sat in the doctor's waiting room, she began to hear the sounds of people suddenly moving very quickly in the procedure room. The room she was in was locked, and people were not permitted to leave. After what seemed a very long time, the doctor emerged and told Carmen, "She died." Carmen said, "I don't know if you've ever had that terribly weak feeling in your legs like they're rubber, and you're just going to slide to the floor, and I thought I was sliding to the floor." It seemed to her another long time before the doctor added, "But we saved her." The patient was farther along in her pregnancy than she had reported—fourteen weeks—and the doctor said that the anesthesia had caused such a violent reaction that her vital signs had stopped briefly. The activity that Carmen heard had been people rushing to find oxygen, which had not been available in the procedure room. When Carmen went in the procedure room, the girl was alive and conscious, but making wild movements, not in control of her body. Carmen insisted on making a phone call to the CCS medical advisor in New York, who conferred with the Puerto Rico doctor and then told Carmen that the treatment was appropriate. Carmen said, "I was somewhat reassured, except that, as soon as we hung up, that doctor in Puerto Rico asked me whether he should give the abortion again, and I couldn't believe it, that any doctor would ask a lay person after what [the patient] had been through, whether he should gamble with her life again, should *he* try it again, because she was still pregnant. Of course, I said no, and took [the patient] back to the hotel and stayed with her." The young woman's father came to accompany her home.[13]

The CCS never again referred to that doctor. "That taught us a lesson that we didn't know, and that was that we couldn't trust a woman's memory about how far along her pregnancy was. Until that point, we had simply asked for evidence of possible pregnancy, we didn't know very much about weeks and how important an examination would be," she recalled. Within hours of the procedure, she called New York to ask the Judson Church secretary to change the outgoing message on the CCS answering machine to say that every woman had to have an examination by a gynecologist and arrive at her counseling session with a doctor's note indicating the length of her pregnancy in weeks.

Counselors would not refer another woman without knowing at which stage of pregnancy she was.[14]

Carmen recalled that the young woman emerged from the experience physically fine. Because the New York group had not yet made connections in England or Japan, where later abortions were performed legally, the girl wound up in a home for unwed mothers and gave the baby up for adoption. "I wrote to her once," she said, "and couldn't maintain the contact because it was too much for me — there was a guilt there that I carried for a long time, about what happened to her."[15] But Carmen heard of her progress from her doctor, who also was a member of Judson Church and served as one of the CCS medical advisors.

When the CCS began to insist on notes from gynecologists, simply stating that the woman had been examined and how many weeks along the pregnancy was, they ran into unexpected resistance. Women who had been patients of the same gynecologist for years found that their physician refused to give them such a note. Carmen recalled, "We couldn't believe it. . . . Somehow they thought they'd be implicated in something. We never could understand what they thought they'd be implicated in, because they'd do that kind of a note for anybody else. If your employer needed that note, they'd gladly give a note saying you were found to be pregnant." So the CCS developed what Carmen called a "snotty letter" for doctors who refused. It read in part, "We are quite willing to continue handling problem pregnancies until doctors themselves are ready to deal effectively with what is, after all, a medical problem. However, we are upset when physicians refuse to cooperate in such a small way and we fail to see any possible harm that could come to a doctor. As a consequence, the woman is forced to undergo a second examination by a cooperative physician, thereby incurring additional expenses at a time when she can least afford it." The letter asked the doctor to reconsider their refusal in the future. Meanwhile, they referred women to the Margaret Sanger Bureau on 16th Street, where they could be examined quickly and the staff doctors were willing to supply the needed note. It was still an added delay and expense.[16]

If the letter to unwilling physicians sounded rather sharp, it reflected the clergy's disappointment and anger at the lack of cooperation from doctors. They had hoped for greater support, if not actual participation, from the medical community, in view of Robert Hall's 1965 survey showing that 87 percent of OB-GYNs favored abortion law reform.[17] Certainly doctors referred women to the CCS; by 1970, half of referrals to the New York CCS came from women's personal physicians.[18] That theoretical support did not translate to great outspokenness or activism; most physicians were not willing to put their reputations or careers on the line as the clergy were—even in the small matter of writing a note for a patient. A 1969–70 survey of Philadelphia OB-GYN physicians by the nonprofit Metropolitan Associates of Philadelphia found "evidence of considerable ignorance about current abortion law and practices" and that the "feeling that abortion practice is 'emotionally distasteful' is widely held among OB/GYNs."[19] Opposition by physicians was sometimes quite active. In 1969, for instance, the Medical Society of New Jersey asked the state's attorney general to investigate the New Jersey CCS; if there was such an investigation, it did not result in any interruption in the group's referral work.[20]

The counselors also had to match women with doctors who were willing to perform an abortion at their stage of pregnancy. A doctor in Washington, DC, would take women only under ten weeks, which, for most women by the time they had realized they were pregnant, seen a physician, and had a counseling session, was unrealistically early.[21] (In the 1960s, pregnancy tests had to be performed by a physician or laboratory, took at least a day, and were not perfectly accurate; the first home pregnancy test—which still involved a test tube—was marketed in 1978.[22]) Most of the CCS providers would perform abortions up to twelve weeks. Abortions later in pregnancy were more complicated, more expensive, and might even require overseas travel. In 1969, a doctor in London, England, would perform later abortions at his clinic at a total cost (including travel from Chicago) of up to $1,100 (about $7,480 in 2017) for women whose pregnancies were close to twenty weeks along.[23] For a while, two doctors in Japan, where elective abortion had been legal since 1949, would perform abortions through the twenty-eighth week of pregnancy. In 1970, the round-trip travel from Chicago cost $900 and required a passport, a visa to enter Japan, and a smallpox vaccine to return to the United States; the procedure, if performed that late, could cost more than $650 and require four nights in the hospital. In spite of the cost, travel challenges, and time required, one Japanese doctor was so inundated with CCS referrals for very late abortions that he began to get protests from his staff. He eventually "discouraged" cases later than twenty-two weeks, according to a note to the Chicago CCS from the U.S. missionary minister who headed the CCS group in Japan. The minister made arrangements for women whom the CCS referred to Tokyo, worked with Japanese colleagues, and coordinated eleven international volunteers who provided transportation from and to the airport.[24]

Even if women had the funds, out-of-state and international travel was new to many. As the CCS became more experienced, counselors provided as much travel information as possible—about flights, ground transportation, hotels, and sometimes sight-seeing opportunities. Internationally, in addition to the referrals to England and Japan, many women from the West and Midwest were referred to Mexico; from northern states, some women went to Canada— beginning in 1968, when Dr. Henry Morgentaler began to offer illegal abortions in his Montreal office, and in greater numbers after Canada legalized abortion in 1969.[25] The Chicago CCS warned women who traveled to Mexico that they had received reports that U.S. border agents, particularly in San Antonio, were "rude and taunt the women on occasion" when they returned to the United States. The CCS told women that they were not at legal risk, but "if they are particularly rude be sure to get their name and badge number and we will file a formal complaint on your behalf."[26]

If the clergy had any doubts about whether women needed and wanted their help, the response could not have been clearer. The calls for help continued to come in large numbers. The clergy on call found their schedules filled with problem pregnancy counseling. During a week on call, each clergyperson might have to fit up to twenty—and sometimes more—counseling sessions into an already busy schedule. Those few ordained women who served as CCS counselors were particularly inundated. A young woman minister had been meeting with the CCS group from early on.[27] As soon as she began working with the CCS and her name came up on the answering machine message, she was flooded with calls. Women were "waiting all over our house and out in the street," she recalled in an interview. The house was "like a rathole. Still, they came upstairs, even though the place looked like hell, to talk to me about an abortion. That's how desperate they were." She counseled twenty or more women a week when she was on call. "I think I did get inundated during my 'on' weeks, because I was a woman," she said.[28]

It was also clear that the need for abortion referrals was not confined to New York City. The number of calls from women outside the area—whom the clergy refused to counsel by phone—indicated a vast need nationwide. During its first year, the New York CCS agreed to help a woman from any part of the country if she could come to New York City for in-person counseling. But that was a big burden for the group to shoulder and was not practical for most women in distant states. The group was committed to face-to-face counseling, so the idea of referring women by phone was dismissed.[29] The CCS soon sought clergy elsewhere who could start counseling services in other regions. Moody heard from clergy who had seen the need in their own areas and wanted to connect with the New York group. As chapters formed around the country, the New York office created the National Clergy Consultation Service as a clearinghouse for information—including approved doctors—and protocols. Rather than commit those instructions to a paper handbook, clergy came to New York and Howard Moody and Arlene Carmen traveled around the country conducting training sessions for clergy counselors. The administration of the National CCS organization consisted essentially of Carmen.[30]

Arlene Carmen

In fall 1967, several months after the launch of the CCS, Judson Memorial Church hired Arlene Carmen as church administrator. Carmen had met Howard Moody in 1965 when she was raising funds for the Mississippi Delta Ministry and through the Village Independent Democrats—part of the reform movement that fought to give black people, immigrants, and women a greater voice and later made New York more amenable to abortion law reform.[31] She began working with the CCS group before its public launch and well before she was hired by Judson. Almost immediately, her work at Judson went far beyond the usual role of church administrator; she shaped and led the CCS with Moody.

Carmen grew up with two sisters in a secular Jewish family in a working-class neighborhood in the Bronx. Her father, Jack, was a postal worker who was not especially political. Her mother, Minna, was an intense woman who managed the household on very little money and revered Franklin D. Roosevelt; after her daughters left home, she became a social worker.[32]

As a child, Carmen contracted a bad case of whooping cough, and respiratory problems continued throughout her life. She attended city schools and majored in English literature at City College. She was funny, smart, and attractive. After college she worked at the National Conference of Christians and Jews—"just because there were jobs, it was not a deliberate choice on my part," she said—then at Jewish Theological Seminary of America. She knew in her last year there that she would be taking the job at Judson Memorial Church, but she stayed on to finish a project. Meanwhile, she participated in many of the meetings leading to the formation of the CCS in May 1967. It was her involvement with Judson, she said, that brought the issue of abortion to the center of her attention.[33]

Carmen was politically active—she had canvassed for the Village Independent Democrats and shared an apartment at one time with the feminist writer Susan Brownmiller—but she was not a part of the women's movement. Of Moody, she said, "I suspect he was a much earlier feminist than I was. And it's hard to come to terms with that. Probably it's true." In the 1970s and 1980s, Carmen was at odds with Brownmiller and other feminists, including the National Organization for Women and the radical Redstockings group, over pornography (which Carmen saw as a civil liberties issue) and prostitution. Carmen and Moody both worked on the Judson Prostitution Project, a program that offered health care, legal advice, and support to "working women," as

Carmen and Moody called them in the title of a 1985 book on the project, not to "save" them from their careers.[34]

In November 1967, when Carmen officially joined the staff of Judson, she was thirty-one. "I'm probably the only Jewish administrator of a Baptist church in the United States of America," she joked in 1976. She had an ambivalent religious relationship with the church. At first, Moody said, "she wouldn't tell her mother that she was going to work for a church."[35] Although hers was a secular Jewish family, Carmen quoted her mother as saying that "being Jewish is all in here." Members of Judson remember her attending Sunday services there—but often she was standing at the back, in the doorway, or on a side balcony, chain smoking. After twenty years of working at Judson, she realized "how irretrievably intertwined my life is with this place and this people," and she joined the congregation—though, she said, "In large measure who I am was determined by generations of Jews whose genes I have inherited. And that will never change. Nor would I want it to."[36] A number of Jews had joined the church, which was a uniquely ecumenical Baptist/UCC congregation; under Moody's leadership, Judson had never required Jews to undergo baptism to join. They remained Jewish *and* members of Judson Memorial Church.[37]

The woman minister who was an early member of the CCS said of Carmen, "She was very articulate, she was clear, she was organized, she was a good strategist. . . . She had a kind of businesslike look about her, her hair all kind of skimmed back in a tight bun. . . . Everybody liked her." Rabbi Bogage recalled Carmen as "Very able. Very. Just one of these people who was way ahead of her time. A woman who could really move things around."[38]

Carmen lived in a church-owned apartment just around the corner from Judson on Thompson Street. She was a loving and indulgent aunt to her sister Jewel DeRoy's daughters, although they lived in California (they visited as often as possible and were quite close). DeRoy recalled, "The family joke about Arlene . . . was that Arlene, whose life was centered in the Village, never went above 14th Street except for a protest. But she would go uptown to very luxurious stores and buy very luxurious, adorable dresses for these kids when they were little, when they were babies. She was very pampering in every way she could. So she made an exception. And she wouldn't have done it for herself . . . but she did it for the girls." She enjoyed camping, an occasional gambling visit to Nevada, and, inexplicably to DeRoy, "she had a great taste for hillbilly music." DeRoy remembered her sister as strong-minded but often retiring in manner, and church member Abigail Hastings recalled her as "a private person."[39] Yet Carmen's work with the CCS called on her to be anything but retiring. In a classic example of mustering courage and boldness on behalf of others, Carmen took tremendous risks and ruled the administrative end of the CCS with an iron hand.

When the CCS began, Ephraim London, the group's volunteer attorney, advised the clergy to counsel women and make referrals, but never to have any communication with the doctors who were performing the abortions. Carmen took on the job of maintaining connections with doctors, from checking on their credentials, offices, and bedside manner to arranging how women were to contact them to negotiating prices. She would do no counseling herself. With this strict division of labor, they hoped, conspiracy among the clergy, client, and abortion provider would be difficult to prove. Carmen headed a women's committee to find and evaluate doctors. She and others took tremendous personal risks to ensure that the doctors used by the CCS were capable practitioners and respectful to patients, visiting them in person, usually posing as pregnant women in search of an abortion. When Carmen posed as a potential patient, she was sometimes in the examining room, on a table, with her feet in stirrups before she revealed her real mission and proffered a letter from the clergy. She later told interviewer Ellen Chesler, "I went through all the steps, short of having an actual abortion, before I would make it clear that I was not there for that purpose. Often I never got that far, because something about the situation was so appalling. I knew immediately that it was not a situation I thought we could refer women to . . . if an office was very filthy, for example, or if the doctor was very crude, unpleasant, God knows what."[40] In fact, sometimes Carmen dropped a doctor from the list after the first phone call. She later recalled, "You'd be told, 'Meet me at such and such a parking lot, at such and such a time, at such and such a place.' . . . 'Who is the doctor? Where is the office?' 'Don't worry about it.'"[41]

As Carmen recalled to Chesler, she and the other women who assessed the doctors looked for certain things. The doctor had to be a licensed physician but not necessarily a gynecologist; experience providing abortion care was more important than the specialist credential. They looked for doctors who did the procedure as a sideline in their own communities where they practiced openly. They felt strongly that the procedure should be done in an office or at least in a professional medical atmosphere, not in a motel room—often the preferred temporary location for illegal providers. They also considered the doctor's manner and personality in dealing with patients, "whether it was punitive and judgmental, or whether they were just treated as patients are most often treated." For at least the first year, Carmen said, cost was not a primary consideration, although that came to be a topic for negotiation as the CCS realized how valuable their referrals were to the physicians. Finally, the procedure had to be a dilation and curettage (D&C) done under either local or no anesthetic. Carmen said, "Although we understood that a woman undergoing the procedure without an anaesthetic was going to experience more pain, it was felt that she would be medically safer than she would be having a general anaesthetic in an office setting, especially in an illegal kind of thing, where if something were to go wrong, the doctor would really be in a difficult position" and her life could be jeopardized.[42] As they dealt with more doctors, CCS coordinators realized that experience was much more important than prestigious credentials; doctors who had done many abortions had a lower complication rate.[43]

In one week early in the operation of the service, the committee investigated five Philadelphia-area physicians and rejected them all.[44] Carmen visited many of the doctors herself—probably a couple of dozen or more, she recalled. Many times she traveled by plane, in spite of her fear of flying. She made a visit to Dr. David Sopher's clinic in London in April 1969 to see conditions there for herself; she was very satisfied with them.[45] Carmen dealt with doctors throughout the operation of the CCS, maintaining the roster of approved providers, receiving reports from women who used their services, and eventually negotiating lower fees. Carmen threatened to drop—and sometimes did drop—physicians from the CCS roster if they treated women unprofessionally or charged higher fees than those agreed on. Most were at pains to comply with her requirements.

The CCS was a great advantage to the doctors they worked with, first in sheer numbers of referrals. Those numbers were what gave the CCS economic leverage in negotiating price and quality. Doctors—especially those operating illegally or on the margins of the law—in the United States were also grateful for the clergy's screening process, which checked the dates of the pregnancy, gave women information about the abortion procedure, and reminded women of the risks the doctors were taking. One physician who took CCS referrals in Texas told writer Carole Joffe "that the patients who came to him through the clergy consultation network as a whole suffered less pain than those who came from other referrals. . . . 'They were less scared, they were more confident, . . . they had some issues they had [already] talked about. . . . I certainly became aware that fear was a major contributor to your reaction to the procedure.'"[46]

Carmen also coordinated the clergy, enforcing the service's inflexible rule that women always be referred out of state for their abortions so as to confuse jurisdictions. In fact, some clergy—notably Spencer Parsons in Chicago—did make in-state referrals, but presumably without Carmen's knowledge; she dropped clergy from the CCS for violating that rule or for accepting money for counseling. Moody said, "Anyone that even thought about charging something, they were out, quickly. And Arlene was the enforcer. And she was wonderful. . . .

She didn't mind saying, 'Those clergy are a bunch of shitheads! They don't know from nothin'.' And she would bring 'em around. I mean, they learned that if they didn't follow the rules of our thing, they were in trouble—with her."[47] She clearly did not feel an automatic affinity with clergy; she told Chesler, "Just because they're clergy, I mean, there's a barrier, there's an obstacle for me between myself and a clergyperson, be it rabbi or minister, it doesn't matter. There are very few clergy who have been able to break open that barrier for me, so that I think of them as people. But there are some, and some of them were part of that original twenty-one who participated at the very start. I remember thinking that they were just sort of WASPs, you know, here I was with all these WASPs" (white Anglo-Saxon Protestants).[48] She expressed disappointment and even anger that more rabbis didn't participate in the CCS and recalled that many women called and asked to speak with a rabbi. But clergy remember her admiringly as charming and bright—and fiercely protective of the CCS and the women it served. From her office at Judson, Carmen ran a nationwide network of hundreds of ministers and rabbis and a roster of doctors that extended throughout the United States and into Canada, Puerto Rico, Mexico, England, and Japan, all of whom, clergy and physicians alike, were used to doing things their own way. Carmen made sure that they all did things the CCS way, and she dealt with problems that arose.

In 1968, one of the original CCS clergy referred three women who could not afford to travel to Puerto Rico to a New Jersey physician who was not on the list of CCS providers but whose credentials he had checked himself. In fact, the doctor was loaning his office to an unlicensed abortionist, who took the three women's money and then did not complete their abortions. Carmen and Moody arranged for several imposing men from Judson's congregation to visit the abortionist along with one of the women, and the money was returned. However the three women's pregnancies were now advanced enough that they could not obtain safe abortions, and all three carried their pregnancies to term.[49]

Carmen even dealt boldly with the Mafia. Moody recalled, "New Jersey was the only state in which the Mafia controlled abortion. And we found out about that later, when we started the service, and we were [sending] hundreds of women [there] all the time. They offered us $50 a woman for referrals. And Arlene Carmen turned it down. No way."[50]

Carmen was a guiding force for the CCS, and she and Moody wrote its first history, *Abortion Counseling and Social Change, from Illegal Act to Medical Practice: The Story of the Clergy Consultation Service on Abortion*. It was a slim volume published in 1973, just as the *Roe v. Wade* decision changed abortion politics completely. She was instrumental in founding the free-standing clinic that came to be known as Women's Services. She helped organize the many avant-garde arts events that

Judson sponsored. From 1975 to 1985, she and Moody did pioneering work on the streets with sex workers, and they wrote *Working Women: The Subterranean World of Street Prostitution*, published in 1985 by Harper & Row. Carmen campaigned against censorship and was an organizer of the People With AIDS Health Group. She managed to accomplish all of this before her life was cut short from congestive heart failure in 1994 at the age of fifty-eight.

4

The Network Grows

By the summer of 1967, the Clergy Consultation Service of New York City was well under way, but the number of calls from women outside the New York City area—whom the clergy refused to counsel by phone—indicated there was also a vast need nationwide. The New York group quickly sought out clergy elsewhere who could start up counseling services in other regions. Moody said of the rapid expansion of the CCS that "it was so easy to move from locale to locale because it didn't cost much, and if one church were willing to have the answering machine, then you were in business. In the early days most of the people were Baptists that led these things, because I was Baptist and I didn't know a lot of other people out there. Most of them were campus-oriented people."[1] The first CCS spin-offs were in New Jersey, Pennsylvania, and Los Angeles.

New Jersey

Rev. Charles H. "Chick" Straut Jr., a Methodist minister in northern New Jersey, had been a very public activist since he was first arrested at a February 1965 peace vigil outside the New York Hilton Hotel, where world leaders were meeting to talk about how they could implement Pope John XXIII's 1963 encyclical, *Pacem in Terris*, calling for world peace.[2] Straut had been a stalwart of civil rights and antiwar actions in the New York area and Washington, DC, and he was outspoken. "The press loved me," he said. "Nobody else in the area was so outwardly radical."[3] His East Rutherford church, located in a mainly Polish and Italian Catholic area, was rather conservative. Straut estimated that

43

"the congregation was about one third behind what I was doing, one third were turned off, and one third couldn't make up their mind." He recalled that one day the minister from an even more conservative Free Methodist church in the area told Straut about what Moody was doing in New York. Straut's immediate response was, "'Abortion? That's murder!' That's what I'd always been taught." The other pastor suggested, "Why don't we sit in on a meeting with Moody?" Moody was one of Straut's heroes for his civil rights and antiwar work, and since Straut was aligned with almost everything else Moody said, he agreed to a meeting. They recruited UCC minister John Wightman and another local clergyman, and the four went to New York City, attended a meeting of the CCS, and then spoke privately with Moody afterward. Straut said, "He convinced me. On the ride home, we decided we would do something about this."[4]

They soon recruited thirty-six clergy members statewide, all Protestant or Jewish, divided them into six regions, and set up a rotation with one counselor for each region on call one week out of every six, "so it wasn't too much work if you were working in a parish," Straut said. As an all-male group, they felt it was important to offer a woman's voice for callers, so Straut's wife, Judy, recorded the weekly message on the answering machine. Because Straut had dealt with reporters before, he served as spokesperson and chair of the group. Modeling themselves on the New York CCS, they went to the newspapers with a public announcement in November 1968. They took out listings under "Abortion, New Jersey Clergy Consultation Service" in telephone books throughout the state.[5] In the first year, the New Jersey CCS counseled 1,100 women, 50 percent of whom — and they knew "almost exactly," Straut said, because the clergy asked women to fill in anonymous surveys — were Roman Catholic. They began referring women to doctors in Puerto Rico, Japan, and Great Britain.

Unlike the New York group, the New Jersey clergy dealt directly with doctors. Straut recalled, "I got invited to come to Mexico City to meet with some doctors, inspect their clinics, and approve the cleanliness and safety standards. That expanded our reach." But his independence from the rules and standards set by Moody nearly led to at least one serious problem. On his own, Straut located an abortion provider in Brooklyn, and the New Jersey clergy began referring to him. Then a woman who had used the Brooklyn doctor called the clergy to report that she had suffered a serious infection after her procedure. Straut said, "She didn't want to make trouble or damage our operation because it was doing so much good, but she thought we ought to know. So I visited the doctor and told him we would have to stop using him."[6]

Meanwhile, Straut's activities and outspokenness were causing problems in his congregation and with his bishop. As a Eugene McCarthy alternate delegate to the 1968 Democratic Convention in Chicago, Straut was at the front of the closing-night protest march. The group was stopped by a phalanx of police and National Guard troops, some in tanks. The lead forty protesters, which included the Chicago Seven and Straut, were arrested for defying police orders not to step off the curb. As they were hauled away in paddy wagons, they looked back to see the police and troops blasting the crowd of protesters with tear gas. Judy Straut was in the crowd and, as he later learned, "ran like hell" back to the hotel where Democratic Party workers gave her $25 bail for her husband. They caught the red-eye flight that night, and he woke up in the morning to front-page headlines and pictures of himself in the paper. Although Straut had supporters in his congregation, the net effect of his activities made his parish work difficult. His bishop recommended that he move into social justice work. Straut left his parish in December 1969 to become director of the Brooklyn division of the New York City Council of Churches.[7]

The New Jersey CCS carried on through a transition period. Rev. Orrin T. "Ted" Hardgrove of the Community Baptist Church of Parsippany, already a counselor in the group, set up the counseling rotation for northern New Jersey and attended meetings. He recalled that there were then only four or five clergy participants in his area. He served a rather conservative congregation, most of whom did not know of his abortion referral work, so unlike Straut, he did not serve as a public spokesperson, and he did not advertise the group.[8] Statewide, the group had thirty-one members in 1969.[9] In November of that year, Rev. John Wightman, a UCC minister, took over as state chairperson. Early on, Wightman said, when the group made most of its referrals to Puerto Rico or England, "Most women who came to me had access to money somewhere. I'm not aware of anyone who didn't go" because of money, he recalled, but added, "It was a relief to send women to New York" after abortion became legal there in 1970.[10]

By 1972, the New Jersey CCS had about forty-five members, and it continued its work, with Wightman as chair, until after the *Roe v. Wade* decision. Wightman told the *New York Times* that before *Roe v. Wade*, the CCS received an average of thirty calls a week just from Essex County, but during the whole summer after *Roe*, they received "only four or five calls."[11]

Pennsylvania

Finding that many women were coming to the New York CCS from Philadelphia, Howard Moody called his friend Rev. Allen J. Hinand, whose Central Baptist Church was actually in Wayne, Pennsylvania, one of the old-money Main Line suburbs of Philadelphia. Hinand told historian Joshua Wolff, "Howard called me and said, 'This is ridiculous; starting in about two months

I'm going to tell these [Pennsylvania] women to call you!'" Hinand laughed, adding, "That was an incentive!"[12]

Hinand had grown up in the mine country of Butte, Montana, the son of a railroad union organizer. He belonged to a socially conscious Baptist church that counted both mine management and mine workers among its members. Hinand said he had never met a Republican or experienced a conservative church until he attended a Baptist college in Oregon. After graduation, he traveled east for the first time to enroll in Andover Newton Theological School in the Boston area; as a seminary student he attended his first national American Baptist conventions. "The Baptist circle of liberal clergy is very small, so you become acquainted with each other at the annual convention," Hinand said in a 2010 interview.[13] Moody and Spencer Parsons became mentors for Hinand and other young, liberal Baptist ministers. After graduating from seminary in 1963, Hinand was called to Central Baptist Church in Wayne, Pennsylvania, as director of Christian education and two years later became co-pastor with Rev. Richard Kech. With the national headquarters of American Baptist Churches located in nearby Valley Forge, Central's congregation at that time included some fifty ordained Baptist ministers, Hinand recalled.[14] Hinand saw the church as a place to prepare people to improve their community, and he was active in many social justice issues, holding debates on the Vietnam War, establishing a youth center, and working on fair housing issues.[15]

After Moody's call, Hinand phoned five or six close Baptist friends, including clergy from State College, Pittsburgh, and Philadelphia; from an ecumenical group in Wayne, he recruited a UCC minister, a Presbyterian, two Episcopalians, and three rabbis. Some went with him to an initial meeting with Moody in New York—the same meeting that Straut and the original New Jersey group attended. Then the larger group of Pennsylvania clergy spent an afternoon being trained at Central Baptist Church in Wayne. But Hinand felt an acute absence: "I was a feminist, and I felt strongly that women needed to be involved," he said. He called two women feminist friends. The first was Marilou Theunissen (pronounced Tennyson), whose husband, Bruce Theunissen, was a Presbyterian minister and a founding member of the CCS chapter.[16] The second was Barbara Krasner, who lived in King of Prussia; although she was Jewish, she had been active with Judson Memorial Church in New York City for years. With Judson, Krasner had helped establish a kind of house church that Moody described as being composed of "some Baptist liberals, some agnostic activists, and some strayed Jews." Krasner became an official member of Judson in 1969 without leaving Reform Judaism behind. She was a strong advocate for women's health and, starting in 1970, ran Judson's watchdog group on hospital abortions (see chapter 8).[17] The two women trained as counselors and served as full members of the CCS in spite of their layperson status. They also visited doctors as a team before the clergy made referrals. Theunissen later became director of the Pennsylvania CCS.[18]

The Philadelphia group consulted with five lawyers before beginning to quietly refer women.[19] They went public in November 1968; a *Philadelphia Bulletin* article listed eleven ministers and one rabbi by name and affiliation.[20] By May 1969, they reported that they had fifteen counselors, were receiving fifty to seventy-five calls a week, and were doing thirty to fifty counseling sessions a week.[21] The chapter was unusual in that they sent many women to local doctors, even though the national office strongly advised sending women out of state as a legal precaution. Theunissen asked her neighbor, Dr. John B. Franklin, an associate professor of obstetrics and gynecology at Jefferson Medical College in Philadelphia, to take abortion referrals from the CCS, and Franklin proved to be a crucial advocate with his medical colleagues. He recruited other doctors to take referrals, as well as psychiatrists who could approve abortions.[22]

The Metropolitan Associates of Philadelphia (MAP), an ecumenical, nonprofit lay ministry organization with which Hinand had worked, also formed a task force composed of doctors and others to pressure hospitals and physicians to increase the number of abortions they provided. The members saw part of their task as the education of doctors. When the task force first met, women's right to abortion "on demand" was "rejected by the doctors almost unanimously," but after meeting regularly for a year for discussion and hearing the cases of individuals seeking abortion, "many of these same doctors were performing abortion upon 'request,' i.e., abortions were being decided upon by the women, not the doctors."[23] In addition, a report in *Today's Health* in 1970 said that a survey had shown "that older physicians are more likely than their younger colleagues to favor abortion law reform. Perhaps it's because doctors long in practice have seen a greater number of anguished women with unwanted pregnancies."[24] In other words, doctors were influenced by the individual stories of women, just as the clergy was. As Dr. Robert Hall wrote in 1970, "Now that abortions are actually safer than childbirth, it's no longer within a doctor's purview to decide which women qualify and which do not."[25]

The doctors on the MAP task force were able to carry their new way of thinking to some of their colleagues and greatly increase the number of abortions performed in Philadelphia hospitals. The task force later concluded that employing doctors' networks and applying pressure from outside the hospital staff helped make the change, saying that insiders—in this case, staff doctors—are "greatly aided in attempts to effect change if they are perceived by those in power to be responding to outside pressures for change, rather than initiating change." The report also found that the CCS provided legitimacy to the staff physicians' efforts, eased "the physician's personal doubts, some of which carried over from a religious background," and helped legitimize abortion in the eyes of the public.[26]

By May 1969 the CCS reported that the Philadelphia counselors were sending half their referrals for local hospital abortions. Welfare paid for the procedures of those who qualified.[27] MAP reported, "One teaching hospital assumed an essentially open door policy and its practice increased from 12 to about 800 abortions a year. The number of ward abortions performed at the public city hospital changed from 50 to about 300 a year."[28] In February 1970, the CCS newsletter reported that the Philadelphia chapter, "after numerous meetings with doctors and hospital administrators now manages to put close to 80 percent of their women through local hospitals despite a law which is as restrictive as any in the country."[29] Such strong cooperation with the CCS by physicians and hospital administrators was rare.

California

Moody recruited from among his own contacts, and clergy and others around the country heard about the CCS from friends or news reports and called or wrote to Moody to learn more. One of the calls he received was from Elizabeth Canfield and Rev. S. Huw Anwyl of Los Angeles.

Anwyl was born in north Wales, in a Welsh-speaking Presbyterian family; even in 2006, after living in California for decades, he spoke with a musical lilt.[30] Asked where his passion for social justice came from, he recalled his upbringing as a Presbyterian in Wales, a "very fundamentalist" background. A young woman who became pregnant before marriage was barred from the fellowship until she had gone through a series of steps to return. "She would literally be ostracized," Anwyl said. He recalled such an instance when he was in his early teens. After a Sunday service, at the church meeting, the deacons discussed the young woman's case and decided that she would be permitted to attend services but not participate. One evening, young Huw and his father were walking home from evening services and saw the young woman and her boyfriend. Anwyl recalled,

> The general practice was when that happened she would have to walk on the other side of the street, and nobody would talk to her. So I'm walking with my father, and I remember thinking, well, what's he going to do? He went up to her and he stopped and crossed the road to her and talked to her. Probably that was, as much as anything, what for me implemented what this whole thing was all about. Everybody could see that he was talking to her; there was nothing in the dark about it. I said to him afterwards,

"Okay, why did you do that?" And he said, "Oh," he says, "she's still a person, still a person."

His father's simple, unafraid kindness was profoundly moving to Anwyl, even as he told the story six decades later. His father's action was prayer. "Prayer has to be practical, and I said, if you can do something about it, don't bother praying about it, just get on with it and do it."[31]

Anwyl joined the British air force and was stationed at the air navigation school near Bulawayo, Zimbabwe, then Rhodesia. He recalled,

> My job was as assistant to the station commander, so everything that he was seeing came across my desk. That literally meant that I saw everything that he had to deal with, and a lot of it, apart from the flying issues and the air navigation issues, were human problems—people being away from home, into primarily alcohol issues. My early days in the air force had pretty well tossed out the fundamentalism that I grew up with, because it didn't have answers that I was looking for. And came to one of those turning points where I thought, well, that wasn't doing anything, but what is, and what will do something to help in these situations?

Interested in what connects religion and practical action, Anwyl gave up his early involvement in Liberal Party politics and an offer of a job as a tobacco plantation supervisor to return to Britain and prepare for the entrance exams for Cambridge. There he found himself woefully unprepared academically. A librarian pointed him to the *Encyclopedia Britannica*, he started to read, and he pushed himself through university.[32]

Anwyl came to the United States in 1960 as a UCC minister. In those days, he was known by his Anglicized name, J. Hugh Anwyl. After a short stop in a Michigan parish, he took over Avalon Park Community Church in Chicago. Like many of the CCS clergy, he had a strong personality and a big commitment to justice that had a way of getting him in hot water with congregations. "I ended up being fired from that after three years. Honored by the city for my work in racial integration, fired by the Caucasian congregation, for obvious reasons." He helped with the merger of two churches, Presbyterian and UCC, in Bloomington. Then "I got a telephone call, one of those mythical things, calling me from Hollywood, literally that. It was a church in Hollywood. And so I ended up going out to Mount Hollywood Congregational Church." During his five years at Mount Hollywood, Anwyl became involved in the issue of abortion, and that was the major factor (among many, he said) that eventually got him fired again, in 1969.[33] He joined the California Committee on

Therapeutic Abortion (CCTA), the activist group that met in and around UCLA.

Elizabeth (Liz) Kanitz Canfield was also a member of the CCTA. Like Anwyl, she was an immigrant, having fled Vienna with her parents and siblings in 1938. In the United States, she attended nursing school, struggled to make a living in New York City, and eventually rejoined her family, who were now in California, where her father was a music professor at the University of Southern California. There she met her second husband, who worked in the oil industry, and she lived with him in Colombia and Venezuela. When they returned to California in 1957, his company folded and Canfield took various jobs — babysitting, ironing — to support her family. At that point, she recalled in an interview, "I needed something for the soul. You don't just work and work and work."[34] She volunteered at Planned Parenthood in Los Angeles, where her fluency in Spanish was helpful. She served as interpreter for Spanish-speaking women who came in for contraception.

One day the St. Louis philanthropist Joseph Sunnen came to Planned Parenthood looking to hire someone to take his company's contraceptive product, Emko Aerosol Foam, free of charge to women in poor neighborhoods of Los Angeles and around southern California. Her Planned Parenthood supervisor recommended Canfield. After a one-hour interview, Sunnen hired her and "stuffed my garage with boxes of Emko," she recalled. She visited Los Angeles housing projects and rural migrant labor camps. Canfield educated women about contraception and gave out the foam with "a card with my post office box, and they could reorder it. All free. They never paid anything for Emko." The Emko Program, as it came to be called, was replicated around the United States and in Puerto Rico into the 1960s.[35]

Canfield modestly said, "I did that for years and [then, in the mid-1960s] got a letter from Mr. Sunnen saying, 'I am interested in abortion law reform.' I'd never even thought about it. 'I would like you to explore a group at UCLA . . . who are interested in law reform, and they want my money, but I need to have you look at them.'" Canfield did not feel especially qualified to judge the CCTA, and even less so when she met with them. It was a group of eminent scholars, physicians, and lawyers — "Milton and Ruth Roemer, who were internationally known as public health figures; there was the president of the American College of OB-GYN, Keith Russell; and on and on, and I, little Liz, was going to examine them!" Canfield laughed at the memory. With the help of Ruth Roemer, she wrote a favorable report to Sunnen. "It wasn't very long after that I received a number 10, ordinary white envelope in the mail. With $100,000," Canfield recalled. The money came from the Sunnen Foundation and went to the Episcopal

Diocese of California to support the church's state abortion law reform efforts, including the work of the CCTA.[36]

Using Sunnen's grant, California Bishop James A. Pike pulled Rev. Lester Kinsolving from his parish in Salinas to become a full-time lobbyist for abortion law reform.[37] The CCTA hired a director and launched a powerful education and advocacy program. A new law was passed in the legislature and signed by Governor Ronald Reagan in June 1967, just about the time the New York CCS group went public. The new California law protected doctors who performed an abortion in a certified hospital when the hospital abortion board determined that continuation of the pregnancy would cause mental or physical harm to the woman or in cases of rape and incest.[38] It was a reform that made little practical difference to most women, but it was an improvement. On the day the new law took effect, the CCTA held a celebratory board meeting at which they asked Anwyl and Canfield to contact Moody and find out how to set up a CCS in California. Late in 1967, Anwyl and Canfield flew to New York to learn all they could.[39]

They founded a Los Angeles chapter of the CCS and went public on May 15, 1968—even before the New Jersey and Pennsylvania chapters—under the name Clergy Counseling Service for Problem Pregnancies. As the *New York Times* had done, the *Los Angeles Times* ran a story about the group on the front page, reported that nearly fifty clergy members were participating, and published the names and affiliations of a number of them, noting, "Nearly all the clergy are located in Los Angeles County except for two in Lompoc and one each in Riverside, Upland, Claremont and Oceanside. Eleven Unitarian-Universalist ministers are included, making it the largest-represented denomination in the counseling service."[40] Anwyl recalled, "The day after that story was in the *Times*, I had 293 calls."[41]

Two weeks later, Canfield reported to the national office that the Los Angeles group was overwhelmed. In their first eleven days they'd had more than 1,000 calls, more than 300 phone conversations between women and clergy counselors, and more than 100 counseling sessions; of those, only ten to fifteen "might possibly qualify for therapeutic abortion under the California law."[42] They scrambled to find other medical providers—doctors outside of Los Angeles and clinics in Mexico.

Anwyl also found medical and clergy resources that the CCS used in Japan, where abortions later in pregnancy were legal and safe. The need arose early in the work of the Los Angeles group because of a Canadian woman who came for counseling in 1968. Anwyl recalled that the woman was forty-three and had a heart problem and other medical concerns that made pregnancy a threat to her health. But she was already fifteen weeks pregnant, and she could not get an abortion in Canada.[43] At the time, the CCS was referring to providers who could help only up to twelve weeks, but Anwyl knew that later abortions were available—and legal—in Japan. The woman had funds to travel there but was unwilling to go alone. Anwyl told her he would try to find a travel companion for her. Every day she called back, but he had found no one. So on the third day, a Wednesday, Anwyl agreed to go with her to Japan. He hurried to make arrangements and get a visa in time to leave on Friday. But on Thursday he received another phone call from an Oregon student who had traveled to Tijuana for an abortion. She had thought she was twelve weeks pregnant, but in fact she was further along and was refused an abortion there. Anwyl told her to come to Los Angeles and he would help, on the condition that he speak with her parents. Her parents flew to Los Angeles that day, and on Friday, Anwyl, the student, and the Canadian woman were all on a plane to Tokyo. While the women were in the Tokyo clinic for two days, Anwyl had an idea. He went to a church organization and asked to meet with U.S. missionaries who were in Tokyo. "I said to them very simply, I don't expect you to agree with me on the issue of abortion, but I'm appealing to you, from the humanitarian point of view, to help out American women who come in here, haven't a clue about anything to do with Japan. And I must say, they made a huge difference, because ten or twelve of them responded." After that, when women needed later abortions, Anwyl called the CCS coordinator in Tokyo and gave him their arrival information. "They'd meet them at the plane, take them to the clinic, be with them, probably take them shopping afterwards, put them on the plane, and that was that. So they were key players at that—for a relatively short time, maybe a year or so."[44]

Anwyl recruited or assisted clergy in most of the western states to form new CCS chapters, and he said that he used to joke with Moody that Moody was the bishop of the East and Anwyl the bishop of the West. But the California chapter itself never expanded much beyond the Los Angeles area. That seems to have been primarily because nonclergy abortion referral groups were active in other areas of the state. As of 1969, the Los Angeles CCS was referring San Diego women to the women-run Abortion Counseling Service and northern California women to the Association to Repeal Abortion Laws—Patricia Maginnis and Lana Phelan's group—in San Francisco.[45]

Anwyl's job as minister at Mount Hollywood Congregational did not coexist easily with his work on the CCS and other causes. The congregation fired him in February 1969. The *Los Angeles Times* reported, "Moderator Purcell Brown Jr. said many members find little fault with Mr. Anwyl's positions and his personal involvement in political and social issues, but that many feel the pastor does not keep them adequately informed of his activities or involved in church decisions, nor does he spend enough time on members' personal needs." The article continued, "Mr. Anwyl conceded in an interview this week that he spends 70 to 80 hours a week with the abortion counseling service, which includes 50 ministers and rabbis."[46] His work with the CCS, however, was far from over. He received substantial funding for the CCS—and in March 1969 started a new organization to serve as its base, the Ecumenical Fellowship—from well-known investors and philanthropists Charles Munger and Warren Buffett.[47]

The CCS pushed the only slightly liberalized California abortion law to its limit. The 1967 reform allowed abortion only in cases of rape or incest or where a woman's physical or mental health was endangered. Early on, most of the women the Los Angeles CCS referred had to apply for abortions under the law's mental health provisions. This required one or more commonly two psychiatrists to state that the woman's mental health was in danger. The CCS referred women—and even provided transportation—to psychiatrists who were supportive and low cost. After the September 1969 California Supreme Court decision in the case of *People v. Belous*, which struck down the wording of the state abortion law as vague (see chapter 8), the approval process for abortions became much easier.

Anwyl, other clergy counselors, and supporters like Charlie Munger—who was already on the board of Planned Parenthood of Los Angeles and later joined the board of Good Samaritan Hospital—cajoled and pressed hospitals and doctors to take referrals from the CCS and make abortions more easily available. Initially they faced negative attitudes among doctors that were similar to those found by the Metropolitan Associates of Philadelphia; whereas in Philadelphia doctors were invited to meet for discussion and their minds changed over the course of a year, Anwyl apparently took a more confrontational approach. He recalled that at his first presentation to the Los Angeles Obstetrical and Gynecological Society, the doctors were "antagonistic, hostile." The physicians were shocked that a minister was doing abortion counseling.

Anwyl said the CCS "took over" two underused hospitals—that is, pressured administrators to increase the number of abortions performed. They worked with supportive physicians at UCLA and the University of Southern California and recruited from physician training programs there.[48] In March 1970 Anwyl told the *Los Angeles Times* that since the beginning, when the Los Angeles CCS referred 89 percent of women to Mexico and 5 percent to Japan, they were now referring 84 percent to doctors in California.[49] He said they used "economics, not idealism" to appeal to doctors, and the referral power of the CCS was such that they could negotiate price and insist the doctors do a certain number of procedures for free. "If a physician becomes judgemental or moralistic in his attitude toward the patient, if he charges too much or fails to meet our other requirements, he is immediately dropped," Anwyl told the *Los Angeles Times* in 1969.[50] In June 1970, the Los Angeles CCS, now with 100 clergy members, opened its own ten-room office at 3150 Olympic Boulevard. "Unfortunately, it still costs from $500 to $700 to terminate a pregnancy in California," Canfield was quoted as saying at the time. "However, the poor can get Medi-Cal assistance."[51]

Larry Lader wrote in his book *Abortion II*, "By establishing permanent hospital agreements all over California, Anwyl eliminated the cruel and cumbersome system of abortion committees and processed almost every case in less than two days, mainly for 'mental health' and usually without the cost of psychiatric approval letters."[52] Anwyl later said that the CCS was able to refer women within California even for late abortions, up to twenty-four weeks into pregnancy. The Los Angeles CCS was one of the few chapters willing to provide counseling and referrals to women from out of state. It was also the largest single chapter, with 100 clergy members and some lay counselors (including Canfield) in 1970. At the end of 1970, Canfield moved on to a paid job at University of California, Northridge. By then, the group's negotiations had brought the price of an abortion down from $500 or more to as low as $170.[53]

Hundreds of women came to California for abortions. Anwyl said that many came from the Midwest; the Chicago CCS sent quite a few women who did not want to travel to New York. Many came from Oregon, Arizona, Nevada, and Montana, and Anwyl traveled to Bozeman at one point to start a CCS chapter there. Although Colorado's abortion law had been liberalized, many women there still came to Los Angeles; Anwyl speculated that the resources in Colorado were limited, and some may have sought anonymity in traveling to another state. Anwyl recalled that for women in Washington state, King County Hospital in Seattle and other resources were available.[54]

Initially, Planned Parenthood had not been cooperative with the clergy group in terms of providing abortions. But the CCS had helped create a greater acceptance of abortion by the medical community in southern California, and in 1971 Planned Parenthood of Los Angeles (PPLA)—with CCS supporter Charlie Munger on its board—decided to expand its services to include abortion.[55] In April 1971 the CCS became a division of Planned Parenthood with Anwyl taking the title of associate director of PPLA.[56] In 1972 he became executive director of PPLA, a position he then held for seventeen years. By that time, the CCS counselors included a number of graduate students in psychology and social work.[57]

Following the merger of the Los Angeles CCS and PPLA, word came to the National CCS that the group now charged women $10 for counseling and referral. A 1972 article in *Seventeen* magazine, however, described it as a "strictly voluntary" donation.[58] At any rate, as part of Planned Parenthood, the LA CCS had become involved in the actual abortion process by running clinics and hiring doctors. These practices were perfectly acceptable at nonprofit clinics like those Planned Parenthood operated; but National CCS had set strict guidelines: CCS counselors could encourage donations, but were never to charge for counseling or referral services, and the ministers themselves were not to deal with doctors.[59] A 1972 article in the Santa Monica *Evening Outlook* even accused the CCS/Planned Parenthood of taking kickbacks for referrals, quoting Anwyl as saying, "We have contracts with the hospitals and the doctors (to which patients are referred). We get $20 from the hospital for each patient." The article calculated from Anwyl's estimate that the CCS referred about 1,000 patients a month that the group's income from the referrals could have been about $20,000 a month.[60] In any case, at some time in 1971, the National CCS dropped the California group from its official roster.[61] For women who used the Los Angeles referral service, the only practical difference was the $10; they continued to have access to clergy counselors, referrals, and treatment at a cost greatly reduced from just two years before.

Illinois

In early 1968, Moody contacted his American Baptist colleague, Rev. Dr. E. Spencer Parsons at the University of Chicago, to start a Chicago service.[62] Parsons, a Massachusetts native, had moved from a parish post in Newton Center to become Baptist university pastor for Greater Boston. He served students from Harvard, MIT, Radcliffe, and Wellesley, and ran a group that met in the Old Cambridge Baptist Church in Harvard Square. His wife, Ellie, opened their home every Sunday night of his tenure, sometimes drawing more than 100 students with her warm hospitality. They moved to Chicago in 1959, where Parsons became pastor of Hyde Park Baptist Church. In 1965, under his direction, the church made a second affiliation with the Congregational (now United Church of Christ) denomination so that students at the Congregational seminary across the street would feel comfortable as members (today the congregation is known as Hyde Park Union Church). About the time of the change, Parsons left to become dean of Rockefeller Chapel, the interdenominational chapel for the University of Chicago, where he served until 1979.[63] Under his stewardship, and at an explosive time politically—especially on the University of Chicago campus—the chapel became a center for war protest and other progressive causes.

The issue of abortion was not new to Parsons. In Massachusetts he had been a vocal proponent of changing the laws regarding contraception. Like

Anwyl in Los Angeles, Parsons had been a member of an abortion law reform group. Illinois Citizens for the Medical Control of Abortion was founded in December 1966 by Dr. Caroline (Lonny) Myers and Episcopal clergyman Don C. Shaw. The group organized conferences, ran a speakers' bureau, organized letter-writing campaigns, and testified at state hearings, and it received a grant from the Chicago-based Playboy Foundation.[64] It may seem paradoxical that Playboy, a commercial empire founded on magazines and clubs that put women on display for a predominantly male audience, would find itself allied with feminists and clergy. Social and religious criticism of the magazine, in fact, had led Playboy founder Hugh Hefner to respond by enunciating in the magazine between 1962 and 1966 a "Playboy Philosophy," taking a liberal stance on civil liberties in a society whose mores were changing quickly. Hefner started the Playboy Foundation in 1965 to foster "reproductive health and rights, human sexuality, civil rights and civil liberties, and First Amendment rights," and access to contraception and abortion law reform were two of the first causes it supported.[65] The Chicago CCS also received a grant from the foundation (see later discussion); few if any of the women who benefited from the service would have imagined that connection.

In December 1967, Moody had already been in touch with at least two Chicago-area clergymen who were interested in establishing a CCS there, but nothing formal had resulted.[66] Parsons invited Moody to speak at an April 1968 conference on abortion at the University of Chicago.[67] The following month at the American Baptist convention in Boston, Moody and Parsons spoke in support of a resolution recognizing abortion as "a matter of responsible personal decision."[68] At first Parsons limited his CCS participation to referring Chicago women to the New York group. But throughout that year, Moody pestered him to establish a working CCS chapter in Chicago, and in late 1968 Parsons began to organize.

As Parsons set about recruiting for a Chicago chapter, he knew who would likely be sympathetic. In a 2003 interview, he recalled that as dean of Rockefeller Chapel, he had many contacts among antiwar and civil rights activists. "There's no doubt that the people who are interested in the anti-war movement and the civil rights movement are also interested in the rights of women in terms of the abortion problem," he said. Those contacts resulted in an initial meeting of thirty-five to forty-five clergy members. Gynecologists explained the procedure, and a lawyer outlined the risks. Afterward, "after we picked ourselves up off the floor," Parsons said, about twenty clergy signed up. The group increased to thirty or thirty-five in the first few months.[69]

Clergy members were asked to contribute $10 or $20 each for start-up expenses, including the cost of sending a representative, graduate student

Ronald L. Hammerle, to New York for training (at a cost of $125).[70] The Chicago group began its work quietly in April 1969 and went public in December as the Chicago Area Clergy Consultation Service on Problem Pregnancies. Their telephone answering machine gave the names of four clergy with phone numbers in the 312 area code. As of March 1970, the service was receiving 80 to 125 calls a week.[71]

The Chicago CCS kept paper records on its patients, coded with a case number and a clergy number—no names. These forms give a pretty clear outline of what a session was supposed to cover and asked the clergy to record fairly detailed medical and demographic information about each counselee. (See Appendix B for a 1970 example.) The Chicago CCS continued to collect dues from its counselors (apparently $10 a year) and may have been unique in accepting—and, based on the wording of the interview form, even soliciting—donations from women at their counseling sessions. The New York group was adamant, for legal and ethical reasons, that the clergy handle no money, especially that no money change hands at counseling sessions, although they were grateful for donations that came with thank-you notes after women had undergone safe abortions.[72]

Later in its operation, however, the Chicago chapter actually did handle the money women paid for medical fees and plane tickets. Rev. Donna O. Schaper, who later succeeded Moody as senior minister at Judson, was a seminary student in Chicago in 1973. By the end of January of that year, abortion had been legalized nationwide by the *Roe v. Wade* decision, and legal status may have changed the Chicago chapter's willingness to handle money. Schaper recalled that three or four seminarians—and she was the only female seminary student at the time—had a kind of work-study job staffing a counseling office on Michigan Avenue. "Four afternoons a week, from four 'til seven, I would go down to this office downtown, and meet thirty minutes at a time with women who wanted to [go] to New York to get abortions. . . . They had already had some kind of screening, so I was not helping them make the decision. Somebody else had made the decision with them." Likely an ordained member of the clergy had done the initial counseling. "It would be my job to make sure they were sure, kind of open up the possibility that they weren't sure, and show them the medical procedure that would happen." Schaper had some props and a script for telling women what the procedure would be like. But most of the session involved travel arrangements. She recalled, "These were not people who had ever been on an airplane. *I* hadn't been on an airplane." She would explain the logistics of getting to the airport and how to get to the Women's Services clinic in New York City (see chapter 8). In Chicago these secondary counselors received women's checks for their medical fees and plane tickets.

"We charged $300 per woman, I'll never forget that, because it was a hundred and some for the abortion, and a hundred and some for the plane ticket. And clearly it was subsidized. Sometimes the hardest thing would be that they wouldn't have the money. Or they'd have $98 instead of $300. Every now and then I would just take the money out of my pocket and put it in. I was working for them, and I would just do it. Because it would be clear to me that women were so unbelievably forthcoming and grateful."[73]

Schaper is white, and many of the women she counseled were black. "The most poignant memory I have of it is a generalized memory, which is basically who I was, this dumb white kid, certainly not rich, but in graduate school, talking to mature African American women as if I knew something of what they were saying to me. But I remember feeling: just—just shut up, don't say anything, receive it, and kind of weep. I mean, that was my feeling." Schaper said she did weep with women. "A lot. A lot, a lot. And pray. Because they'd start praying. It was just so—heavy."[74]

Beyond the money transactions, Parsons also flouted—at least from time to time—the National CCS requirement that counselors refer women out of state. Specifically, he often sent Chicago-area women to Dr. T. R. M. Howard, a black surgeon who had been a civil rights leader in Mississippi. Howard had been closely involved in the Emmett Till murder case as a supporter of Till's family and was a nationally known speaker before he moved to the South Side of Chicago, where he opened a clinic, became an ordained Baptist minister, ran unsuccessfully for Congress, and promoted black entrepreneurship.[75] Parsons recalled in an interview that members of the feminist abortion referral group Jane had told him about Howard's clinic, which was only four blocks from Rockefeller Chapel. "I sent him all the people that I felt I could send safely," Parsons said. "You had to judge the person you were talking with, whether they were scatterbrained or whether they were very serious-minded people, and were aware of the consequences for me and for the chapel and the University, and for themselves and for the doctor." If he felt a counselee could be trusted, he sent her to Howard. Howard was perhaps the only resource for poor patients who could not afford either the regular cost of an abortion or the travel expense and time to go out of state. Howard had told Parsons, "I will not do an abortion for free. They can give me something. And I will accept it." But, he added, "I will not turn anyone away." Parsons said he never did. But he asked Parsons not to send only indigent patients, and Parsons made an effort to send a corresponding number of women who could pay the full price of $250 to perhaps $500. Parsons recalled Howard saying, "I'll tell you, if a little black girl comes in here, and she's in trouble, I'm going to do it for nothing. But your white middle-class people, they can pay. And I'm going to charge them." In general, Howard charged white abortion patients double the fee he did for black patients. "He was very frank and open," Parsons said, "and I enjoyed him."[76]

Parsons said that he reserved the risk of making in-state referrals for himself; he didn't want to put other Chicago clergy in greater legal jeopardy. But CCS chapters outside of Illinois referred many women to Dr. Howard as a highly skilled doctor who treated women with dignity. Rev. Carl Bielby, first head of the Michigan CCS, said that in 1968 he visited a Chicago clinic that was likely Howard's. He "put on a mask and went into the clinic and the operating room and stood at the elbow of the doctor and observed everything."[77] Bielby was impressed, Howard received sterling reviews from CCS patients, and no one referred to him by the CCS ever had a complication, according to Parsons. Dr. Edward Keemer, a black physician who did abortions in Detroit—including for women referred by the CCS—wrote that he had visited Howard's clinic in the early 1960s and was also impressed with the facility and Howard's skill. But Keemer, a self-described Marxist, disapproved of the profits that Howard made from his abortion work. In addition to being an exceptionally skilled surgical practitioner, Howard had a reputation for generosity and lavish entertaining. He did live on a grand scale for many years, but he encountered legal difficulties, including conviction on tax charges (he received a fine and a year's probation) and acquittal in an insurance fraud case and a 1968 trial for abortion (in which his acquittal was based on the fact that the policewoman who came to him as a patient was not actually pregnant, and therefore no abortion could have taken place). Howard opened the million-dollar Friendship Medical Center in 1972, where a staff of internists and specialists provided excellent general medical care in addition to the abortion practice. After the *Roe v. Wade* decision in 1973, and Howard's appearance on the cover of *Jet* magazine performing an abortion, public criticism and resignations by key medical staff resulted in financial troubles for the clinic, and Howard was heavily in debt at the time of his death in 1976.[78]

Besides the on-the-spot request for donations and the occasional in-state referrals, the Chicago CCS was different from other chapters in being especially diligent about asking women to report to them following their abortions. They received hundreds of letters and calls. These were very helpful in identifying bad practitioners or dangerous situations; in addition, the statistics were followed closely for research purposes by the graduate student who served as administrator of the Chicago service, Ron Hammerle.[79]

Hammerle was working on a doctorate at the University of Chicago Divinity School in a new program that combined academics and social action, and the link between the civil rights movement and the fight for abortion rights drew his interest. He met Parsons in 1967 through the group Illinois Citizens for the Medical Control of Abortion, and Hammerle became a full-time direct employee of the CCS, with his position funded by a grant from the Playboy Foundation. From an office in the University of Chicago's interfaith program building, he served as administrator of the Chicago CCS and the wider Illinois group, and he organized CCS chapters throughout the Midwest. Hammerle attributed the Chicago chapter's emphasis on follow-up reports from women to its administrative staff, which was larger than those of other chapters and thus able to process all the information that came in. He wrote his 1969 doctoral dissertation on abortion, working with the chair of the obstetrics and gynecology department at the University of Chicago Medical School, as well as advisers in the law and divinity schools.[80]

Other States

A network of Denver clergy had been referring women for abortions since the mid-1960s.[81] Although Colorado's law was liberalized in 1967 to permit abortion in cases of danger to the physical or mental health of the woman, the change had made little practical difference. The state health department reported that during the first year under the new law, only 262 therapeutic abortions were performed in Colorado hospitals.[82] Rabbi Buz Bogage, one of the founding members of the CCS in New York, moved to Denver in 1968, joined the existing network of clergy counselors, and chaired the group when they officially announced themselves as part of the CCS in January 1970.[83] The group started with about twelve clergy, listed by name in an article in the *Denver Post*'s *Empire* magazine, and by early 1972, under the chairmanship of Rev. Jerry Kolb, there were more than forty clergy counselors receiving 1,200 calls a year.[84] Women came from around the state, and Bogage estimated that 60 percent were Latina/Hispanic.

When a group of South Carolina clergy was contemplating starting a CCS chapter there, they invited Moody to come speak to them. He could not go on the date they requested, so he asked his friend Allen Hinand, the leader of the Pennsylvania CCS, to take his place. The group sent Hinand airplane tickets. A couple met him and took him to the board room at Furman University, a conservative school that was affiliated with the Southern Baptist Convention until 1991. "There were all these portraits of the past presidents. My first question was: 'Is the room bugged?' It seemed like a set-up." The group assured him it was not; someone on the faculty had arranged for them to meet there. There were twenty-five clergy from around the state. Hinand trained them in procedures, and in how they had set up the Pennsylvania chapter of the CCS, saying that their experience might be different. He told them, "You must follow the rules. If you're not going to follow the rules, just leave the room right now." By this time, in fact, Hinand was able to tell them the cautionary tale of the arrest of Pennsylvania CCS member Rev. Robert Wallace (see chapter 6). The South Carolina chapter went public in November 1970, with six ministers listed publicly. By 1972 the service had sixty-three counselors; they did not encounter any legal challenges.[85]

As chapters formed around the country, the New York office created the National CCS as a clearinghouse for information—including approved doctors—and protocols. Clergy either came to New York or Moody traveled to meetings around the country to conduct counselor training sessions in person.

The main funding for this expansion work came from GM heir Stewart R. Mott, who was a strong supporter of abortion reform. Mott's foundation Spectemur Agendo gave the CCS $10,000 in 1968, half of which was to be used for the National CCS, and half for the expenses of the New York City group.[86] As it turned out, the local group received enough contributions from grateful women to cover its own expenses, and the entire $10,000 was used for the National CCS.[87]

Apparently this grant made it possible to hire Rev. Bennett Owens in 1968 to reach out to clergy around the country and help them to establish new CCS chapters. Owens was a navy veteran who graduated from Yale Divinity School and served several Baptist churches before coming to New York City and serving as an administrator with the Episcopal Church. The church granted him a year's dismissal to work with the CCS.[88] Owens indicated that the National CCS was initially planned as a short-term project to establish chapters around the country that would then continue independently.[89] He left the group in late 1969, after about a year, but by then Moody and the directors of regional CCS chapters were able to train clergy to run new chapters, and the national office, coordinated by Arlene Carmen, continued to provide training, maintain lists of recommended (and blacklisted) physicians, disseminate information, and run national and regional meetings.

At a national meeting in New York on May 28, 1969—by which time the CCS had had some scares, both medically and legally—the clergy in attendance discussed the need for all the chapters in the growing network to be careful. They agreed to refer only to licensed physicians, check with the CCS in the state where the doctor was located before referring, and share negative reports about physicians. They would also be cautious about referring women who were more than twelve weeks pregnant.[90] That gathering in the spring of 1969 included representatives from CCS chapters in New York City; New Haven, CT; Los Angeles; Michigan; Chicago; Boston; Ithaca, NY; Chapel Hill, NC; New Jersey; Philadelphia; and Cleveland. In October 1969, twenty-four

Bridgeport, Connecticut, clergy started a CCS chapter with the sponsorship of the Connecticut League for Abortion Law Reform. By 1972, clergy had formed chapters—some much larger and more formalized than others—in thirty-eight states, Washington, DC, and Canada; in addition, there was the group in Japan that had formed to assist women referred from the United States.[91]

Hard numbers are elusive, because most CCS chapters did not keep written statistics—or at least we didn't find many. Carmen, who administered the national group, probably had the best overview. She said that by the time the CCS went out of business following the *Roe v. Wade* decision in 1973, there were 3,000 clergy members across the country. She estimated that as of 1970 they were referring 100,000 women a year—10,000 in New York alone. In 1971, at the annual conference of the National CCS in New York, the estimate of "between 125,000 and 150,000 annually" was called "conservative."[92] Taking an even more conservative 50,000 as an average for the early two years of the CCS, and 100,000 as an average for the later three and a half, it is quite likely that the CCS nationally referred 450,000 women for safe abortions.[93] If the average cost of an abortion was $300, the clergy might have brokered on the order of $135 million in fees. In 1969 Ron Hammerle did a similar calculation to demonstrate the clergy's power to negotiate.[94] It is impossible to estimate the numbers of deaths the CCS prevented by offering women alternatives to unsafe practitioners.

5

The Women

The procedure was over shortly, and the doctor patted my hand and told me I had been a good patient and should have no problems. I thanked him and then began to sob. My friend entered and asked the doctor why I was crying. He told her not to worry—that it wasn't because I was in pain. He knew in part why—because I was happy that it was over. But I don't think he realized how thankful I was that so many kind and concerned people had helped me along the way. . . . The operation was Wednesday and today is Saturday, and I'm sure I'll be able to return to teach on Monday. I could emotionally exclaim, "It's a miracle!"— but I am fully aware that it was through the efforts of some very under-standing, trustworthy, and talented human beings that I am now healthy and so happy. Thank-you hardly seems adequate for this truly new year, but sincerely,

Thank you.

A grateful teacher who has learned a great deal.

Letter to Rev. Hayes Fletcher of the Chicago Clergy Consultation Service,
January 3, 1969[1]

Who Used the CCS?

From 1967 to 1973, the Clergy Consultation Services across the country referred hundreds of thousands of women for safe abortions. All kinds of women came to the service, from very young to middle-aged, unmarried and married, of all religions, races, and ethnicities.[2] Recording the experiences of the women who used the service would be material for another book. The clergy remembered some individual women they counseled and in many cases were deeply affected by their interactions. They received feedback from some women after their abortions—by phone, in letters, or through personal encounters. This account of the women who used the CCS, then, is filtered through the eyes of the clergy.

The CCS kept some statistics. Of a sample consisting of 6,455 women counseled by the New York CCS early in its operation, about half were between eighteen and twenty-five years old. Two-thirds were single. More than 80 percent were white. About a third were Protestant, a third Catholic, and about a quarter were Jewish. Half came to their counseling meeting when their pregnancies were eight weeks along or less. Half had used no contraception at all.[3] In April 1970, the Chicago Area CCS reported similar statistics for a smaller sample. Of 1,152 women seen in one year, the group had completed questionnaires for only 78 women. Again, half were age eighteen to twenty-five, all but three were white, nearly half were ten weeks along or less, and three quarters had used no contraception. A higher proportion than in New York—three quarters—were Protestant. Chicago counselors noted who had accompanied each woman to her appointment: a "husband" or "mate" came with more than half; one or both parents accompanied fifteen women; others came with a friend or other relative; only twelve arrived alone.[4] Very few sought abortions for the kinds of mental or physical health reasons that hospital abortion committees usually required; the Chicago CCS estimated that 85 percent gave "family or environmental" reasons.[5]

The clergy did not ask women about their economic status, but at least in the beginning, the services that the counselors recommended were costly. The doctor's fee was several hundred dollars, and because all referrals were out of state or out of the country, travel time and expenses could be considerable. The clergy realized that their counseling, though free, was useless to poor women because the services they referred to were so expensive. Once they recognized their power, they negotiated to lower costs and obtain abortions at very low cost for some women.

The Process

Women were referred to the CCS by friends or by their doctors or family planning clinics; some learned about it from newspaper articles (most of which, starting with the first *New York Times* piece, included the service's local telephone number) or student publications. Popular magazines such as *Seventeen* and *New York* published information on how to contact the CCS.[6] In some cities women simply looked up "Abortion" in the phone book, or they heard about the CCS from feminist groups, their lawyers, or their own clergy. When the first black woman elected to the U.S. Congress, Shirley Chisholm, also became honorary president of the National Association for the Repeal of Abortion Laws (the full name of NARAL at the time) in 1969, she was interviewed widely in print and on television. As a result, she received many pleas for help in finding an abortion, and her congressional office replied with contact information for the CCS.[7]

When women phoned their local CCS, they heard a message listing several clergy names and phone numbers, and in some cases where they were located, so that women could choose to go to a counselor in their own area—or, if they wished, as far away as possible from their own area. Women then called the counselor—usually at a church office—to make an appointment. Many of the services made a point of having a woman record the outgoing answering machine messages to put callers more at ease. Only one chapter seems to have asked callers to leave their number on tape; Rev. Haywood D. Holderness Jr., a Presbyterian minister then in Mobile, ran the Alabama service and recalled that he phoned women back to make counseling appointments.[8]

Counseling

Parents, boyfriends, and husbands often accompanied women to their appointments. Counselors interviewed for this book made clear that their goal was to help women follow through on their own decisions. Sometimes it wasn't clear whether the decision presented to the counselor truly was the woman's own, but perhaps was her parents' or partner's. In such a case, the clergy counseled the woman alone.

Rev. Gregory Dell was a young Methodist associate pastor in Naperville, Illinois, when he began counseling for the CCS. He recalled, "One of the things that they didn't tell us in training but I learned very quickly is to be especially alert when a man called to make the appointment." When that happened, Dell said, he told the man, "I appreciate your calling, and it may be difficult for your wife, girlfriend, or whatever, but I really do need to talk with her, and it's up to her whether she wants to come by herself or with someone else." In one instance, a middle-aged businessman accompanied his young secretary, with whom he had been having a sexual relationship. Dell remembered her as seeming "relatively naive." He said, "It was very clear to me that this woman had very little understanding about herself, about what prerogatives she had, about whether this was something she wanted. *He* was very clear." She was twenty-two weeks pregnant, which meant that the only option for an abortion was going to Tokyo. "That was no problem for him. For *him*," Dell recalled with fresh indignation. He asked the man to leave so that the woman could talk with him in private. For him, an important part of counseling was "to say to a woman, this is a matter of choice, this isn't a matter that someone else decides this is the way you should handle this pregnancy. *You* get to make that decision, not the man involved, not your parents, not someone else, but you get to make the decision." Whether a woman came to the session with her mind made up or was still unsure, Dell said it was important for her to have a conversation about all the options—keeping the baby, adoption or other kinds of legal arrangements, or abortion. "I think that's what becomes empowering, is when people feel they can choose. It's when people feel they have no choice that I think that the tragedy gets multiplied," he said.[9] Dell had graduated from Duke Divinity School, and he discussed some of his formative experiences at seminary in a fond and ironic way during a 2004 interview, saying, "you had to be against the Vietnam War, otherwise you couldn't graduate from seminary." When Dell was suspended by the Methodist church in 1990 for conducting a union ceremony for a same-sex couple, he was also fired by Garrett-Evangelical Theological Seminary; he noted that the seminary was "shifting" in terms of its support for progressive causes.

Minors who came alone to a counseling session were generally urged to confide in a parent or, if that was impossible, another relative. Written policy of the Iowa CCS required that a minor must either be accompanied to her counseling session by a parent "or be able to demonstrate to the counselor's satisfaction that she is 'emancipated,' generally free from the control of her parents."[10] The Milwaukee Area CCS proposed more stringent guidelines, directing that a parent or guardian must be present and give consent.[11] We heard of teenage girls and couples who were counseled by the CCS in many locations; this must have been a judgment call on the part of individual counselors.

Dell remembered a teenager, fifteen or sixteen years old, who had not told her parents that she was pregnant. She seemed very uncomfortable and unsure about what she wanted to do about her pregnancy. Dell recalled, "I encouraged her to consider talking to her parents about it. She said, 'I think they'll kill me.' I said, 'I can imagine that they could be very upset and you would be very upset. But sometimes parents come through in ways that you wouldn't expect.' And she told her parents, and they threw her out." Dell was overcome with emotion at the memory. "Christmas Eve, staying by herself in somebody else's house, eight-and-a-half months pregnant," he said. She stayed in touch with Dell for more than a year afterward. She put the baby up for adoption. But, Dell said, she felt as if she had made her own decision. "It was painful to someone who was involved with her in that decision making. I don't think I would have told her to do otherwise or offered to her the options otherwise, but— that's part of what gets missed as people talk about this, that this is not a simple circumstance for most women."[12]

Rev. Orrin D. Judd was the minister at Central Baptist Church in East Orange, New Jersey, when two college students came to see him. He discerned that something was not right, so he spoke with them separately. The young woman told him "No, I really would like to keep the baby, and hopefully it will keep us together." But when Judd spoke to her boyfriend alone, "he said, 'I was on the verge of breaking up with her, but I'm willing to support her through the abortion.' I called them together and said, 'You two have some things you need to talk about. She's operating on an assumption that's not valid. Talk it out, and if you decide for the abortion, come back and I'll give you the information.' They came back and I gave them the information." Judd remembered another young girl who came in with her parents. "The parents were pushing her for the abortion, but she seemed indecisive. So, again, I split them up. She wanted to keep the baby, but she was expecting her mother to help her with the baby. I told them to go home and talk it over. They came back and she decided she wanted the abortion. I feel like I did a real service, just helping people be clear about what they really wanted—what's right for them, not what's right for me. I was helping them to make a decision that they could live with and feel good about."[13]

Even affluent adult women with many resources sought the help of the clergy. Rev. Robert Pierce, an American Baptist and a founding member of the New York CCS, was working at the National Council of Churches office in the youth department in 1967. He recalled his surprise at the very first woman who came to him for counseling. She was in her mid- to late forties, with a substantial career, wanting to terminate a pregnancy. Although her sister was a doctor, she felt she couldn't talk with her about it. What surprised Pierce was not that she didn't have her own resources to find a safe abortion. "It was that she was so alone. Here she was, such a professional woman, and felt so alone. There was no place to turn." Pierce recalled thinking at the time, "Well, we're doing the right thing, we're doing some of the right stuff."[14]

Not every woman needed this kind of sensitive and at best empowering counseling, nor did every counselor feel the need to provide such detailed counseling in every case. One Conservative rabbi was in his mid-thirties and leading a congregation on Long Island in 1967 when he read about the CCS in the *New York Times*. He immediately called Howard Moody and asked to join the group. He estimated that he counseled a total of 500 women up to 1970, meeting them either in his office or at his home. He later wrote that the largest identifiable group was about twenty nurses who were Catholic. "I imagine the guys thought nurses were knowledgeable enough to take care of their own contraception, but the gals disbelieved in birth control; at least until they got pregnant." He recalled a forty-nine-year-old Holocaust survivor who said she would kill herself rather than bear another child. He remembered "a fourteen-year-old whose mother lamented she had left her child alone for Thanksgiving eve, and berated herself over and over. The pregnant daughter, when I talked with her alone for a minute or two, exclaimed, 'My mother is an idiot! She thinks you can only get pregnant at night!'"

The rabbi said, "I learned to stay out of their business. They needed help, not counseling. They universally didn't like the idea of having an abortion, but having a baby seemed crazy to them. They needed a name, address and phone number."[15] As he pointed out, many women came to the counseling meetings with their minds firmly made up, needing the valuable referral information, and they rejected counseling. Rev. Allen J. Hinand, who founded the Pennsylvania CCS, estimated in 1969 that "95 percent of the women who come into this office already have made up their minds that they want an abortion."[16]

Rev. Tom Davis, then chaplain at Skidmore College in Saratoga, New York, and his wife, Rev. Betsy Davis (who died in 2002), were members of the Capitol Area Clergy Consultation Service on Problem Pregnancies, which served a large area around Albany. As an undergraduate at Dartmouth College, Davis got involved with the student Christian movement, which was "pretty radical at that time" and took up the cause of civil rights. Davis went on to study under Reinhold Niebuhr (1892–1971) at Union Theological Seminary in New York City. Niebuhr developed a philosophical perspective known as Christian realism, which Davis summarized as "Human beings could indeed be rotten at the same time that they could display sacrificial love." This approach was developed in the context of World War II and the Holocaust. Davis's theological outlook was also influenced by his experiences as University of North Carolina chaplain from 1960 to 1963. His campus work during those years was focused on the civil rights movement. Following the completion of his Ph.D. in 1966, Davis went to Skidmore College to teach religion and serve as campus chaplain to the 1,400 women students. He said that Niebuhr's course on the history of ethics opened his eyes to religion's treatment of women. He recalled Niebuhr teaching that in Neolithic times hunter-gatherers regarded women as touched with the sacred due to their childbearing capability. When men became jealous of this, they invented religion to control women's reproductive capabilities. "Women . . . are going to have abortions. When women were dying because they could not—and right next to the hospitals where a safe procedure was available and they couldn't give it to them—that was evil. That was a moral evil." Davis also said of the reformer John Calvin's (1509–1564) role in developing Protestant theology, "You have to have a theology that accepts the wisdom of what human beings learn about life, and incorporate them. And Protestantism at its best has always done that." Davis held up as an example Calvin's development of divorce laws in Geneva, using his experience, with some Roman precedent, to tailor laws that fit the contemporary situation.

Davis said that most of the women he counseled had given their decision careful consideration before coming to talk to him. "You know, you go into this thinking that women are going to need a lot of conversation with a wise minister like you. Well, that's baloney. They've thought about this a long time." He remembered one or two sessions with women "who were concerned about the status of their soul" and a few calls from women after their abortions, who feared they would go to hell. But in general, he said, "I was educated by these women as to how clear they were about what they were doing, and they'd thought it through, and it was very matter-of-fact in some cases. Not that they were taking it lightly; it wasn't lightly; it was a serious matter for them. But they really didn't need any of my worldly wisdom. They knew what they wanted." Davis recounted his most memorable counseling session: "There was a woman who was working in a factory somewhere, she was in a blue-collar job, a very burly woman. [She] came in, and she just said, flat-out, 'I ain't interested in any sermons here.' And I said, 'Okay.' And she said, 'Do I look like a friggin' mother to you?' I said, 'Here's the number.' And she left. She was very angry that she was pregnant, and very determined that she would not have the child."[17]

Davis later headed the Clergy Advisory Board of the Planned Parenthood Federation of America and wrote a history of Planned Parenthood's relationship with clergy.[18] He spoke in an interview about a 1955 Planned Parenthood conference on abortion, perhaps the first public discussion of abortion by mainstream physicians in the United States. The gathering included doctors who had been prosecuted—and even gone to prison—for performing illegal abortions, because they knew the most about the subject. Almost all the attendees were men and some of their attitudes toward women were sexist. But Davis was particularly impressed with one doctor who stood up and said, "The determination of a woman who wants a child and is infertile, her determination to have a child is really amazing and strong. It does not even begin to compare with the determination of a woman who is pregnant and doesn't want the child." Davis said that it was remarkable at the time for a physician to say publicly that it was useless to try to dissuade women who want to end a pregnancy. "You're not going to persuade them; they'll even risk their lives," Davis said. As a counselor, he said, "my sense of it was that the women who came to see me were pretty determined, pretty understanding, some of them were older than I was, and they knew what they wanted to do."[19]

One woman who had an abortion while a first-year student at Central Michigan University expressed her frustration with the CCS in an interview for the 1992 film *Back Alley Detroit*. She complained that she and her boyfriend had had to travel some seventy miles from Mt. Pleasant to Lansing to speak in person to a clergy counselor who, she said, "could have given us a number over the phone." She recalled that the counselor told the couple "we were bad kids, and then gave us the number."[20] Although the founders of the CCS intended to remove barriers and stigma for women who sought abortions, participating clergy counseled in their own styles. Their encounter with a judgmental CCS counselor was the only such report we uncovered in our research, but of course there may have been others.

Abortion Experiences

Women's experiences of the abortion itself were as different as the women and the practitioners to whom they were referred. No matter how certain they were of their decision, and how much the counselors tried to prepare them, the procedure and all that led up to and followed it could be surprising—for good and for bad.

The CCS counselors asked women to report back on their procedures. Most women did not contact their counselors again, but many of those who did clearly knew that the information would be helpful to other women. Carmen and Moody wrote that 40 percent of the women referred by the New York CCS reported back. When the New York group started using a new doctor, just one counselor made those referrals and urged every woman to report on whether the quality of treatment and the price were exactly as she had been told to expect. Only after a few weeks of good reports was the doctor's name added to the list of approved practitioners for all counselors to recommend.

Some of the letters that were mainly thank-you notes still conveyed information about a woman's experience. An undated typewritten letter to Spencer Parsons said, "I felt so much better after talking with you. I was still nervous about it but not quite as afraid. Everything followed through exactly as you said it would." The writer reported that the doctor was competent, "kind and patient," and she returned home the following day with no complications. She asked Parsons to thank the doctor again for her and concluded, "Let me tell you again how grateful I am for kindness and your help. When I left your office that day I didn't feel like such a low person. I appreciated your understanding as much as anything."[21]

Some of the very detailed letters conveyed affirming and positive abortion stories. For example, a Chicago-area woman who traveled to Mexico City with her husband for her abortion sent a typewritten note dated April 7, 1970, to her CCS counselor reporting on her experience. Her husband had been asked to wait for her at their hotel, "probably for lack of room and also for the morale of those who came alone." She described the ride to the clinic with the fourteen other women seeking abortions that day, saying that it "induced a spirit of community among us all which helped to diminish the fright." As the women went upstairs two at a time for their procedures, the driver set out cookies and coffee cups to serve the first two when they returned. The writer said, "None of us could believe that they would be in any condition to eat, but within fifteen minutes after her operation the first girl was fully recovered, with appetite intact. The anesthetic caused temporary nausea and vomiting in some of us, but within an hour, all had recovered." The procedure took only five to seven minutes, she said, so three hours later all fifteen women were ready to return to the hotel. Some flew home that evening.[22]

On the other hand, we found a far from ideal experience in another letter written to Rev. John Mendelsohn of Chicago's First Unitarian Church after a woman's abortion in 1970. Mendelsohn had referred her to Dr. Jesse Ketchum, who was then in Buffalo, New York. She described arriving with a friend at a hotel in Buffalo and waiting two hours to see Ketchum. She was then called into Ketchum's "office" suite—an inner waiting room with plush carpeting and crystal chandeliers, two small procedure rooms, a dressing room, and a bathroom. She said the doctor injected her with medication; nonetheless the procedure "was extremely painful and I was terribly scared, but I sobbed quietly so as not to disturb the goings on." Immediately after the procedure, she continued, "the receptionist walked in with a bucket of water and a sponge and asked me to cleanse myself from the pool of blood I lay in and that I get dressed right away. I was very tired. I asked her for help, but I don't think she wanted to get her dress stained." The writer could hear a young girl in the next room screaming in pain. "Feeling rather faint, I got up to get dressed, still crying, when the receptionist came back in and asked in her heartwarming sweet smile, but with all the sincerity of her false eye lashes, 'Isn't *this* what you wanted?'" The woman stayed at the Buffalo YWCA for two days before returning to the Chicago area. "I stayed home for three weeks and returned to work. On my second day back to work, I was overcome with pains similar to those of that long, past hour, and I fainted." Her family physician diagnosed an inflammation, but not a serious infection, and she stayed home for another week. In spite of her bad experience, she concluded her letter by saying, "At this date, I feel pretty good. But I wanted to tell you of my experience. I do believe that Dr. Ketchum is probably a very capable abortionist; it is just that what I saw did in no way meet what I expected. . . . I would like to thank you, though, ever so much, for helping me when I needed it most. Thank God, it's all over now.[23]

The CCS took women's negative reports very seriously and acted on them. A major complication, mistreatment, or repeated overcharging resulted in a doctor being dropped from the referral list. Carmen and Moody wrote, "Usually within several days the doctor would be on the phone wondering why we had stopped sending patients. If our only complaints had to do with overcharging, we would usually give him another chance if he promised to stand by the agreed-upon fee."[24] On the other hand, the need to find enough competent doctors in many areas of the country forced the clergy to compromise a little on their standards for providers. They preferred those who worked in their own clinical office setting; nonetheless they referred to Ketchum, who performed procedures in hotel rooms. Although they avoided physicians who were known to be physically or sexually abusive and sought those who treated women with dignity, there still were instances of doctors or their staff who were shaming or insensitive (as Ketchum's assistant was) or patronizing—as in the letter that opens this chapter, describing a doctor who patted a woman's hand and said she had been "a good patient." The doctors' competence and the women's safety were clearly the priorities of the service.

In spite of the counselors' efforts to enable women to reach decisions that they felt comfortable with, some did report complicated feelings of regret. In 1971, Spencer Parsons, then chair of the Chicago CCS and dean of Rockefeller Chapel at the University of Chicago, received a letter from a woman he had referred to Kansas City for an abortion. She found the caregivers pleasant, but she developed an infection that made the experience "quite painful." For her, however, the infection was not the only repercussion. She wrote, "Although the procedures for the operation are quite simple, I'm afraid that the after effect is not quite as simple. Doctors can administer a drug for just about every symptom, and can relieve most pain with various types of drugs, but it's really a shame that there is nothing that can help eliminate the pain inside a person (i.e., emotional) except time itself." Nevertheless, the writer thanked Parsons for his help and for the ease of making arrangements. She wrote, "I would like to say that I'm grateful for your organization which will be able to help so many other girls like myself, but I wish for all girls that they would never have to experience an abortion. In my opinion, there is no greater loss than giving up your baby." She concluded the letter, "Again, my appreciation is extended to you, and I honestly don't know what I would have done without your help. Please don't think that because I stated that I wished that no girl would have to undergo an abortion, that I am not thankful for myself. I had to learn the hard way, but at least I learned."[25] The CCS gave follow-up counseling in many such instances, and some services were able to refer Catholic women to a sympathetic priest or nun if their misgivings were based on their religion.

Of the women's letters that are preserved, most are simple thanks. One such sample was a handwritten note to Spencer Parsons from a Michigan couple: "It is difficult to put into words how thankful we are for the help you gave us last month, when we so desperately needed someone to turn to. We used the Chicago number you gave us and your confidence in that doctor is certainly justified. He was very good—there was no pain and no complications. Our family physician told us he did an excellent job. As we look back it seems like a miracle that we were given your name to contact. You're doing a wonderful service and we shall always be grateful to you."[26]

But the service that the clergy provided to women who were accessing abortion providers entailed a legal risk, which is the subject of the next chapter.

6

Brushes with the Law

O n the Monday morning in May 1967 when the *New York Times* published
the intentions of the Clergy Consultation Service on its front page, the twenty-
one clergy named in the article half expected to hear police knocking at their
doors. They had set out precautionary guidelines—counsel only in person,
refer women out of state to confuse jurisdictions, keep minimal paper records,
and never charge a fee. On the advice of their legal counsel, the group had decided against meeting with the district attorney's staff ahead of time to clear up
questions of legality. Howard Moody recalled that lawyer Ephraim London
told them, "Don't admit that you're breaking the law, *ever*. That's not your
place." Contacting law enforcement before the service began might have implied
that they had doubts about their own legal status.[1] In spite of such precautions,
there were some notable instances of clergy running into trouble with the law,
including Rev. Bob Hare in Cleveland and Massachusetts, Rabbi Max Ticktin
in Chicago and Michigan, and Rev. Robert Wallace in Pennsylvania. None of
these men were successfully prosecuted.

Relations with Police and Prosecutors

In Michigan, a group of clergy met in Lansing with state police to sound them
out and set ground rules before the service started work, according to their
founder, Rev. Carl Bielby. Bielby, then working for the Detroit Council of
Churches, and campus pastors from the University of Michigan and Michigan
State University asked state police representatives, "How can we do this so that
you can't arrest us?"[2] The Michigan CCS may have been the group described
by Ronald L. Hammerle as receiving the help of the state police to write its

74

public statement, "advising the clergymen on certain legal words to avoid!" The state attorney general and governor were also informed.[3] No member of the Michigan CCS ever encountered legal problems, but the Michigan state police did target an Illinois clergy member—a story told later in this chapter.

All the clergy interviewed for this book were well aware that their work with the CCS was at least on the edge of the law (if not illegal) at the time, and we asked whether they had feared arrest or other legal repercussions. Very few said they had. In fact, a few—including Rabbi Balfour Brickner, who was arrested many times in his long career—snorted at the very idea.[4] Many of the CCS clergy had been involved in civil rights and antiwar demonstrations, and some had been arrested long before the CCS work began. Moody was arrested in a 1963 civil rights demonstration. Rev. Chick Straut of the New Jersey CCS was arrested with other peace protesters outside the 1965 *Pacem in Terris* conference in New York City. Rev. Finley Schaef of the original New York group said he was arrested perhaps a dozen times over the years. Rev. Robert Pierce told us, "I was arrested trying to integrate Glen Oaks Park in Baltimore, I was in Selma, I did lots of protests with Howard [Moody] in the school and education stuff, we took our kids in strollers to protest in New York City [in support of] integrating the schools, and we had a rent strike in my apartment building that I organized. So I've had a long history of—I call myself a professional provocateur. . . . I have a deep commitment to social justice, a passion for doing the right thing. So this [working with the CCS] was a no-brainer for me."[5]

Some of the original group of clergy in New York felt strongly that they should make a point of committing civil disobedience as a way to force change in abortion laws. But a more compassionate principle prevailed; the ministers couldn't help women from jail.[6] So the group set out to "be absolutely open about our aims, intentions, and goals, stating those as explicitly as we could in order to mitigate against any appearance of an underground or illicit activity."[7] As Rev. Farley Wheelwright of the Cleveland CCS told the *Wall Street Journal*, "This is no abortion underground. . . . We're helping to bring abortion above ground, to make it open, respectable and eventually legal for any woman to end her pregnancy whenever she and her doctor feel it's the best course."[8] The clergy cast their counseling as a natural expansion of their pastoral responsibility to women. They hoped this view would suggest an added traditional legal protection: confessional privilege. In New York state, the 1813 case of *People v. Phillips* had established that clergy could not be compelled to reveal information received from parishioners as part of their confession. As of 1968, all but six states had enacted some statutory protection for communications between clergy and communicants, and the 1958 decision in *Mullen v. United States* had established such protection nationwide.[9] Of course, it was by no means certain that a court would view CCS counselees as parishioners or communicants (most were not members of the counselors' churches or synagogues) or their counseling sessions as taking place under the seal of confession, but the counselors hoped that law and tradition would offer some protection to themselves and the women who came to them.

At first, a courtroom defense didn't look necessary. To the group's surprise, the police left the CCS alone or at least took no direct action against them. They weren't watched in any obvious way. A few days after the service began, however, with the answering machine and counselors flooded with requests, staff at Judson Memorial Church found that their office phones—not the line dedicated to the answering machine—were tapped. They could hear unusual clicks on the line, and their suspicion that the sounds came from a police tap was confirmed by a tip from a contact in the police department. For a time, the group did not discuss any substantive CCS business over the Judson phone lines; Moody recalled using a public phone several blocks away for a while. Schaef, of nearby Washington Square Methodist Church, said that his church's phone lines were checked for taps, but he didn't think anyone was monitoring his CCS work.[10]

No word came from the district attorney's office, either. Moody recalled, "The district attorney of New York, Frank Hogan, every time he was asked about this group, the clergy that were breaking the law, he said, 'No comment.' Because he didn't want to do anything."[11] In Cleveland, Cuyahoga County Prosecutor John T. Corrigan told the *Wall Street Journal* that his office was unlikely to target the CCS as long as it was simply giving women information and not "actually serving as the agent through which an illegal Ohio abortionist gets business"—a statement that affirmed the wisdom of the CCS policy of referring out of state.[12]

The clergy concluded that the police, nothing if not realists, recognized that the CCS counselors were doing a service in keeping women safe from dangerous back-alley abortionists. Ronald L. Hammerle quoted a local CCS organizer who said that a former chief of detectives had told him, "Look, we've got murders, rapes and robberies where people get victimized. We're not interested in arresting people who help people. The only abortionists we're interested in are those who charge a thousand dollars and leave the woman dying."[13] Arlene Carmen commented in a 1976 interview, "I don't believe that the authorities would have touched us. . . . They were kind of, in their own way, grateful because they knew that we were sending women to very safe places, so that the women wouldn't come back here to New York and wind up in the hospitals with botched abortions. At least we were helping to alleviate some of that problem in the city."[14]

In fact, the police sometimes came to the CCS for help. "We served all," Moody said. "Lots of police wives, judges' wives and daughters, we saw many of those. And I remember one federal judge from Minnesota came with his daughter, and I counseled her, and he did not want to break the law. Naturally, a judge. So he took his daughter to Japan. Afterward he sent the CCS a donation."[15] In their book, Moody and Carmen told of the experience of Rev. Lyle Guttu, one of the original CCS members and a Lutheran minister who then worked in Brooklyn. A couple came back to thank him after the wife's abortion. "The man was so grateful that he wanted Pastor Guttu to feel free to call him if he could ever be of help in his line of work. Asked what his line of work was, he replied that he was a captain in the New York City Police Department."[16] In Missouri, CCS coordinator Judy Widdicombe's mother-in-law—who had the same last name—received a call meant for Judy from the county sheriff's office. Widdicombe, assuming there was a warrant out for her, called an attorney and spent the night at a friend's house to avoid immediate arrest. The next day, having learned that there was no warrant, Widdicombe's husband answered their home phone. He told her, "That was the sheriff's office. . . . Somebody there wants your *services*. Their girlfriend's daughter is pregnant."[17] In Detroit, a car with a license number that Rev. Carl Bielby recognized as a police plate pulled up outside his office for an appointment. Bielby suspected he had been set up, but in fact the officer was bringing his daughter for counseling.[18] Spencer Parsons recalled a similar experience in Chicago: "A police officer came in one day and said, 'Mr. Parsons, I'd like to talk with you. I'm a police officer of the City of Chicago, and if you don't wish to talk with me, I fully understand. But my daughter's in difficulty, and I'd like to talk with you.' And that kind of opened up [an] above-board kind of relationship with some of the Chicago police. It was really very, very satisfying to me."[19]

Moody recalled one instance in which the New York district attorney's office and police helped protect the CCS. He received a phone call from a man who said that his girlfriend had gotten an abortion through the CCS. The caller followed this not with the usual thanks for the clergy's help but with a threat to expose the doctor who performed the abortion unless the CCS gave him $5,000 in cash. Moody asked the man to call back in an hour, during which time he alerted the district attorney and police. They put fake money in a brown paper bag and fitted Moody with a wire. When the blackmailer called back, Moody arranged to meet him near the restrooms in Washington Square Park. Moody was to come by himself. The man approached Moody as he entered the park. In his 2009 memoir, Moody wrote that before he handed over the fake money, "I said to him, 'How do we know that you won't be back again to extort more money?' He replied mockingly, 'You don't. You will just have to trust me.' So I gave him the brown bag, and as he turned to walk away, two plainclothes officers intercepted him." The man, who was the nephew of a well-known New York clergyman, didn't have a chance to expose the doctor. Moody said, "That was the one and only unpleasant response to our work."[20]

For all the publicity that the various chapters of the CCS received—and most of the chapters didn't just operate publicly but actually sought to make their service known to women through newspaper interviews, advertising in campus papers, listings in the Yellow Pages of phone books, and more—nowhere did police or prosecutors make the CCS a primary target of investigation or prosecution. The group's few run-ins with the law generally came in the course of legal actions against doctors.

Two Difficulties in Cleveland

In Cleveland, the CCS went public in January 1969.[21] The chapter's chair was Rev. Farley Wheelwright, a Unitarian minister who had been an early member of the New York City group. By late May, Wheelwright had recruited about twenty clergy, and the group had counseled and referred some 500 women.[22] Then news came from England that a young Ohio woman, Jo Ann Michael, an eighteen-year-old who had been married just a month earlier and then separated from her husband, had died at an abortion clinic in London and the CCS had made the referral.[23] A coroner's inquest was called, and Scotland Yard investigated. The physician involved was not Dr. David Sopher, to whom many CCS chapters referred women, although the clinic was Sopher's—Lady Margaret Nursing Home.[24] Moody sent out a memo to counselors reminding them to refer only to Sopher.[25] At the time, Wheelwright would not confirm publicly that any member of the CCS had counseled Jo Ann Michael, but years later he recalled, "Of the at least several hundred women who we provided consultations to, this was the only one that died. I personally made a trip to London to investigate. . . . The abortion went off perfectly and the death was due to an anesthesiologist who left the client alone post-operatively and apparently had not done her job properly. I believe that she was dismissed from the clinic but not prosecuted for negligence."[26] Indeed, the inquest concluded that Michael had died of respiratory obstruction during anesthesia. No legal action was taken against the CCS or its members.[27]

The death was still fresh in the minds of Clevelanders when on June 10, 1969, a member of the Cleveland CCS was indicted by the state of Massachusetts in a completely separate case. Rev. Robert Hare, then thirty-five, was a Presbyterian minister and a native of Pittsburgh. Hare's forebears had been part of a dissident Presbyterian group from Scotland. He had graduated from McCormick Seminary in Chicago and taken a job as associate chaplain of

North Carolina State College in 1962. At that time Hare, who is white, frequently worshiped at Davie Street, a black Presbyterian church whose new minister was the dynamic Rev. J. Oscar McLeod. McLeod and Hare worked with black students from nearby colleges to desegregate theaters, restaurants, and other public places in Raleigh—work that eventually resulted in Hare losing his job. After serving a black Presbyterian church in Richmond, Virginia, and continuing his civil rights activism, Hare and his family moved to Cleveland in 1968. Hare's job was to establish, as he later described it, a "social-activist kind of free-floating house church, possibly capturing the interest of some people who were tending to be turned off from the church. . . . We met in people's homes. One of our participants was a manager of a TV station, and we'd meet in the TV studio. We'd meet wherever we could find space to meet."[28] Although he had never addressed the issue of abortion, he was known as a social activist, and Wheelwright approached him about joining the just-forming Cleveland chapter of the CCS.

Wheelwright arranged training sessions for the Cleveland clergy. At one of these, a local lawyer spoke to the group. "The attorney said we weren't violating the law," Hare recalled. "Not far from the edge of it, but we weren't violating it. . . . We would not hand [counselees] anything. No sheets, no cards. . . . I, as a counselor, and the Clergy Consultation Service, would say, 'If you wish to, you may write down [the doctor's] name and phone number.' They would, of course. But I wasn't giving it to them, I wasn't handing them anything that could get passed on. Attorney's advice. We're only exchanging speech."[29]

The Cleveland service handled many calls. Hare said, "The three or four [clergy] who were on in a given week were *busy*. . . . It took time."[30] Abortion providers were at a premium, and the clergy counselors were always looking for good out-of-state doctors. Wheelwright wrote to us in 2007,

> Half of our job was interviewing and reviewing women in search of an abortion. The other half was attempting to locate doctors willing to perform abortions who resided in other states. Most doctors came from New York and Michigan. We never referred a patient to Mexico because we had no means of checking their qualifications. I personally went to Canada to a medical society meeting and recruited a doctor from Massachusetts who had set up a clinic about 20 miles outside of Boston. I visited the clinic and it looked like an ideal set-up, and we sent many women to him.[31]

The provider was Dr. Pierre Victor Brunelle, a McGill University Medical School graduate who practiced in Chelmsford. Reports from Cleveland women who went to Brunelle were uniformly positive. Wheelwright was un-aware that Brunelle had lost his license to practice in Massachusetts as a result of an earlier abortion case and apparently was being watched by authorities.[32]

One night in April 1969, one of Brunelle's patients, a woman from the Cleveland area, was driving home after her procedure when she felt severe cramps. She stopped at the first building she saw to get help. Moody and Carmen later wrote, "In one of those strange quirks of fate, the building happened to be the headquarters of the highway patrol. Before providing her with medical assistance, the police demanded that she tell them what had happened; she did, including the names of both doctor and minister."[33]

The investigation apparently revealed the names of many Cleveland women who had been patients of Dr. Brunelle. At least a dozen were questioned, and two testified before a grand jury in Massachusetts, according to the Cleveland *Plain Dealer*.[34]

In June, Cleveland CCS chair Wheelwright learned of a problem. According to Hare, Wheelwright called all the local CCS members to tell them that Brunelle had been arrested. He told them that investigations might include them and asked them to go through their files to find any counselees they might have referred to Brunelle. Hare found five women who had taken Brunelle's contact information, and he called to alert them to the investigation. "One, two, three, four, they were appreciative, said if they got visited they'd stand on their rights; number five said, 'They were here.' [The police] had already been there the evening before." She was a young schoolteacher who lived at home, taught at the school where she had grown up, and was engaged to be married. Hare had counseled her and her fiancé; they had been worried about the effect a pregnancy would have on her relationship with her family and her career as a teacher.[35]

When Hare heard that the woman had already talked with the police, he sought an attorney. Gerald A. (Jerry) Messerman was already well known as a social justice and free speech lawyer. As Hare remembered it, Messerman told him not to worry—that Brunelle was in trouble, but that the woman happened to learn of him through Hare was "ancillary" and probably of no interest to a prosecutor. That evaluation turned out to be optimistic. At 7 o'clock the next morning, Hare recalled, his home phone rang. It was the Associated Press asking, "'Will you confirm for us that you've been criminally indicted in the state of Massachusetts yesterday?' I said, '*What?*' I'd not heard from any courts. I could hear the tickertapes going [in the newsroom]; he said, 'Well, it's on the wire service: you and Dr. Pierre Victor Brunelle. Do you know Dr. Brunelle?' I said no. Literally, I didn't know him." The reporter told Hare that the wire service story said that Hare and Brunelle had been indicted on a unit indictment;

in other words, the two men had been indicted as one for the same crime, performing an abortion, with Hare aiding and abetting. Hare called Messerman, who was both surprised and dismayed. As he recalled, Messerman told him, "We're in very deep trouble. A unit indictment is rare. We have a big choice to make fairly quickly. If we just let them do it, you're going to get arrested by the Ohio State Police, on behalf of the Massachusetts [police], and they're probably out looking for you now, so watch your step." Sure enough, wherever Hare went that day, people told him that police had been looking for him.[36]

Hare considered the alternatives: fight extradition to Massachusetts, which would be expensive and not necessarily successful; wait for police to arrive, possibly at his home, to handcuff him and haul him off to jail, probably subject to a great deal of press coverage; or, as he decided to do, appear in court in Massachusetts voluntarily. Hare and Messerman flew to Boston and appeared before a judge in Middlesex County, Hare in a dark suit and clerical collar.[37]

Messerman contacted William P. Homans Jr., whom Moody called "one of the finest civil liberties lawyers in Massachusetts," to handle the case locally.[38] Hare and Messerman returned in a couple of weeks and, with Homans, filed a motion to split Hare's indictment from that of Brunelle. Because a unit indictment was rare, Hare's attorneys speculated that the grand jury had suspected Hare of a larger role, or perhaps a payoff, indicating a conspiracy. But Hare said later, "Our functions were distinctly different, and I'd by no means been an aider and abettor." In fact, he had never met or talked with Brunelle—nor had he visited Massachusetts before he answered this charge.[39] The judge who heard the motion agreed that the unit indictment didn't make sense, and the two men were charged separately. Brunelle was eventually convicted on charges of violating the state abortion law—not for the Cleveland woman's case but for an abortion he performed a few weeks later on a university student—and served sixteen months in Norfolk Prison.[40] Hare said he never did meet Brunelle.

Meanwhile, friends and supporters in Ohio had organized the Committee for Bob Hare's Defense to raise money for his legal and travel expenses. Rev. James L. Grazier, the executive of the Presbytery of Cleveland, the regional unit of the Presbyterian church, and Bishop John H. Burt of the Episcopal Diocese of Ohio were co-chairs, indicating that the CCS had the support of mainstream religious institutions.[41] The defense fund raised $16,000.[42] Hare's lawyers, both devoted to various justice causes, accepted minimal fees, but the case took much longer than anyone expected.

Not all individual clergy supported Hare. Pressed by some of his fellow ministers, the Presbytery of Cleveland assigned a committee to investigate Hare's counseling activities and whether his ordination should be revoked. In

February 1970 the committee reported in Hare's favor, finding that his counseling was well within the scope of appropriate activities for an ordained minister;
in fact, the committee's motion included the statement that "any further prosecution in the case at hand should be carried out against this Presbytery also,"
since the presbytery had been informed about his activities. Seventy-five percent
of the voting body of the presbytery supported the committee's report, and
Hare remained a minister in good standing. The church body's strong support
surely came in part from an awareness that if a clergyperson could be charged
with aiding and abetting merely for counseling a person who was later prosecuted for a crime, church freedom would be threatened generally.[43]

Hare's legal team filed motions to dismiss the charges against him—that
he had aided and abetted in the performance of an abortion, and that he had
been an accessory before the fact. Messerman based Hare's defense on the First
Amendment's guarantee of free speech: he had a right to counsel women and
impart information to them, and women had a right to know the information.[44]

Court arguments for dismissal began on a Monday before Easter in spring
1970 and continued the next morning. Back in Cleveland, Hare got word that
the judge had dismissed the indictment on the facts of Hare's behavior, saying
that a person who counsels a woman who is seeking abortion "does not by
doing so commit the crime of aiding and assisting the abortionist." The decision
avoided the stickier issues of jurisdiction, constitutionality, and church freedom.
Hare celebrated with a victory party.[45]

But the celebration turned out to be premature. A week later, Hare recalled,
"we got a communication that the prosecutor had filed an appeal to the Massachusetts state supreme court against the dismissal order, arguing that the judge
who had ordered the dismissal had done so on erroneous technical grounds.
Well, now we're in the appeal mode. *That* takes a long time." Over the next year
and a half, Hare's church work continued, but he stopped counseling for the
Cleveland CCS while the case was under way. Others in the group continued
to counsel and make referrals.[46]

At last, in late 1971, the Massachusetts Supreme Judicial Court took up
the prosecutor's appeal to reinstate the case. Hare's team argued the appeal.
Hare recalled, "Ordinarily in appellate court, the court renders an opinion up or
down. In this case, they intentionally attached a memorandum of opinion in
which they said, essentially, the court grants the argument against the dismissal;
however, on exploration of the data or the evidence, this court feels that there is
no further cause for prosecution. . . . But it's just a memorandum of opinion.
[The prosecutor] re-indicted me," Hare recalled with a laugh.[47]

The prosecutor reinstated the indictment in March 1972. Meanwhile, Hare
had been interviewing for a job as minister of a church in Natick, Massachusetts.

A lawyer on the church's search committee had looked into Hare's case and assured the committee that the charges were almost certain to be dropped. Hare was hired, and he and his family moved to Natick. News of his re-indictment came to church members—most of whom knew nothing of the case—during his first week on the job. In spite of the initial shock, Hare said, the congregation dealt well with the news and he went on to have a good experience in Natick. The legal case dragged on. By the end of 1972, there wasn't even a date set for a new trial. Then, unexpectedly, a resolution came from higher up the judicial ladder: the U.S. Supreme Court handed down its decision in *Roe v. Wade* on January 22, 1973, striking down abortion statutes throughout the country. The Massachusetts prosecutor's case against Hare evaporated for good.[48]

Charges in Michigan

Hare was not the only clergy counselor who was swept up in legal action against a doctor. Chicago Rabbi Max Ticktin was the target of a police sting that aimed to convict a Detroit physician. Ticktin was a graduate of the University of Pennsylvania and Jewish Theological Seminary in New York. He and his wife spent the tumultuous years of 1947 and 1948 in Israel. In those years after World War II, the student population at the University of Wisconsin was growing rapidly, and Ticktin was recruited to run Hillel House in Madison. He raised money for a new building and brought top intellectual speakers to the campus. He later said he enjoyed campus work and was not interested in a job with a congregation, where he would be "working for those who also pay your salary." He stayed in campus life.[49] In fact, when we interviewed Ticktin in 2006, he was in his eighties and still a popular professor at George Washington University, where he energetically climbed the stairs to his third-floor office and spoke with sharp intellect and detailed recall.

In 1969 Ticktin had been head of Hillel at the University of Chicago for five years, and he directed Hillel chapters throughout the Midwest. He had already been counseling conscientious objectors to the Vietnam War, and he and Hillel associate director Rabbi Daniel Leifer were among the first clergy Spencer Parsons recruited to Chicago's CCS. The group started quietly in April 1969, and Ticktin recalled that at first the group referred most of the women they counseled to England or Japan, and soon to California and a hospital in Kansas City. Then the group received from the Michigan CCS the name of Dr. Jesse Ketchum in Detroit—much closer for Chicago women, but still out of state to confuse jurisdictions. (This was the same Dr. Ketchum who later practiced in Buffalo, New York, and was the subject of the letter quoted in chapter 5.) Parsons later wrote that Ketchum was "hesitant to work with the Clergy Consultation Service in Chicago because he did not want to jeopardize his general practice and the reputation of the small community hospital which he owned just outside of Detroit. However, after a meeting in my home in Chicago, Dr. Ketchum agreed that we could send patients to him and that he would use his best judgment as to whether the procedures would be done at the hospital or elsewhere."[50] The Chicago CCS began to refer to him. According to Parsons, in the summer and fall of 1969, Ketchum provided abortions for more than 100 women referred by the Chicago CCS, with no complications beyond a few minor infections that were treated with antibiotics by local physicians.[51]

Ticktin recalled in our interview that he and Leifer had agreed to take calls during Christmas week of 1969, when the Protestant ministers were busy. During that week, a quiet one for counseling, Ticktin met with a couple who raised his suspicions, but only slightly.[52] In a statement that he prepared in mid-January in case he was deposed, but which he never had occasion to use, he detailed what happened.[53] On December 23, he wrote, a woman called asking for "help on a personal problem"; she said that Ticktin had spoken with a friend of hers who had been pleased with his help. Ticktin clearly understood that the "personal problem" meant a problem pregnancy. He was surprised when she refused the offer of an almost immediate appointment and said she could wait a week to see him. They set an appointment for 3 p.m. on December 30, and he asked her to call on that day to be sure he was in town and not delayed by snow in Milwaukee, where he had a commitment the previous day. On December 30, the woman called, and she told Ticktin that she would be accompanied by the man involved. There was nothing unusual about that or about most of the counseling session. Ticktin said that any suspicions he might have had about the woman's willingness to delay meeting and the fact that she had not given him her phone number were offset when she answered his first question, about how she had heard of the CCS. The woman named the friend who had referred her, and Ticktin recognized the name as someone he had counseled on November 14. He gathered that they were from "near Chicago." They discussed the medical facts of the pregnancy and Ticktin suggested options. Marriage was out of the question, the couple said, because of legal difficulties, which Ticktin took to mean that the man was already married. The woman rejected the idea of adoption. As he usually did, Ticktin stressed that he did not advocate abortions and that he was there to help them "explore the alternatives."[54]

"If they were to reject all other alternatives and decide to terminate the pregnancy," Ticktin wrote, "I felt that they ought to give special consideration of the possibility of going to London," as the safest and legal choice, though the travel cost would be expensive. Ticktin had a prepared sheet of contact information and instructions for women going to London. As a second choice, he offered Puerto Rico. "We then came to talking about Detroit, and I had mentioned

Dr. K. [Ketchum] as a man who I had never met or spoken to, but who came with the highest recommendations which had been verified, as an experienced obstetrician. He was known to us to be a man who had access to a hospital, which was another way of underlining his professional reliability. I explained very clearly that I had nothing to do with the money and that no money passes through my hands nor through the hands of any other person on this counseling service." Ticktin explained how to make an appointment with the doctor, how much the procedure would cost, what to expect, and how to prepare for it. "We closed by my asking them whether they had any other questions and then indicating to them that there really was no need for them to be in touch with me again," he wrote.[55]

The counseling session didn't raise any further suspicions, and on January 4, 1970, he left for Israel on a trip with a group of other rabbis. Ticktin recalled in our interview that not long after they arrived in Jerusalem, he received a call saying that his office had been raided and there was a warrant for his arrest. There was nothing Ticktin could do where he was. "Little did I know that there was a great deal of stir in Chicago," he said. His colleague, Rabbi Leifer, was doing everything possible to protect him. Leifer found Ticktin an attorney, Leon Despres, a civil rights lawyer who was also a city councilman and a longtime opponent of Mayor Richard J. Daley. Leifer also called the Chicago police captain involved in Ticktin's case and learned that the Chicago police were acting on behalf of police in Michigan. "They were after the doctor and his wife, and what they ultimately wanted to do was get more evidence. The people who'd come to see me [for counseling] were a policeman and a policewoman who had been sent to do that. Of course I didn't know that," Ticktin said.[56]

On January 6, a Michigan judge had charged a Detroit-area doctor, his wife, and Ticktin with conspiracy to commit abortion, an offense that carried a possible four-year prison term.[57] That same night, the Circuit Court of Cook County, Illinois, approved a search warrant for Ticktin and his Hillel office, seeking evidence of the conspiracy, including documents giving the names and addresses of both abortion providers and "individuals who have in the past received abortions from these individuals, also names and locations of individuals who are awaiting abortions."[58] "That is the funniest part of it all," Ticktin said, "because whoever issued that warrant didn't know state statutes—that the [Illinois] state legislature had just passed some kind of legislation protecting the privacy of files of psychotherapists and clergy people. So whoever was the lawyer for the police department either had not been consulted or goofed, because by the time I got back, they withdrew their warrant for my arrest."[59]

Nonetheless, when Ticktin landed in the United States, a friend was waiting with $2,000 or $3,000 in cash, in case the New York police swooped in to arrest him. The authorities left Ticktin alone. "But my files *had* been tampered with," he said.[60] As the *Chicago Daily News* put it, "Chicago police raided the Hillel Foundation headquarters, 5715 S. Woodlawn, early Wednesday [January 7, 1970] and reportedly confiscated some of Rabbi Ticktin's files, which were turned over to Michigan authorities."[61] The clergy had been asked to devise a code for their own files, and Ticktin and Leifer used either Hebrew names instead of English or some other code, plus a date and time. The evidence would have been partial at best. By the time Ticktin returned, the police had backed off, "perhaps because their lawyer realized that he'd gotten in too deep, or perhaps because Despres scared the blank out of them," he said.[62]

As he traveled home, Ticktin had been forewarned about the warrant, but he was not expecting to step into the great tumult of press and public notoriety that awaited him. The case had been page one news in both Chicago and Detroit.[63]

Ketchum, then fifty-two, was a suburban Detroit physician who worked with the assistance of his wife Judith, twenty-three. Women who had been sent to him gave him mostly favorable reports. Ticktin said he had never met Ketchum and that apparently the CCS had not checked him out adequately; for one thing, when the woman sent by Michigan police to Ticktin called to make her appointment with Ketchum, she was told to meet him at a motel. That should have ruled him out as a provider for the CCS, but with competent abortion providers in short supply, the CCS sometimes did compromise on what could be thought of as a "house call," and Parsons had agreed that Ketchum could use his judgment. The group was aware of Ketchum's arrangements, because they gave women information about the five hotels where they could meet him. In any case, the motel venue sounded sleazy in the news articles.[64] In addition, the police found that Ketchum had done at least one procedure across the river from Detroit in Windsor, Ontario. "So," Ticktin recalled, "there was even one headline which—we burst out laughing like mad—which said, 'Rabbi Seized in International Abortion Ring.' International! All because of this Windsor thing."[65]

As the *Detroit Free Press* reported, "Ketchum was arrested at the Northland Inn in Southfield Monday night [January 5, 1970] after he had gone there with a female State Police undercover agent and a state policeman posing as her boyfriend. Police later searched Ketchum's home and confiscated records and about $150,000 in cash," which would have been an unusually large sum, even for a physician who did a great deal of work on a cash basis. The paper reported that Ketchum had offices in Royal Oak, Michigan, and owned a small seven-bed hospital there. The two were also known as Dr. and Mrs. Chalmers, and Judith Ketchum sometimes used the name Miss Morgan.[66] To many of the CCS women he treated, Ketchum was known as Dr. K.[67]

The Ketchums were charged in Michigan with conspiracy to commit abortion. Oakland County Prosecutor Thomas Plunkett said that he brought the charges reluctantly because he was "in full favor of repeal of the present abortion law."[68]

Meanwhile, in Chicago, Ticktin recalled, "Somebody at the University of Chicago had set up a place to get signatures—'We are backing Ticktin'—and they ended up with fifteen hundred names!" With a touch of amusement he added, "And I was a big hero in the campus newspaper, faculty people were calling me, and—But at this point we were laughing already."[69] As the Chicago news coverage died down, the spotlight there eventually left Ticktin. In Michigan, however, the press continued to follow the case, and Ticktin's name continued to appear. At the end of January, the *Detroit Free Press* ran a major feature on the front page of the women's section headlined "Campus Rallies Behind 'Little Rabbi.'"[70] Although Ticktin later laughed about the article—"My stature isn't that short!"—the reporter, Jean Sprain Wilson, drew a sympathetic portrait of Ticktin and his family. She visited with them at their home, met with Ticktin at his office, and wrote of his concern for students, his popularity on campus, and his modest demeanor, all of which undoubtedly helped counterbalance the sensational headlines. As the hubbub in Chicago died down, Ticktin's Detroit lawyer continued to track Ketchum's case; he told Ticktin that he was still at some risk of arrest and should not set foot in Michigan until he received definite word that the charge against him had been officially dropped. Ticktin said, "So that was a limit on my professional responsibilities [as Hillel director for the Midwest], because I had to get to East Lansing occasionally, or to Ann Arbor, where we had two posts. As I recall it, between January or February '70 and May '72, I may have snuck into Michigan once or twice. I didn't take it too seriously."[71]

At the end of March 1970, a district judge dismissed the charges against the Ketchums, ruling that the Michigan law allowing abortion only "when necessary to preserve life" was unconstitutionally vague. He based the decision on the similar California court decision in the case of Dr. Belous—a case whose appeal the U.S. Supreme Court had refused to consider the previous month. Many hoped the decision would result in passage of a more liberal state law in the Michigan legislature, but it did not. When New York state legalized abortion that summer, the Ketchums relocated their practice to Buffalo (see chapter 5 for a letter from a woman referred there by the CCS). The death of one of Ketchum's abortion patients in June 1971 led to his 1973 conviction on charges of criminally negligent homicide. He was sentenced to three years in prison and released on parole after just over one year. His license to practice was revoked in Michigan and New York, but he later worked for a time without a license at hospitals in Florida.[72]

Ticktin never received official word that the charges against him had been dropped. He moved to Washington, DC, in 1972, and in January 1973 the *Roe v. Wade* decision removed the potential legal threat against him, as it did for Bob Hare.

Close Calls

The only other clergy counselor who faced legal charges—and the only one whom police arrested at his home—was Rev. Robert B. Wallace of State College, Pennsylvania.

Wallace grew up in Arizona, began his ministry in Los Angeles, and then went into campus ministry at Arizona State University. From 1965 to 1973, he was the minister at University Baptist Church in State College. In a telephone interview, he recalled that he had met with women who needed abortions before he joined the CCS, but he had not known of doctors to whom he could refer them. As a fellow Baptist, Wallace knew Howard Moody, who probably recruited him to the CCS. There were several other CCS members in State College, including some of the campus ministers at Pennsylvania State University.[73]

In 1970, the CCS coordinator for Pennsylvania was Rev. Allen Hinand, who ran the group from Wayne's Central Baptist Church. Hinand was careful about following the guidelines the New York group had set out. Arlene Carmen, in the New York office, clearly viewed some of the clergy as loose cannons, Hinand recalled in an interview, but Hinand was not one of those; she and Moody knew he felt as strongly as they did about how important the CCS procedures were. In the Philadelphia area, where Hinand was based, "We knew there could be some legal action, so we were very careful with record keeping," he recalled. "At the end of the week [on call], counselors would submit all their forms to me, and I kept them in the parsonage in Wayne."[74] That may not have included all counseling forms from around the state.

One morning in September 1970, Penn State campus police, coordinating with Pittsburgh police, came to Wallace's home before he had left for the office. They took him to his office, searched his files, confiscated some, and later returned them. As Wallace recalled the incident, he was released on his own recognizance and did not spend time in jail. He soon learned that he had been arrested simultaneously with a Pittsburgh gynecologist, a well-known, well-established doctor and the only doctor to whom the State College CCS referred women for abortions. Though the national CCS strongly discouraged referrals within states, the Pennsylvania CCS had developed good relationships with physicians based in hospitals, and Philadelphia counselors referred many women locally (see chapter 4). The State College group had received the Pittsburgh doctor's name from the CCS and had felt safe enough because the doctor was in a different county. Apparently a woman Wallace had referred had given his name and the doctor's to police. Wallace believed it was a woman who had contacted him after her abortion. She "had real remorse and reported it. She came from a Catholic background and had made confession. She felt she had done a terrible thing and wanted to prevent this from happening to anyone else," he recalled.[75]

The physician involved must have been one of the three doctors charged on October 5, 1970, with conspiracy to commit an unlawful act. All three were eminent OB-GYN specialists on staff at several hospitals in Pittsburgh, including Magee-Women's Hospital, where some 900 abortions had been performed that year.[76] A State College attorney, a member of Wallace's church, took his case pro bono and kept in touch with the doctors' Pittsburgh defense attorney.[77]

Wallace said he feared repercussions in his job; his CCS counseling was not public knowledge, even within his congregation. He recalled, "I had done it on my own, not as a ministry of the church, but exercising clergy privilege," which ensured confidentiality. Perhaps one or two people in the congregation knew he did abortion counseling, he said. Wallace pointed out, "You don't ask permission from the congregation as to who you can counsel." When Wallace was arrested, "I was fearful how the church would handle it, but they handled it very well," he said. "They couldn't understand all the issues, but they trusted me." Baptist church polity is based in the congregation, so as long as he had his congregation's support, he didn't fear repercussions from the larger church hierarchy.[78]

Meanwhile, the Allegheny County district attorney, Robert Duggan, subpoenaed Magee-Women's Hospital to provide records, and three women who had had abortions at the hospital requested an injunction to block the subpoena. Their request came before a panel of two county judges who ruled the Pennsylvania abortion law unconstitutional on January 5, 1971. (The law read, "Whoever with the intent to procure the miscarriage of any woman, unlawfully administers to her any poison, drug or substance, or unlawfully uses any instrument or other means with the like intent is guilty of a felony," but did not define *unlawfully*.) Without access to the hospital evidence, Duggan's case against the doctors and Wallace was effectively over.[79]

In the three cases in which CCS members faced charges—those of Hare, Ticktin, and Wallace—the physicians, not the clergy, seem to have been the primary targets of the police investigations. In Wallace's case, the woman who reported her experience to the authorities may have implicated him and the physician, and charges were brought against both, but the ensuing prosecution focused entirely on the doctors.

In 1971, an investigation of Douglass Hospital in Kansas City, Kansas, threatened to involve the CCS. Iowa counselors routinely referred women to Dr. Lynn Weller, a white doctor who practiced at Douglass, a black-owned facility. In the summer of 1971, the CCS was pressuring the administration at Douglass to reduce its patient load, upgrade its equipment, and reduce prices. On July 24, 1971, the car of an Iowa woman was stopped by Kansas City police after she left the hospital.[80] The woman was taken for a medical exam and asked to sign a release for her medical records from Douglass Hospital. A detective presented the hospital with the release form the same day, and the county district attorney, a devout Catholic, indicated that he intended to send investigators to Iowa. The CCS warned its counselors who were not clergy, medical professionals, or lawyers to stop counseling for the time being, since they might not have the legal protection of confidentiality. Counselors who continued to send women to Douglass Hospital were asked to warn them of "possible political harassment."[81] Soon Douglass was in fact ordered to stop abortion services because it lacked accreditation.[82] Weller practiced for a while in Washington, DC, then returned to practice in Kansas City once Douglass was accredited.[83] The CCS continued to refer to him at Douglass, but in September 1973, after receiving death threats and having talked about a contract on his life, Weller was shot dead at his home. The killing was apparently for personal reasons, not because of his work providing abortion care.[84] Ideological violence against abortion clinics and providers started later, after what began as peaceful protests following *Roe v. Wade* gradually escalated to harassment, sit-ins, and blockades at abortion clinics, leading up to a clinic arson in 1976 and bombings in 1978; the first murder of an abortion provider for his work took place in 1993.[85]

Only one of the counselors interviewed remembered police action against the CCS that had no known connection to an investigation of a practitioner. Rev. Donna Schaper, now a UCC minister and head of staff at Judson Memorial Church, was one of several seminary students who worked part-time as counselors for the CCS. They staffed an office in downtown Chicago where, Schaper recalled, "We were raided twice. And we were closed down more than once. . . . We were arrested. We were kept downtown, in jail, at one point for about forty-eight hours. But nothing happened to us. We were arrested and let go. Nobody ever booked us, even. I don't think we have a record." If those arrests were part of a larger investigation, Schaper never heard about it; they stand as an anomaly in the otherwise tolerant attitude of local authorities nationwide. They also challenge Parsons's statement that the Chicago CCS, which he headed, enjoyed cordial relations with the police force (perhaps he had forgotten those raids when we talked, but we were not able to resolve the apparent contradiction before his death in 2013).[86]

There was one other close call with the law that did not result from the investigation of a doctor, but it did not start as a police investigation of the CCS, either. Early in the operation of the CCS, probably in 1968, there was a fire in the New York apartment building of one of the clergy counselors, who asked to remain anonymous, and her husband. She recalled in an interview,[87] "We were living next door to a drug pusher. So the night before this fire, somebody had had a big fight with somebody, I'm certain a customer, out in the hallway, and this guy said, 'You motherfucker, I'm going to see that you pay for this!' That's what we heard outside our door. And then, later on that night, the hall had been doused with gasoline and the whole thing was on fire. We're sure it was directed toward this guy." Fortunately, the clergywoman and her husband woke up about 4 a.m. They found the apartment full of smoke, and their front door was hot. They climbed down a fire escape into the parking lot behind their building. She and her husband fled the apartment with sheets around them and nothing else. They ran to the nearby fire station.

The clergywoman realized that she had been counseling CCS referrals the previous day, and all of her files—files on women, doctors, and the CCS network—were on her desk where she had left them. The files on the women contained questionnaires with details about their situation, no names, but clear evidence that she was making abortion referrals. Because the fire was suspicious, the police searched the building and confiscated her files, thinking there was an abortion ring in the apartment. "I said, damn, they're going to arrest me, and I've got a sheet on," she recalled with a laugh. "But they didn't." A firefighter brought the couple some clothes from their apartment, and as soon as the clergywoman could get into her church—she didn't have her keys with her—she started telephoning. She wasn't able to reach Moody, but she did reach Schaef at Washington Square United Methodist Church. She recalled saying, "We've got to call the ACLU pronto. . . . We're in doodoo here. This whole thing is going to come crashing down on us because the cops think I'm running an abortion ring. And I'm going to probably be arrested within the day." Schaef said he would come right away. "So he dashes out here with his collar on and everything, and he goes into the precinct house like gangbusters, says, 'You have confiscated private clergy files. I want them back *immediately*!' And they said, 'Oh, okay, Father,' and handed it to him." The clergywoman worried that the police had already made copies of the files and that she would be arrested at any moment, but apparently they had not done so, and there were no further repercussions from the incident.

Grand Jury Investigations

Clergy from two of the largest CCS chapters also found themselves swept up in grand jury investigations. Both were based at least in part in political motivations, and in each instance the threat of indictment was real.

On a Friday afternoon in May 1969, New York City police raided an apartment in the Riverdale section of the Bronx. When they arrived, a seventeen-year-old was on the operating table, and her mother was in another room; police ignored pleas from the girl and her mother and would not allow the doctor to finish the procedure. Two women were in a bedroom recovering from their abortion procedures, and several other people, including a thirty-year-old college professor and her husband, also a professor, were in the waiting room. Police detained the clients and their family members—all from out of state—as witnesses. They arrested the doctor—a physician from the Dominican Republic who turned out to be unlicensed in New York—and three others involved in running the clinic, and they were charged with abortion, second degree. Police learned of a second location used by the group, and two others, including another doctor, were also charged. Bronx District Attorney Burton B. Roberts said the raid was the result of a three-month investigation. They had learned that twenty women a day had abortions at the apartment, and that many had been referred by "prominent individuals, including clergymen," according to Roberts.[88] CCS chapters in other states were indeed referring women to the Riverdale group. Activist and NARAL founder Larry Lader wrote in *Abortion II* that several months earlier the Philadelphia CCS had sent clergy to check on the Riverdale group; they found it to be clean and well equipped and approved it for referrals, but they had neglected to ask for the doctor's license. Lader called it "the most expert clinic on the East Coast" at the time, so its closure was a devastating loss to the CCS. Lader himself had referred many women to the Riverdale group. Even more disturbing was the threat to the entire CCS system of referral if the district attorney indicted clergy for their counseling role.[89]

Roberts said of the arrests, "As long as the abortion law is on the books, we shall [act] according to the spirit and letter of the law. However, the fact is that the law needs modification and liberalization so we can face the problem realistically and allow the medical profession to perform abortions in appropriate circumstances."[90] But his stated view on the need for change did not deter him from pursuing a five-month grand jury investigation—a drive that Lader viewed as political grandstanding. Otherwise, Lader asked, "with dozens of backstreet abortionists in the Bronx, why hadn't he gone after the hacks and incompetents? Why close down the one clinic of proven standards?"[91] Although the focus of the investigation seemed to be the medical practitioners, Roberts called a roster of sixty witnesses, including Moody, Schaef, and Rev. Jesse Lyons, all founding members of the New York CCS. Lyons, a Methodist minister on the staff of Riverside Church, was on the board of NARAL. He had resigned from the CCS in late 1968 because he wanted to be able to refer in-state to doctors—including the Riverdale group—that he had heard about from another non-CCS minister. Up to the time the practice was shut down, he had referred four or five women to Riverdale. Lader was also called before the grand jury in September 1969. He told the grand jury that careful referrals by the CCS and himself had raised safety standards for women seeking abortions, that they had brought the need for change in the laws to public attention, and that, indeed, laws were changing. He pointed out that in California, in the case of Dr. Leon Belous, the state supreme court had just declared unconstitutional an abortion law that was very similar to New York's.[92] Schaef and Lyons expressed their intention to say nothing, but Schaef later said he told the grand jury, "You people just don't understand how much suffering women go through."[93]

The grand jury handed down its indictments in October 1969. There was none against the clergy or Lader; only the two doctors and four others involved in running the clinic were charged. The cases never came to trial; according to Lader, the defendants pleaded guilty to misdemeanor charges and paid fines.[94]

In the midst of his appearances before the grand jury, Lyons brought suit in federal court against the state of New York in *Lyons v. Lefkowitz* (state attorney general Louis Lefkowitz). Lyons was represented by NYU Law School professor Cyril C. Means, one of the original legal advisers to the CCS. The suit asserted that the state abortion law restricted his right to offer pastoral counseling that referred women to qualified physicians. The suit was consolidated with three others under *Abramowicz et al. v. Lefkowitz*—one brought by a group of physicians, one by a group of more than 100 women (the *Abramowicz* suit), and one by a group of women, physicians, and social workers, particularly on behalf of poor women—attacking the constitutionality of the abortion law. The suits came before a panel of three federal judges, who in early 1970 received Lyons's deposition and heard dramatic personal testimony from women who had had abortions—including author Susan Brownmiller—and others who had sought abortions unsuccessfully. The case, whichever way it was decided, looked likely to be appealed to the U.S. Supreme Court. But before that could happen, the New York legislature voted in March 1970 to repeal the state abortion law. What might have been historic cases, including that of Lyons, became moot.[95]

In 1971 a Chicago grand jury was convened after Rev. Dr. E. Spencer Parsons, head of the CCS there, testified before the state legislature in support of legalizing abortion. His testimony included the statement that he knew twelve men and one woman in Illinois who had performed abortions and that one doctor had performed more than 20,000 abortions. The Republican majority leader in the state house was Rep. Henry Hyde, an opponent of abortion who went on to U.S. Congress and later sponsored the 1976 Hyde Amendment to restrict Medicaid funding for abortions. (Hyde also served as chair of the House Judiciary Committee during the impeachment trial of President Bill Clinton.) Hyde wanted Parsons to name the abortion providers. Parsons later recalled, "When Henry Hyde asked me to name the doctors that I knew were doing abortions in Chicago, I said, 'I can't do that, because that would violate the confidential character of my pastoral ministry.'"[96] The state bill to legalize abortion failed to pass, and Hyde promised to press for a grand jury to investigate Parsons and the practitioners he knew about. "That is a case of mass criminality," Hyde said. "Abortion is a felony with a one- to ten-year sentence."[97]

Hyde's attack on Parsons was prominent in the news, and soon Parsons received some unexpected support. He recalled,

> About a week and a half after Henry Hyde made his big speech about taking me down . . . [I heard from] the bank where I did my checking. I just did checking; I didn't have any great amount of money, probably had about $3,000 or $4,000 in the bank. . . . One day a bank person came to my house and said, "Mr. Parsons, it's our estimate that they'll arrest you on a weekend. And you won't have any cash, and the bank will be closed, and we don't want you to be stranded, so here's $500. Keep this cash readily available, your wife can take care of it. And if you need it on any weekend or holiday, when they usually come to arrest people," he said, "you'll have that for bail." I had not asked for that. They arrived at my door.

That was unusual full-service banking in the era before ATMs and weekend banking hours.[98] Moral support included a telegram from the directors of the YWCA of Metropolitan Chicago saying that the YWCA "strongly deplores the grand jury investigation" of Parsons "for his refusal to divulge the names of Illinois doctors performing abortion." The telegram expressed support for abortion law reform and opposition to "the intimidating tactics used by the anti-abortion group."[99]

Cook County state's attorney Edward V. Hanrahan did call a grand jury to force Parsons to talk. Parsons remembered exactly how he received his grand jury subpoena: at the close of the University of Chicago's commencement exercises at Rockefeller Chapel, where he was dean, he followed all the other dignitaries just ahead of the president of the university, who was last in the ceremonial recession. In front of the hundreds gathered for the graduation—and the university president—Parsons recalled, "three police officers stepped out of the aisle that we were walking down, and handed me this subpoena to appear before the grand jury" two weeks later.

Parsons said, "I couldn't use university counsel because corporate counsel cannot handle individual cases. So Ralph Brown was my personal lawyer, and he guided me through the grand juries." He was called twice, about three weeks apart, during which time he was instructed not to leave Chicago. Although Brown prepared Parsons for his grand jury appearances, he was not allowed to accompany him into the courtroom. "You have to walk in alone—which is really kind of intimidating," Parsons recalled.[100]

Between the court appearances, the chief counsel for the University of Chicago called Parsons in unofficially for a chat. He told Parsons that he thought the grand jury might say that he could not claim protection as a clergyman because he had made a public statement about his counseling when he testified to the state legislature. Parsons pointed out that when Hyde had asked him to name doctors he knew who were performing abortions, he had declined, saying, "That would violate the confidential character of my pastoral ministry." The university attorney was skeptical about whether the grand jury would see abortion counseling as a function of a church, but Parsons said that he and Moody had long before sponsored a resolution at the national meeting of American Baptists, "calling upon our clergy to give counsel and advice and assistance to women in matters of personal reproduction, and specifically including abortion." He recalled the lawyer advised him, "Well, stick to it. You may make it." As predicted, the second grand jury did suggest that Parsons had been acting as an individual, not as a pastoral counselor, but Parsons's reply defused that line of questioning.

Parsons was nervous about his recollection that Dr. T. R. M. Howard had told him that he had paid police some $10,000 on two or three occasions to be protected. Brown had advised Parsons that since he hadn't witnessed the payoffs himself, this was merely general information or rumor that he was not obligated to impart to the grand jury. Parsons recalled that he was indeed asked whether he knew of anyone who paid a police officer for protection. He replied, "No, I never knew that firsthand."

The grand juries did not bring charges against Parsons, but Hanrahan continued to pursue abortion practitioners, raiding the Chicago women's abortion group Jane the following year.[101]

Controversies in Illinois and Florida

The Illinois Clergy Consultation Service found itself in legal news and public controversy in early 1972 when it came to the aid of a fifteen-year-old ward of juvenile court who had threatened suicide if she did not get an abortion. Four psychiatrists recommended an abortion, and a juvenile court judge granted permission for the girl to get a legal abortion in Illinois based on the threat to her life. A physician agreed to perform it. But before the procedure could be done, Hanrahan—by now Illinois state's attorney—appealed the ruling to the Illinois Supreme Court.[102] The CCS saw the hand of the Catholic Church in the matter. A four-to-three decision by the court barred the abortion and the girl was released from state custody because she was not receiving appropriate psychiatric treatment at the state home.[103] At that point, with the girl now in her mother's custody, the CCS conferred with the mother, who provided information about her daughter's psychiatric problems and said the girl still wanted an abortion. The CCS arranged and paid for the girl and her grandmother to travel to Park East Hospital in New York, which was equipped to perform abortions up to fifteen weeks into pregnancy. The chair of the Chicago CCS at the time was Harold Quigley, leader of the Ethical Humanist Society of Greater Chicago. Quigley wrote in a memo—and was quoted in the *Chicago Tribune* as saying—that the girl, a Catholic, had been "a pawn of the ideology of the Catholic church," and Quigley noted that in turn the Chicago news radio station WBBM accused the CCS "of exploiting a sick girl."[104] He pointed out that the CCS came into the case very late and at some potential legal risk, since their legal advice indicated that the girl might still technically have been a ward of the court. No legal repercussions ensued, and the girl's attorney announced that she was "in very good spirits" after the abortion procedure and overnight stay at the hospital in New York. A later memo by Quigley said that he had offered the services of a friend, a child psychiatrist, to care for the girl, but the girl had decided to seek treatment through the juvenile court. The CCS followed up with a letter to John Cardinal Cody of the Archdiocese of Chicago; Quigley wrote in the memo that he felt that the Catholic Church had exploited the girl's "ordeal . . . to ideologize the issue."[105]

In Florida, clergy counselors turned the tables on prosecutors with their own lawsuit. In Tallhassee, Rev. Dr. Leo Sandon, a campus minister at Florida State University (FSU), and Rev. Charles N. Landreth, then associate minister at First Presbyterian Church, were part of the CCS there. After Sandon became CCS state coordinator in 1970, he stopped doing counseling himself and sent Tallahassee callers to Landreth.[106] After Women's Services opened in New York in July 1970, they sent most of their referrals there.

In May 1971, Florida State Senator Richard Deeb, a Republican from St. Petersburg, told the committee overseeing state colleges that he had learned that medical personnel and even a campus chaplain were giving students information about where they could go for abortions. He also objected to a freshman orientation program called "Sex on the Campus," which he said told students that "if you need either contraceptives or pills we can get them for you without your parents' consent." Deeb said that young Florida women were endangered by treatment at New York abortion clinics, that the referrals would be investigated as felonies, and that he could provide five witnesses to testify about "illegal abortion counseling" at FSU.[107] Later the wife of one of Deeb's aides came forward to say that she had called the FSU counseling line posing as a woman with a problem pregnancy. Landreth had an extensive counseling session with her and gave her a printed handout about the New York clinic—which she later passed on to Deeb. The woman, a teacher, later told a district court judge, "I had had pictures in my mind of, you know, being kind of a slip-shod organization on campus and I personally felt like maybe I was doing a community service." However, she said, "After talking with Rev. Landreth and ever since, I felt badly. I hope I have not done anything to injure either of the people involved, because I was impressed with their sincerity," she testified.[108]

The threat of prosecution hung over Landreth and Sandon for several months. State Attorney William Hopkins of Leon County—where Tallahassee is located—convened a grand jury, hoping to indict them, and the teacher Landreth had counseled was called to testify.[109] The two stopped counseling in early July 1971, and they also took action, filing suit with three of their counselees against Hopkins in U.S. District Court to challenge as unconstitutional the Florida law against advising on, advertising, or distributing printed information about obtaining an abortion. They alleged that Florida's 103-year-old law violated their First Amendment right to freedom of speech and religion. In an August pretrial agreement, Landreth and Sandon stipulated that they were doing abortion counseling, free of charge, and referring women for abortions in New York, where the procedure was legal. On September 22, a three-judge federal panel ruled that the three counselees—all of whom had already obtained abortions in New York—lacked standing in the suit, and that Landreth and Sandon had not proven that Hopkins's intent to prosecute them if they were indicted constituted a great enough threat of "immediate and irreparable injury" to warrant the federal court's intercession. The clergy's case was dismissed.[110]

Landreth and Sandon were not indicted, and the Tallahassee CCS was soon back in operation.[111] Meanwhile, a flurry of lower court cases found the Florida law unconstitutionally vague, and campus journalists tested the law forbidding "advertising" abortion by publishing lists of legal abortion providers in student newspapers. In February 1972, the Florida Supreme Court struck down the Florida law as "vague, indefinite, and uncertain" in the case of a physician in Miami who was performing abortions.[112] The court called on the legislature to reform the state law, and seven weeks later it did pass a more liberal statute permitting physicians to perform an abortion when a woman's physical or mental health was in danger.[113]

In Pennsylvania, the CCS filed as amicus curiae to a 1971 suit, *Phyllis R. Ryan et al. v. Arlen Specter, District Attorney of Philadelphia*, seeking to have the state abortion law declared unconstitutional. The suit was modeled on a successful class action brought in Connecticut, *Abele v. Markle*, sometimes called Women versus Connecticut. Similar suits were filed in New York, Illinois, and other states. The *Roe v. Wade* decision in 1973 made the Pennsylvania case moot before a decision had been handed down.[114]

In the CCS's five years of operation, with an estimated 3,000 counselors making referrals quite openly in states with legal restrictions of varying severity, only three counselors faced formal legal charges, and not one was convicted. Grand juries declined to indict any CCS member. This was attributable to the legal advice they had received, the care the counselors took in vetting doctors and sending women out of state, and the recognition by law enforcement that the problems with illegal abortions had more to do with questionable medical practitioners than with the clergy's compassionate counseling. In their dealings with authorities, the CCS also made full practical use of all the privilege associated with who they were: mostly highly respected white male clergy.

7

A Different Kind of Radical Group

The Counselors

The 1960s gave rise to many radical movements and many feminist groups. The Clergy Consultation Service on Abortion was unique. It was overwhelmingly a white, male, middle- and upper-class, middle-aged group of mainline Protestant and Jewish clergy. Yet it really was a radical, feminist, populist group: radical in that it sought an overthrow (not just amendment) of existing abortion laws; feminist in that it worked to return to women power over their reproductive choices; populist in that it strived to serve women of every socioeconomic status, race, and religion. They saw their clerical status as useful to women's fight for abortion rights even if most of them were men, just as many of the same clergy had found their status useful in the civil rights struggle even if they were white.

In 1972, the national office estimated the total number of CCS members at 3,000.[1] That seems quite possible; we have tracked down the names of just over half that number, 1,547 counselors (even as this book went to press, we were discovering additional names). Of those, we know that 1,068 were clergy; the other 479 were either laypeople—social workers and nurses, for example—or clergy who did not use their title. A majority of CCS clergy whose affiliations we know came from mainline denominations: Presbyterian, Methodist, Baptist, Episcopalian, UCC or Congregational, Unitarian, and Lutheran—roughly in that order. Jewish clergy were less well represented, and nearly all were from the Reform tradition, with just a few Conservative rabbis. There were also clergy from the Disciples of Christ, Church of the Brethren, Reformed Church, and five listed as Roman Catholic. We found one or two representatives from each of the Friends (Quaker), Associate Reformed Presbyterian, Ethical Culture, Christian Methodist Episcopal, and Swedenborgian Church.

Of all the names we found, only twenty-four were female clergy, a manifestation of the small number of women who were ordained in those days. When the CCS began, few denominations called women ministers, and there were no ordained U.S. women rabbis. The Society of Friends (Quakers) had always accepted women as ministers, and the Congregational Church (by the time of the CCS, part of the United Church of Christ) had been ordaining women since 1853. Presbyterians—that is, the predecessor of the Presbyterian Church (USA)—and Methodists began ordaining women as full ministers in 1956, and the Church of the Brethren did so in 1958. But by the 1960s and 1970s, even in those denominations, the percentage of clergy who were women was small, and the number of women who headed their own church congregations was minuscule. Many seminaries accepted female students, but most female seminary graduates in the 1960s and before became religious educators or music leaders, not pastors of congregations.[2]

As a result, a clergy group in that time was bound to be mostly male. Although they used their own respectable status and power to advance the work of the group on behalf of women, they acutely felt the lack of women participants. Starting with the New York group and again in almost all the chapters across the country, the male clergy made special efforts to recruit female clergy counselors. They felt the injustice that in their efforts to make safe abortions accessible to women, men were still controlling that access. They knew that many women felt more comfortable confiding in a female counselor. The woman minister who was among the original members of the New York group found herself inundated with calls in greater numbers than the male counselors.

Around the country, women were active participants in, and even founders of, CCS chapters. Rev. Peg Beissert, although she herself was Presbyterian, was serving as assistant minister at Christ Church, a UCC congregation in Summit, New Jersey, when her head of staff, Rev. Allen Tinker, recruited her to the CCS. The day after her ordination service in June 1971, he took her to a meeting of the New Jersey CCS in Rahway. Beissert recalled, "We got there. It looked like a hundred men. Really, it was packed with, I think, every clergyman from [the New Jersey CCS]—it was men then. And I was very unusual as a woman. They all stood and applauded when he introduced me. And I said to Allen, 'Why do they do that?' He said, 'Peg,' he said, 'These are all men! They're dealing with a problem that's innate with women. And now, thank God, you're here!'"[3]

Rev. Allen Hinand, head of the Pennsylvania CCS, recruited two feminists he knew, Marilou Theunissen and Barbara Krasner, even though they were not clergy members. The two women visited doctors together, worked closely with Hinand, and did counseling. Theunissen became director of the Pennsylvania CCS and continued its work for several years after the *Roe v. Wade* decision in 1973.[4] Laywomen like Arlene Carmen took strong noncounseling roles in many of the chapters, checking out doctors and dealing with them, doing administrative and coordinating work, and helping train clergy counselors. In spite of the national group's proscription against nonclergy counselors, laywomen and laymen did counsel for some chapters. A doctor who had been a volunteer counselor with the CCS when she was a medical student told writer Carole Joffe that she transported women to their abortion procedures. The young woman was galvanized by her volunteer work and went on to become a staff physician at the Women's Services clinic immediately after it opened.[5]

Judy Widdicombe, a nurse, was the founder of the St. Louis CCS, and from the start she recruited both men and women as counselors, including nurses and other nonclergy volunteers. Widdicombe also recruited a layperson, Georgie Gatch, to start a chapter in Columbia, Missouri. Then working at the campus ecumenical center at the University of Missouri, Gatch looked for people who were involved in campus ministry, men and women, clergy or lay. She considered their political leanings—looking for people who were involved in the civil rights and antiwar movements—and whether "they could be supportive and helpful to women."[6]

Elizabeth Canfield was the co-founder of the CCS in Los Angeles. She recruited clergy, raised funds, was the administrator for the group, vetted doctors and clinics, and counseled. She was a layperson, but she had volunteered with Planned Parenthood, educated women to whom she distributed Emko contraceptive foam, and, as one of the founders of the Los Angeles Free Clinic, had done extensive counseling for women with unplanned pregnancies. In her time with the Los Angeles CCS, she recalled, they did not use any other nonclergy counselors.[7] After she left the group and the Los Angeles CCS merged with Planned Parenthood, a number of CCS counselors were social workers, psychiatric nurses, or graduate students in those fields.[8]

Diana March was a member of a women's group at her Unitarian church in Elgin, Illinois, a suburb of Chicago, when she trained as a lay counselor for the Chicago CCS. "Women who were pregnant appreciated talking to another woman," she recalled, and they came from far and wide to talk to her. March visited the practice of a woman physician on the west side of Chicago, and she said one could "smell fear" in the waiting room, and the anxiety level of patients was very high. She asked the doctor if she would want to have a support person in the waiting room to provide comfort and reassurance and to answer questions; March herself acted in that role that day and wound up working with the doctor for a couple of days a week for several months as a patient advocate and counselor.[9]

One of the cases seen by this doctor was a young couple who had driven from Ohio. The young woman's pregnancy was too far along for the procedure to be done in the office. The doctor tried to convince them to go to a hospital, but they had no money and were very frightened. The doctor decided to go ahead and do the procedure, against her better medical judgment, and it "did not go well. There was tissue left inside," March recalled. The couple still refused to go to a hospital, so the doctor made arrangements for them to stay at the doctor's mother's home so the woman could stay under the physician's care. Instead of following the doctor home, the couple drove back to Ohio. The patient's condition worsened. The physician sent money for the girl's hospitalization in Ohio via March and Spencer Parsons, head of the Chicago CCS.[10]

March continued to counsel women as a CCS volunteer and wound up making a career of it. In 1973 she helped to start a private, nonprofit family planning clinic, Crossroads Clinic, in Palatine. At first they offered contraception and testing for sexually transmitted infections for teens, but eventually provided pregnancy counseling, low-cost prenatal care, and abortion services.[11]

Seminary students, men and women, counseled for the Chicago group, too, even though they were not yet ordained. Donna O. Schaper was a student at University of Chicago Divinity School, not yet ordained, when she and other students counseled for the Chicago CCS (see chapter 4). In fact, this was a triple flouting of the original guidelines: they were not ordained, the CCS paid them for their counseling work, and the counselors actually handled the money for the travel and procedure.[12] Those were flagrant violations of the rules that Arlene Carmen tried to enforce most strictly on a national basis, but Schaper was counseling relatively late in the time of the CCS, 1972–1973, when abortion was legal in New York and then legalized nationally by *Roe v. Wade*. In any case, Parsons ran the Chicago service—very successfully, with only minor legal repercussions (see chapter 6)—his own way.

In Michigan, the CCS included many counselors who were nonclergy therapists and social workers, both men and women. In 1971, Lauretta (Lauri) Talayco Holmes was a counselor at Family and Children's Services of Lenawee County in Adrian, Michigan. Social workers and family counselors were uniquely placed to witness a change in attitudes during the late 1960s and early 1970s. Holmes said, "We did problem pregnancy counseling, and I was the main problem pregnancies counselor. I was seeing the changeover in attitudes. In

1969, girls said, 'I've got to go someplace so no one knows.'" The pressure to give up an out-of-wedlock baby was strong, especially for white women, in the 1950s and 1960s, when, as Rickie Solinger has written, "pregnancy became fundamentally a moral issue."[13] The shame of pregnancy outside marriage was enormous, whereas there was much more anxiety than shame attached to seeking an illegal abortion, a retrospective psychological study found.[14] But the sexual revolution and feminist movement of the 1960s, the civil rights movement, and the welfare rights movement changed attitudes about single mothers, according to Solinger. In particular, the legalization of abortion gave women new light in which to consider all of their options. "Thousands of mothers reasoned then [when abortion was legalized] and afterward that if they could, with dignity and legal standing, choose to end their pregnancies, surely they could, with equal dignity, make an alternate choice and decide to be the mothers of the children they gave birth to," Solinger wrote.[15] Lauri Holmes recalled, "In 1971 or '72, I had my first client who said, 'My friends are all telling me I should keep this baby.' It was a sea change." Childbearing outside of marriage was becoming socially acceptable, "shotgun weddings" became rare, and in 1972 federal law prohibited schools that received federal funds from expelling pregnant students.[16] Holmes said most of her counseling then involved the question of whether to keep a baby or choose adoption. She was named as a member of the Michigan CCS as one of three trained lay counselors at her agency in a 1971 letter to national coordinator Arlene Carmen. When asked, Holmes said she did not remember being a part of the group; the CCS training (which may have been just a short workshop or information session) and list of recommended abortion providers would have been a small part of her routine work. She did remember counseling one upper-middle-class family who took their daughter to New York for an abortion. She didn't see the daughter afterward, but the mother came in, "expressing great surprise that it was so simple. She [the daughter] felt as if she'd never been pregnant. . . . I suppose she thought that it would be horrible and traumatic," but the experience had been a good one.[17]

Although the clergy considered themselves feminists and were joined by many laypeople who were feminists, some women-led feminist groups looked upon the CCS with attitudes ranging from suspicion to outright scorn. The clergy, however well meaning, were still men who were controlling women's access to abortion, placing themselves in paternalistic roles in relation to the women they counseled. Patricia Maginnis, who had given classes in self-abortion and freely handed out referrals to doctors in Mexico since 1966, was at the scornful end of the spectrum. Author Cynthia Gorney reported that Maginnis drew a cartoon that she had printed on postcards. "Hominy Dominy Counseling

Service," it read, and the drawing showed "a balding little priestly man with his hands over his face and a second caption that read, 'Women's Counseling for Problem Clergymen.'"[18] Nevertheless, Maginnis provided Canfield with information about abortion in Mexico, which Canfield used for both the Los Angeles Free Clinic and the Los Angeles CCS.[19]

The clergymen themselves were products of their era, and their well-meaning support of women didn't mean that all CCS members were consistently progressive in the way that radical feminists of the time would have respected. Some clergy may have taken a paternalistic view of their counseling, and many probably continued to use a vocabulary that revealed their age and upbringing—calling women "gals" or "girls," for example.

But some women's groups respected the CCS for its work. In Chicago, Jane was a group that at first referred women to a capable abortion practitioner; when they discovered that he was not a doctor, as they had thought, they realized they could learn to perform abortions safely, and they did so. The group organized in February 1969, started their referral work, and in October became part of the newly formed Chicago Women's Liberation Union, after which many more women started calling them.[20] The Chicago CCS was forming at about the same time: Parsons called its first organizational meeting in March 1969; the group started to make referrals in April; and it went fully public in December.[21] The two groups had a respectful relationship.

Parsons had been in contact with one of the founders of Jane in spring 1968. Before Jane had formed and before Parsons had started any abortion referral work, he received a call from a fellow Baptist minister in Bloomington, Indiana, asking for his help in finding an abortion for a young couple, both graduate students. The minister had called Howard Moody, who was a friend, for advice, but the couple could not afford to travel to New York for counseling. Chicago was within reach, however, and Moody suggested that the Indiana minister call Parsons for help. Parsons agreed to try to find an abortion provider in Chicago.[22] As Laura Kaplan wrote in *The Story of Jane: The Legendary Underground Feminist Abortion Service*, "He contacted a woman he knew in the [University of Chicago] dean's office, thinking, if anyone knows, she'll know. She was a member of WRAP [Women's Radical Action Project], the campus women's liberation group. She was also helping Claire [a pseudonym for one of Jane's founders, who made abortion referrals before the group organized] with her abortion referral work. She gave him Claire's number. 'I made the contact and the couple went and had the abortion,' he recalls. 'They came back to the chapel office, and told me they thought it was great that it could be done. Then they went back home and I never heard from them again.'"[23]

As more women came to Parsons seeking abortion referrals, he generally sent them to his fellow clergy in the New York CCS. Kaplan writes, "He thought out-of-state referrals might shield him from prosecution and he felt more comfortable with the clergy network than with the contact he'd made in the dean's office."[24] Later that year, Moody prevailed on Parsons to start the Chicago chapter. One of the local resources to whom Claire and other counselors for Jane had also referred women was Dr. T. R. M. Howard. Kaplan wrote that the members of Jane decided that cooperating with the CCS would be beneficial, since their mission was the same. A member of Jane (called Miriam in Kaplan's book) contacted Parsons and learned "that Jane was only reaching the tip of a huge iceberg. They [Jane] were getting ten calls a week, but the clergy was getting ten calls a day." They agreed to share information, but Kaplan wrote that Parsons felt it would be wise to keep some distance between the groups and for them to avoid using the same Chicago doctors. "As clergymen they had a certain protection that Jane didn't have. It had to be the clergy who took the public role and announced what they were doing, since, unlike Jane, they were people with stature and no one thought of them as subversive. Each group continued to operate on two different levels and kept in touch through regular meetings" between Miriam and Parsons.[25] After July 1970, when abortion became legal in New York and the Chicago CCS was referring as many women as possible to Women's Services, Jane continued to provide local abortions to women who could not afford the trip.[26] The relationship between the radical feminists of Jane and the clergy of the CCS was respectful and recognized the particular strengths each group had. Jane had contacts and experience and could provide abortions locally; the clergy had a status that was both protected and influential and had connections around the country.

Theology of Protestant Counselors

Of course religion was not just a protection and status enhancement for the CCS. The members felt genuinely called to act on their beliefs. Moody felt keenly that organized religion as well as the law had oppressed women, and he wrote an essay in 1967 called "Man's Vengeance on Woman: Some Reflections on Abortion Laws as Religious Retribution and Legal Punishment of the Feminine Species."[27] He laid primary responsibility for punitive antiabortion laws at the feet of Protestants, not Roman Catholics. He wrote, "If the Catholics seemed to be unnaturally obsessed with the future salvation of an unbaptized fetal soul, the Protestants were preoccupied with removing the visual product of woman's immorality and sin. . . . Protestants do not share with our Catholic brothers any belief in the instant animation of the fetus, so the only reasonable justification that we can give for the present abortion law is some innocuous defense of the 'sanctity of life.'" Moody went on to condemn the law as forcing women to seek dangerous illegal abortions. "It is hard to draw any other conclusion from the background and history of the present law than that it is directly calculated, whether conscious or unconscious, to be an excessive and self-righteous punishment, physically and psychologically, of women. . . . Forever the suffering victim of our double standard sexual hypocrisy, the law seems to guarantee that she will not only suffer for her error but will also be denied even the right to correct her mistake." Moody called on Protestants, as the most responsible for the law, to take up the fight to repeal it. "The time is long overdue for a crusade by the Christian church against the outrageous injustice of the present laws. Our silence and timidity have been to condone the law and acquiesce in the suffering."[28]

In a 2005 interview, Moody said, "To me it was an obligation that I felt the church owed, like I think—same way in the art field, we owed it never to censor anything done at Judson—in the theater, or dance, or whatever. Never to censor it. The church, all of its life, has been censoring every damn thing it could put its hands on, you know. And I just felt that was one place where we might do a little recompense, is not to censor, and to support and help."[29]

Moody felt that the recompense had to be active. He called the German theologian Dietrich Bonhoeffer his "spiritual mentor," quoting him: "We will not know what we will not do."[30] The work that Moody did with the CCS woke in him an awareness of a general discrimination that women suffered in medical care; his answer was, with Judson Church and Arlene Carmen, such projects as an outpatient breast biopsy clinic—where such biopsies had previously required an inpatient hospital stay—and a health clinic for sex workers. Moody saw sex workers as another group of "invisible women," like those who had sought illegal abortions, "either ignored, pitied or whispered about . . . suffering silently and profoundly in a sleazy, dehumanizing underworld. . . . When the light finally shone on them, we saw that they were our mothers, our sisters and daughters."[31]

Theologically, Moody argued that free choice is essential to being human. He wrote in his memoir, "My understanding of free choice is that the right to choose is a God-given right with which persons are endowed. Without choice, life becomes a meaningless routine and humans become robots. Freedom of choice is what makes us *human* and *responsible*. And for women, the preeminent freedom is the choice to control her reproductive process." He viewed "the deification of the *conceptus*" as heretical, saying that in his theology, being born is not a right but a gift of God and a woman. "*Rights* begin with birth—they are a birthday present—hence *birthright*. Now we are born and have rights, but even then the rights are not absolute or indisputable. Even after birth our rights are fought for, denied and balanced against those who are already here and whose own rights limit and confine our own."[32]

Huw Anwyl, head of the Los Angeles CCS and coordinator of many of the western chapters, felt strongly that the group's work was good and was needed. He said, "It didn't take me long to be very comfortable with the idea that the only one who should make the decision about a pregnancy was the person involved." However, when he gave public talks, opponents of abortion argued with him. "They'd tell me a lot of things, that the Catholic Church and other churches had been opposed to this for centuries, and who do you think you are to say otherwise? So I said, well, I should find out. And you know the consequences of that kind of research: None of that was true."[33] He almost certainly had in mind theologians such as Augustine (354–43), Anselm of Canterbury (1033–1109), and Thomas Aquinas (1225–1274), who believed in delayed ensoulment of the fetus, before which abortion should not be considered murder.[34]

Lyle Guttu, the only Lutheran pastor we spoke with, discussed the tradition of Lutherans in social services but not "when it comes to protest or advocacy." Guttu speculated that Martin Luther (1483–1546) was a "total medieval man. Calvin thought that things could be done, and Luther thought the world was as the world had been created." Guttu studied at Harvard with Paul Tillich and with Reinhold Niebuhr at Union Theological Seminary. Tillich (1886–1965) was a Lutheran theologian who is regarded as particularly influential in twentieth-century theology. He was an early critic of Hitler and the Nazis and left Germany after being barred from teaching. He taught at both Union Theological Seminary (1933–55) and Harvard (1955–62) and was a major influence on the Rev. Dr. Martin Luther King Jr. King credited Tillich's work on his thinking and referred to Tillich's cautionary view that "sin is separation" to illustrate the evil of segregation in the United States.[35] Dietrich Bonhoeffer (1906–1945), Lutheran pastor and martyr at the hands of the Nazis, was an important influence on the theological thinking of both Moody and Guttu. Guttu's involvement with the CCS was influenced by Bonhoeffer and Tillich, his study of progressive movements, and his pastoral work in East New York with a predominantly black congregation. In addition, he was interested in the work of Saul Alinsky, and he wrote his thesis on community organizing, which he took up in his role as a pastor at a storefront congregation near two large housing projects. Guttu was recruited into the CCS through Al Carmines, a former classmate and roommate, who was serving as the associate pastor at Judson Memorial with Moody. Guttu's volume of counseling was two to three women a week from the CCS founding until 1971, when he moved into other church work and settled at Wagner College. Guttu said of the women he saw, "By the time I saw somebody . . . they knew what they were after. . . . They fundamentally wanted to know if we would help. And we would."[36]

In January 1971, Parsons, speaking at Christian Theological Seminary in Indianapolis, said,

> As a Christian minister, the most compelling reason why I regard abortion as a morally acceptable procedure is that I believe the Christian faith essentially affirms the primacy of the human spirit over the biological processes of nature. That is to say, the quality of personal and family life, the goals, purposes and welfare of particular persons have a prior claim over the accidents of biology. . . . The Biblical commandment, "Thou shalt not kill," was obviously directed toward our treatment of other living human beings, and only by ignoring the original context can it be made to apply to a fertilized ovum.[37]

Many of the pastors we interviewed expressed the opinion that their pastoral counseling necessitated a commitment to compassionate care for women with unwanted pregnancies—their CCS work was simply part of their job as ministers. As we have noted, they were also involved with the social movements of the day, particularly in civil rights and antiwar organizing, and women's rights seemed a natural part of that work. Clergy including Howard Moody, Lyle Guttu, and Robert Hare talked about their internships or first church appointments in the communities that helped radicalize them. Finally, the most influential liberal Protestant theologians of the day taught at Harvard University (Tillich), Yale University (H. Richard Niebuhr), and Union Theological Seminary (Tillich and Reinhold Niebuhr), where many of the clergy to whom we spoke had studied.

The Rabbis

The CCS rabbis we interviewed, and those who wrote on the subject, believed that Jewish teaching permits abortion: the living person (the mother) takes precedence over the potential person (the fetus). A founding member of the CCS, Reform Rabbi Israel Margolies of Beth Am Congregation in New York, speaking at an Association for the Study of Abortion conference in 1968 said, "Until a child is actually born into this world, it is literally part of its mother's body, and belongs only to her and her mate. It does not belong to society at all, nor has it been accepted into any faith. Its existence is entirely and exclusively the business and concern of its parents, whether they are married or not. It is men and women who alone must decide whether or not they wish their union to lead to the birth of a child, not the synagogue or church, and certainly not the state."[38] Rabbi Morton Bauman, a member of the Los Angeles CCS, told the Los Angeles *Herald-Examiner* much the same thing, adding, "I think it's criminal for any child to enter this world unwanted. Having a child doesn't teach a lesson or solve a problem. Religion, not the state, is the institution which teaches ethics and morality, therefore each individual should abide by the teachings of his church and not call upon the state to impose those teachings on others."[39]

Reform Rabbi Balfour Brickner strongly criticized any Bible-based argument that the fetus be considered a full person, saying Exodus 21:22–55 addresses the issue directly. He said,

> Two people are fighting, and a woman is standing by. In the middle of the fight, she is wounded. The ax head falls off, or a rock hits her, and it hits her in her belly, and she's pregnant, and she miscarries. Or she loses the fetus. So the question is raised and answered: Are the people involved in the fight guilty of murder? And the answer is, of course, no. And the reason they're not guilty of murder is because the fetus is only a fetus, and not a living person. So you can't hold the people who were in the fight responsible for murder, because it's only a fetus. Now, nothing could be more specific.[40]

He wrote elsewhere, "According to Jewish law, a child is considered a 'person' only when it has 'come into the world.' The fetus in the womb is not a person until it is born. The Rabbinical principle is *lav nefesh hu*—'It is not a living soul.'"[41] In general, Brickner told us, Jews were very willing to be involved with Planned Parenthood and family planning. "Jewish women were the best practitioners of birth control in the world—still are. I remember I once had a conversation with my then-mother-in-law, who was at that time in her late seventies or eighties, and I once said to her, 'Ethel, what did you folks do when you got pregnant?' And she laughed at me, and she said, 'Why do you ask such a dumb question? Everybody had a doctor'—and she was a New Yorker—'everybody had a doctor in Brooklyn.' Which was to say there wasn't a time when abortion and abortion services were not considered as a viable option and used and practiced as a viable option, certainly among lots and lots of Jewish women."[42]

A Conservative rabbi (who asked that his name not be used) looked to Talmudic teachings. "The theoretical basis for Roman Catholics and Protestants is different. They ask, 'When does quickening take place? From birth? 40 days?'" In the *Roe v. Wade* decision, the U.S. Supreme Court took viability into consideration. The rabbi said,

> The Jewish position is entirely different. It's not whether the fetus is alive. The question is, in Jewish law, as it is concerning Arabs who want to kill Jews. The Talmud says if a person is coming to kill you, get up earlier and kill him first. There's the concept of the chaser and the chasee, the person who is coming to harm you and the person who is going to be harmed. . . . The fetus is endangering the life of the mother. Until the fetus's head emerges intact, or the body emerges, the fetus is coming to kill the mother. You can kill it at any stage to save the life of the mother. The question in Jewish law is what constitutes threatening the life of the mother. I believe emotional health is threatening the life.

The rabbi said he thought that some rabbis might not have wanted to join the CCS because they questioned whether emotional health counts as threatening the life of the mother. He added that as a Conservative Jew, "I'm bound by Jewish law, as I interpret it." Indeed, most of the Jewish clergy members of the CCS were Reform rabbis; few were Conservative, and we found the names of no Orthodox rabbis.[43]

Of the 1,068 clergy members of CCS whose names we found, only 61 were rabbis. The small number of Jewish clergy participants was a sore point for national CCS administrator Arlene Carmen. In a 1976 interview, historian and women's rights activist Ellen Chesler asked Carmen about this. She said,

> I really felt angry over the years over the fact that rabbis would not participate in this. I'll tell you what they said. First of all, it wasn't a problem for their congregations. There's a certain difference, I think, between the Protestant ministry and the rabbinate that I wasn't aware of, but became aware of, as time passed. In the Protestant ministry it's not unusual or uncommon to counsel somebody who's not a member of your particular congregation. It's quite different for a rabbi to be put in that position. There's less of a tradition of outside people coming in for help. Now there could have been a lot of other reasons, and I guess I think that there probably were rabbis wanting to be involved . . . and a couple who really got in trouble with their congregations over it. . . . I used to make up the schedule for the [New York City] clergy . . . I'd schedule their days on the telephone tape recording that gave out names and numbers . . . and, I think that we never had a rabbi more than one week a month, but there were three other weeks in that month. The women would seek counseling, and when they called and asked for a rabbi, I'd have to say no.

Even Rabbi Brickner, a public member and staunch supporter of the CCS, had not actually counseled a lot of women, Carmen said.[44]

Outside of major cities such as New York, Chicago, and Los Angeles, the existing clergy networks that naturally fostered recruitment for the CCS may have been less ecumenical. Reform Rabbi Stephen Forstein recalled that he was the only rabbi in Topeka, Kansas, at the time of the CCS and was not generally included in local clergy groups. He did make abortion referrals on his own but was not aware of nor asked to participate in the Topeka CCS. The Topeka chapter was very small in any case; we know of only two members, both Protestants.[45]

Black Clergy

Loretta Ross writes that the majority of abortions available to black women in the 1950s and the early 1960s were provided by doctors and midwives operating illegally. Black midwives provided most of the abortion and contraception services for black women in the deep South. Ross says that in the 1960s "underground abortions were facilitated by churches and community-based referral services" but does not mention the CCS by name.[46]

Relatively few black clergy joined the CCS, and probably for different reasons than the rabbis. Many in black communities were suspicious of the white medical establishment, especially regarding reproductive health, for good reasons going back to such horrors as Dr. James Marion Sims's experimentation on enslaved women and children. The eugenics movement in the early twentieth century openly advocated advancing "superior" (white) genes and repressing those of "inferior" races, and Margaret Sanger, the founder of Planned Parenthood, at least for a time used the scientific-sounding language of the eugenics movement to promote women's right to contraception.[47] She argued that the use of birth control was both moral and eugenically beneficial. Legal scholar Mary Ziegler writes that to win support for Sanger's version of eugenics, between 1920 and 1928 the *Birth Control Review* (established and edited by Sanger) featured "racialist and anti-immigration" articles. Though she was never a proponent of abortion, Sanger wrote that birth control and "its general, though prudent, practice must lead to a higher individuality and ultimately a cleaner race."[48] In the United States, the racist eugenic legacy played itself out in the Tuskegee experiments that began in 1932, in which black men suffering from syphilis believed they were in a treatment program but in fact had treatment withheld (finally ending in 1972). Additionally, black women were far more likely to undergo forced sterilization than were white women; in fact, in the South especially, black women sometimes went to the hospital to give birth and were sterilized after the delivery. Hospital abortion committees imposed sterilization as a condition of providing an abortion more often for black women than for whites. In the 1960s, as the civil rights movement grew, this history of abuse by white medical providers became more public, causing some black leaders—mostly young men—to conclude that the white-controlled political system had a stake in suppressing and oppressing the black population.[49]

The Black Panther Party was the only nationalist group to support free abortions and contraception, although not without controversy within its own ranks. In 1967, the Black Power Conference held in Newark, New Jersey, resolved that birth control was a form of "black genocide."[50] Nkenge Toure and Angela Davis both made comments about women in the party wanting access to birth control and abortion, but noted that some men tried to shut down family planning clinics in New Orleans and Pittsburgh.[51] Black congresswoman Shirley Chisholm wrote in 1970, after she became honorary president of NARAL, that "there is a deep and angry suspicion among many blacks that even birth control clinics are a plot by the white power structure to keep down the numbers of blacks, and this opinion is even more strongly held by some in regard to legalizing abortions. But I do not know any black or Puerto Rican *women* who feel that way. To label family planning and legal abortion programs 'genocide' is male rhetoric, for male ears. It falls flat to female listeners, and to thoughtful male ones."[52] Many other women of color also fought for contraception and abortion rights, often combining the fight with that against sterilization abuse to complete their contention that they should have full reproductive control of their own bodies—to reproduce as well as not to.[53] Of course, some of the women who sought abortions through the CCS were black.

However, suspicion of the motives of family planning clinics and abortion providers may have been one reason relatively few black clergy—most of whom would have been male—were involved in the CCS. Evangelical black churches, like their white counterparts, would also have tended to disapprove abortion. We don't have good statistics on the race of CCS participants and have been able to identify just a handful as black; of those few, we have not been able to interview a single one. Since many of the white members of the CCS had been active in the civil rights movement and recruited through those connections, it is safe to assume that white members of the CCS were acquainted with black ministers. However, C. Eric Lincoln points out in *The Black Church Since Frazier* that while there was some coming together of white and black clergy at the height of the civil rights movement, the war in Vietnam "became the major competitor for the interest of white activists."[54] We found evidence of that from our own sample of CCS clergy. The segregation of mainline Protestant churches and majority black-serving churches was a legacy of slavery and institutionalized racism in the United States that was not overcome by the civil rights movement and is reflected in the lack of participation by black clergy in the CCS.[55]

The Catholic Church and the CCS

Before *Roe*, the strongest opposition to abortion came from the Roman Catholic Church, whose bishops issued formal statements on the subject and whose clergy publicly advocated stronger legislation against abortion. But views within the Catholic Church differed. Father Robert Drinan, a Jesuit priest, lawyer, and theologian, argued in 1967 from an antiabortion stance *for* the repeal of abortion laws, saying, "repeal would not mean that the state approves of abortion but only that it declines to regulate it."[56] At the parish level, some priests were sympathetic with girls and women who sought birth control or abortions. Presbyterian minister David McFarlane, then in the Rochester, New York, area, had a friend who was a priest at a church that served many college students. McFarlane said that in the late 1960s and early 1970s, "the priests certainly were opposed to abortion, there's no question about that, but you could still go to your priest and talk and not get a doctrinaire lecture. I'm sure there were lots who gave doctrinaire lectures, just like there were lots of Protestants who did— maybe the majority, I really don't know. But at [his friend's church] in those days, you'd at least get some pastoral care." The two young clergymen used to go the bars where the students hung out, each having been given a small allowance by their churches for drinking. McFarlane laughed and said, "I am the first Presbyterian minister I ever knew with a drinking allowance." In fact, the bars were so glad to have them there that they usually drank for free. Students would bring up theological and personal questions, and if a student asked about contraception or abortion, the priest would indicate McFarlane and say, "Talk to him!" McFarlane always had condoms in his pocket to hand out and could refer students to Planned Parenthood, even before he became part of the CCS.[57]

The CCS clergy had contacts among priests and nuns who were sympathetic. Most did not appear on public lists of CCS members. One who participated openly was Sister Barbara Voltz of the Catholic Newman Center at University of Wisconsin–Milwaukee. She spoke publicly in 1972 as a representative of the Milwaukee Area CCS. Although she regarded herself as a nun, she had resigned from her order, the School Sisters of Notre Dame, and became a member of the noncanonical organization Sisters for Christian Community.[58] Parsons said that at least one Roman Catholic priest who later left the priesthood and two nuns, one the prominent feminist theologian Anne E. Carr, were members of the Chicago CCS, and although they did not make referrals, they met with Catholic women who wanted further counseling following their abortions. "When [women] felt very badly about being Roman Catholic and having had an abortion, she was very helpful. And I had priests in Chicago who did the same thing. They said, 'Don't send me anybody initially to counsel, because this would be very awkward for me. But if you have anybody who needs to reflect on this and think about it, I'd be glad to be of help,'" Parsons recalled. Carr also attended counselor training sessions to educate the Protestant and Jewish clergy about Catholic beliefs and explain some of the struggles that Catholic women would be going through when they came for counseling.[59]

Moody said that he had referred Catholic women who had doubts to a priest from the Newman Center at New York University. "A lot of Catholic women, there was an ambivalence. They knew that they'd be excommunicated, they knew—they loved the church, they went to church, they did—but they couldn't do this. They couldn't have the child. But when there was an ambivalence, I knew that I could refer to him, and that he would be as gentle as he could be. I knew how he'd handle it," Moody said.[60] The Los Angeles group included psychologist and counselor James Kavanaugh, then of Chula Vista, who joined the CCS in early 1969, not long after he had written the bestselling book *A Modern Priest Looks at His Outdated Church* and left the priesthood. Kavanaugh was a colorful guest on television talk shows. He became a prolific and popular poet with books such as *There Are Men Too Gentle to Live among Wolves*.[61] The Philadelphia CCS chapter also had two priests on their lists to whom they could refer Roman Catholic women who wanted counseling following their abortion.[62]

The Columbia, Missouri, CCS chapter, based at the University of Missouri campus ecumenical center, "worked closely with the Catholic college ministry [Newman Center]," recalled Georgie Gatch, the CCS chapter coordinator at the time. "They had a counseling service for women who wanted to keep their child; they would sometimes—not *directly*—refer to us, and if we had someone who decided they wanted to keep their child, we would refer them there."[63]

Some active Catholic priests referred parishioners to the CCS. Rev. Wayne Conner was a Presbyterian minister who came to First Presbyterian Church in Kalamazoo, Michigan, in 1971 as a youth minister. He was active in many local ministries dealing with drug use, racism, and other social justice issues, and he was quickly recruited to the local CCS. He recalled in an interview, "On two occasions a Catholic priest I knew . . . placed a call to me saying, 'I won't describe the situation, but there's someone you need to talk to.' It wasn't that he was referring them to me for an abortion, but 'I don't feel free discussing that with them. You'll have a discussion that I can't have.'" One couple went to New

York for an abortion. Another couple, both about eighteen, referred by the priest, came to talk about their wedding. The bride was pregnant, and the priest couldn't perform the wedding because, he told Conner, "'it's not a free choice if the bride is pregnant.'" Conner recalled,

> The boy was virtually silent, and the girl did all the talking. I finally said to the boy, "You're acting like you're feeling pushed into this because she's pregnant." With great hesitation he shook his head very minimally, yeah. So I talked with her—with them both, but mainly with her—about what that means. Would you resent the child? Would the marriage last? What about all the complications if you separate? The boy finally had the courage to say he wouldn't marry her. We talked about taking care of the child. I said, "You are the father. Marriage doesn't have to be the way you take care of the child, but you have responsibility." He didn't think there was a way out. She was madder than hell. Two or three years later, I got a phone call. For some reason I recognized the voice before she'd identified herself. I didn't remember the name, but I knew exactly who it was. She had had the kid and was ready to get married. She really appreciated what I'd done. She was ready to marry—and would I do that for her? She brought the kid to our first meeting—the cutest little kid. I asked about the father. He had stayed in her and the kid's life, and he was not an issue with the new husband.[64]

Conner happily performed the wedding.

CCS members counseled many Catholic women, generally in proportion to the number of Catholics in the general population. Reports from CCS chapters in 1969 said that in Cleveland, 40 percent of CCS counselees were Roman Catholic; New Jersey CCS reported that slightly under half were Catholic.[65] A Chicago CCS spreadsheet dated April 15, 1970, showed that just over a quarter of their counselees at the time were Catholic.[66] During eight months of 1972, women who consulted the Jacksonville, Florida, CCS were about 10 percent Catholic.[67] Parsons recalled asking Catholic counselees if they had used birth control and some replying that they had not because they viewed contraception as wrong—although they were now seeking an abortion.[68] Rev. Benjamin Bohnsack, then a young associate minister at a church in Livonia, Michigan, said that he always asked about religious background because it was important and especially difficult for Catholics. "I would say, 'Your church says this is wrong. How will you feel if you go ahead?' Sometimes they had good answers. If they had poor answers, I would help find other ways for them to think about it. 'Do you agree with all your church says and does?' Or, 'It's a private matter and you don't have to tell anyone about it.' Or theologically: 'God places a lot of decisions into our own hands. That's part of human freedom.'"[69]

Congregations and the CCS

Few of the clergy we spoke with suffered negative repercussions from their congregations or denominations—at least for their abortion counseling. Of the Protestant or Jewish denominations represented among the CCS clergy, none had official proscriptions against abortion. The U.S. Episcopal Church was supportive of abortion law reform and the CCS, although the international Anglican Communion had declared an "abhorrence of the sinful practice of abortion" in 1930. Some individual evangelical Protestant ministers had opposed abortion in the 1930s and 1940s; it is safe to say that there weren't many fundamentalists among the CCS clergy. In 1961, the National Council of Churches declared general opposition to abortion except in case of danger to a woman's life or health.[70] Beginning in 1963, the Unitarian Universalist Association of Congregations passed a series of resolutions supporting "the right to choose contraception and abortion as a legitimate expression of our constitutional rights."[71] In 1968, Moody and Parsons both spoke at the American Baptist Convention in favor of a resolution stating that "abortion should be a matter of responsible, personal decision," and that legislation should permit termination of pregnancies before the twelfth week. That resolution—though it was not official church policy and was not binding on any member or congregation—was adopted.[72] In 1971, Rev. Charles N. Landreth, associate minster of First Presbyterian Church in Tallahassee, Florida, and a member of the CCS, preached a Sunday sermon on abortion. He quoted from the previous year's Presbyterian General Assembly paper, which said that "the unborn fetus must be respected for its own worth, regardless of the period of gestation. However, the needs of the mother may at times take precedence over the needs of an embryonic and unformed child, and the rights of the individual woman, her family, and society, as well as the rights of the fetus, should be considered in each individual case." The statement called on the church to provide pastoral care for women with "problem pregnancies" and to help in finding counseling about alternatives.[73] Again, the statement did not form church policy but was accepted by most of that year's clergy and lay delegates. Many other denominations issued statements supporting changes in abortion laws, including the Greek Orthodox Archdiocese of North and South America (1966), the Episcopal Church (1967), the Union of American Hebrew Congregations (1967; now known as the Union for Reform Judaism), the United Church of Christ (1970), the United Methodist Church (1970), and the Moravian Church of America

(1970).[74] Even the Southern Baptist Convention, representing one of the more conservative of the mainline denominations, approved a national resolution in 1971 accepting in principle the reforms of the ALI model; after the *Roe v. Wade* decision, the Southern Baptist news service viewed the decision as one that advanced "the cause of religious liberty, human equality, and justice."[75]

Evangelical Protestants had long opposed both contraception and abortion, although they seldom spoke or wrote about either publicly in the first half of the twentieth century. Preachers such as Billy Sunday and John Roach Straton alluded to abortion, and Henry Stough preached against it at women's meetings, but it was not a central public issue.[76] After World War II, the secular issues that most concerned fundamentalists were the Cold War, New Deal social welfare programs, and the civil rights movement, issues that led to a focus on states' rights and an antipathy to federal judicial decisions.[77] On the topic of abortion, most evangelical Protestants in those days were relatively silent. As Daniel K. Williams writes in his history of the pro-life movement, "Evangelicals remained on the sidelines [in the 1960s] because they were suspicious of Catholics and because they lacked a clear theology of when human life began."[78] Changes in state abortion laws in the late 1960s disturbed evangelical Protestants, however, and began a backlash against "abortion on demand." A 1971 statement by the National Association of Evangelicals explicitly rejected legislation that made possible "abortion on demand for reasons of personal convenience, social adjustment or economic advantage," but recognized "the necessity of therapeutic abortions to safeguard the health or the life of the mother," and in the case of rape or incest only after "medical, psychological and religious counseling of the most sensitive kind."[79] Jack and Barbara Willke's 1971 *Handbook on Abortion* provided a blueprint for opposition to more liberal laws; it sold 1.5 million copies in eighteen months and was very popular among evangelicals. For the first time, evangelical Protestants began to ally themselves with Catholics and the right to life movement.[80] Then in 1973, with evangelicals already starting to mobilize against abortion, *Roe v. Wade* struck directly at their antipathy to liberal federal judicial decisions that overrode state laws. Evangelicals have formed a major and vocal part of the opposition to abortion ever since. At the time the CCS began in 1967, however, evangelicals were essentially silent on the subject in the public sphere. Williams also points out that some Orthodox Jewish rabbis and Eastern Orthodox churches spoke against abortion at the time, but their political influence was limited, and we know of no CCS clergy participants from either group.[81]

Beyond denominational policy, most of the CCS clergy we interviewed said that at the local level their congregations—to whatever extent they knew of their clergy's CCS activities—were supportive.

Judson Memorial Church, where the answering machine for the New York group and the national CCS office were located, was a combined American Baptist and UCC congregation, and Moody was an American Baptist, but church members included people of diverse religious and nonreligious backgrounds. Judson's inclusivity and its social justice focus were what drew the congregation together, and it fully supported Moody and the work of the CCS. Moody said, "There was real backing there." There might be women in the congregation who wouldn't choose abortion for themselves, but they didn't want to make it illegal, Moody said. "I was doing things illegal, of course. [Abortion referral] was illegal, and I was facing a year in jail and a thousand-dollar fine. All the clergy were when we started this. And this wasn't the only time I was breaking the law. . . . No, the church was incredible. We [were] doing so many things out in left field, especially in the art field, in theater, in dance, and all that stuff. . . . When I came here there was like twenty members at Judson at that point, and we grew up together. . . . People *came* because the church was doing what they were doing."[82]

At Washington Square Methodist Church, Finley Schaef had attracted a younger congregation that supported his civil rights, antiwar, and feminist activism. "The congregation when I went there [in 1966] was kind of old and feeble. It changed, with younger, more radical people and they loved all of that," Schaef said. About his involvement as a founder of the CCS, he said, "I'm not so sure I told the hierarchy [of the United Methodist Church], but it was in the *New York Times*. They never said anything to me about it."[83] Schaef's church also hosted the feminist Redstockings group's famous speak-out on abortion, "Abortion: Tell It Like It Is," on March 21, 1969. It was a truly radical event at the time; Susan Brownmiller later wrote, "Back then, personal testimony was a political act of great courage."[84]

Most of the clergy we interviewed spoke of strong support from at least a few of their parishioners. In some instances the governing boards of individual congregations voted to support a clergyperson who was participating in the CCS; in Pennsylvania, for example, the vestry of St. Martin's Episcopal Church in Radnor voted its support of Rev. James C. Blackburn, and the board of deacons at Central Baptist Church in Wayne did the same for Rev. Allen Hinand.[85] Most of the clergy did not seek prior approval from the governing bodies of their congregations or from the hierarchies of their denominations. Most genuinely viewed their abortion counseling work as an extension of the pastoral care that was an ordinary part of their job. Rev. David McFarlane went further, saying, "In that church in Pittsford [New York], I was associate, I was not the head of staff, but we all were expected to minister to the whole community. And I never had to ask any permissions. The reverse would have been true. If someone ever thought I was backing away from engagement in issues or caring for a person who came, I would have been asked on what basis I was doing that."[86]

In Los Angeles, the Mount Hollywood Congregational Church fired Huw Anwyl, at least partly over his involvement in the CCS. He had been fired before, from Avalon Park Community Church, in 1963 for his outspoken work on racial desegregation. The job at liberal Mount Hollywood seemed a better match for Anwyl's activist leadership, and he followed the forty-year tenure of a committed pacifist, Rev. Dr. Allan Hunter. Anwyl became more activist than ever and on an international scale. Traveling on his British passport, he visited Cuba in 1966 and called for the resumption of trade between the United States and Cuba, a stance that got him disinvited from speaking at the Easter sunrise service at the Hollywood Bowl on his return. He chaired the Los Angeles chapter of the peace organization Clergy and Laymen Concerned About Vietnam. In that role, he recalled in an interview, he had raised $20,000 to charter a flight to Washington, DC, with a group of eighty ministers, and he traveled to Vietnam as he had earlier traveled to Cuba. The Religious News Service gave him press credentials, which allowed him to ride in military helicopters to see the country. "Going to Vietnam didn't change my views about what we need to do, but, on the other hand, it gave me some insights into the complexity of that situation, instead of us against them. . . . So I had a few things to say when I came back. That caused a fair amount of flak, as well."[87]

Anwyl resigned from Clergy and Laymen Concerned in April 1968. The *Los Angeles Times* reported, "Mr. Anwyl said an impasse had developed over whether the chapter should concentrate heavily on draft counseling and the resistance movement or deal with broader questions related to Vietnam and the church, which Mr. Anwyl favored."[88] At the same time, Anwyl was organizing the Los Angeles CCS and by early 1969, as he told the *Los Angeles Times*, he was spending seventy to eighty hours a week on it. A significant number of his congregants were upset that he was neglecting the church in favor of his outside activities.[89] By starting the Ecumenical Fellowship (see chapter 4) Anwyl could spend his time on the CCS as he chose.

Rabbi Buz Bogage, one of the founding members of the CCS in New York, also found that in addition to his activism in civil rights and antiwar campaigns, his CCS work—taking large amounts of time at his office counseling hundreds of women, mostly from outside the congregation—was the last straw with the senior rabbi and board of the venerable Central Synagogue. As sympathetic as some of them may have been individually with his views, the institution found his public activism disruptive, and Bogage left for a liberal congregation in Denver in early 1968.[90] In New Jersey, Rev. Chick Straut moved to Methodist denominational work because his radical political activity (not specifically his CCS work) made his congregation uncomfortable.[91]

In Chicago, Spencer Parsons, an American Baptist, was dean of Rockefeller Chapel at the University of Chicago, and the university community was supportive. He was outspoken in the political arena on a number of issues, and he took on repeal of the abortion laws as one of his main causes. The strong advocacy course that the Chicago group took eventually troubled one of the members, the only CCS counselor with whom we spoke who quit the organization while it was still in full operation. Parsons had recruited an associate of his at the University of Chicago, Rev. Bernard O. Brown, then a program director at International House and associate dean of Rockefeller Chapel. He had been a Methodist, but in 1970 he was ordained in the Episcopal Church, in whose liturgical tradition he had a strong interest. Brown said that the CCS work had the "immediate appeal to me as a pastoral kind of relationship that was needed." He recalled that initially he felt good about his work with the CCS and saw it as a helpful form of pastoral care, especially with students, including international students. "I saw no real conflict between my work as an advisor and pastor to foreign students, as I was until 1970, and what we were doing. The illegality part of it didn't bother me much, because I thought that was on the way to being resolved. And I just thought you don't turn people down when they need help. It was similar to the help I gave to people during the Vietnam time, when they were AWOL and so on. So I was active, and appreciated some of the relationships that were built that way, and felt like I was doing something that I could affirm," he said in a 2004 interview.[92]

After their abortions, women sometimes stayed with Brown and his wife at their home. But as the Chicago group's advocacy seemed to take center stage, Brown felt that the seriousness of the choices women were making was being trivialized in the increasingly polarized political discourse. Brown recalled, "I became disenchanted when, in my view, the work that . . . I'd entered as a counselor and pastor became a question of being a policy advocate. . . . Not because I was wholly opposed to the decriminalization of abortion, because I was and am in favor of decriminalization of abortion, but because I thought it was scanting in important kinds of concerns, and becoming kind of routinized, if that's a word that I could use, in a way that I couldn't participate in anymore." Soon counseling sessions lasted only twenty or thirty minutes, which did not allow the formation of the kind of pastoral relationship that Brown felt women deserved. Meetings and public talks by the group became, in Brown's view, "overly exuberant" in pushing for change, "something that I thought needed a lot more care and thought." Brown was working on a Ph.D. in social ethics, and that training informed his position that "women need to be able to be supported in whatever they had to do . . . but it's not an ethically responsible or morally responsible action that is based solely upon an individual choice. There have to be some resources that include the dimensions of a life that we all have with one another." Brown felt that the polarized camps excluded understanding of the other's position and prevented conversation about what lay between the two extremes. "It became an us-and-them kind of thing, and I didn't feel that way," Brown said.

Although Brown loved Parsons, "he became *really* caught up in this, and thought, I think, that it was part of his administration *and* ministration to people who needed this help to make as easy for them as possible. And I still felt that there's a kind of tragedy, a tragedy about this that people together needed to live through." Abortion, Brown said,

> I believe, and continue to believe, is a violence against a life *form*, not a life in the full sense. I began reading in classical texts that had to do with justified violence. . . . I know that you cannot force a woman to bear a child, and when all is said and done, it will be her choice—but not all is said and done much, and that bothered me, because I felt we were becoming involved in something more crude than I was interested in. . . . So I went in to see Spencer [Parsons], and I said, you know, Spence, I can't really do this anymore, and I told him why. He was very understanding.[93]

Brown continued his work at the University of Chicago and at Rockefeller Chapel, finished his Ph.D. in 1973, succeeded Parsons as dean of the chapel in 1979, and retired in 1995.

To some degree like Brown, many counselors undoubtedly saw the need for their work with the CCS and shared in their counselees' doubts and ambivalence. Rev. Wayne Conner of Kalamazoo said, "A lot of social justice issues are a lot clearer in my mind. Women should certainly have control over their own bodies. No one should tell them what to do or control them. But it's still a little uncomfortable. Some [who have had abortions] still have some discomfort about it—that something, some small part of them, that was alive now is not."[94] Other clergy who may have had doubts about abortion counseling at the beginning, or who were recruited to the CCS without any prior experience with—or perhaps even thoughts about—abortion generally became much more committed to the work as they began to counsel. Benjamin Bohnsack, who had very little counseling experience before joining the CCS, said, "There was never any coercion. I saw women who had their minds always fairly made up. It was never a matter of talking them into anything. They wanted to know what was the possibility of having an abortion, what would that look like, where would it happen, and what would it cost. There was always some degree of upset if not desperation. If I started out with any qualms about the rightness of what I was doing, these were soon gone in the experience of talking with women whose situations were so difficult that I wanted to be on their side."[95]

Clergy and Abortion Law Reform

Pressed by the resolutions of Vatican II in 1965 to take a more active role in contemporary issues, Roman Catholic clergy were early and vocal opponents of liberalizing abortion laws at the state level. They testified before legislative committees and issued public statements.[96] Before the formation of the CCS, political advocacy by Protestant and Jewish clergy on behalf of abortion law repeal and reform lagged behind the antireform activity of the Catholic clergy. Howard Moody and others in the original New York group had been optimistic that the New York State legislature would reform state law in early 1967. But their vocal support for reform came late: Moody's article in _Renewal_ magazine, "Man's Vengeance on Woman," came out in February 1967, just about the same time the New York reform bill was quashed in committee. The failure of the bill was the impetus for the clergy group to take direct action and make abortion referrals themselves, starting in May. When the New York service began in 1967, most of the clergy participants favored reform of the state abortion laws.[97] Moody said later that the group had resolved to learn from the women they counseled, and one of the things they learned was that reform was not enough. "After six months [of counseling] we were for repeal of that law." The group had learned that having to justify certain abortions as opposed to others was an "odious" position. "Reform is the enemy of real social change," Moody said, so the group began working in earnest to repeal the existing abortion law.[98]

As Rosemary Nossiff points out in _Before_ Roe, "the CCS challenged the Catholic Church's role as the exclusive moral and religious authority on the abortion issue in a way no other group could." The very existence of a high-status, religious group advocating for abortion rights opened up political dialogue and encouraged other advocacy organizations—the American Civil Liberties Union, for example—to act on abortion law reform. Nossiff quotes Aryeh Neier, then the head of the New York Civil Liberties Union, as saying that the CCS "challenged the political sanctions and put itself on the line. It helped to take [abortion reform] out of the shadows and made it a respectable issue."[99]

The clergy founders of the other two very large CCS chapters, Parsons in Chicago and Anwyl in Los Angeles, also were involved in political reform efforts before they founded their regions' referral services—Parsons as a founding member of the Illinois Committee for Medical Control of Abortion and Anwyl as a member of the California Committee on Therapeutic Abortion.[100] Public statements by Catholic clergy against abortion demanded an answer from clergy on the other side of the issue, and progressive Protestant and Jewish clergy came forward or were recruited in political efforts to change state laws. The CCS provided a roster of clergy who not only wanted the law to change but also had experience in its effects on the women they counseled. They could give a powerful and personal as well as theological counterargument to the Catholic clergy's testimony in state legislatures, and they had up-to-date statistics. In addition to Moody, Parsons, and Anwyl, many CCS members served as spokespersons for abortion law reform and/or repeal and testified as legislatures considered reform bills. Leaders of the Michigan CCS testified at a state senate legislative hearing on abortion in December 1969.[101] Rev. John G. Wightman, chair of the New Jersey CCS, spoke before the state assembly in 1970.[102] Rev. Arthur Kuehn, then associate minister at Central Baptist Church in Hartford, Connecticut, and a member of the CCS and the Connecticut League for Abortion Law Reform, testified in Connecticut in 1971.[103] The Philadelphia CCS was a partner in bringing suit against the state in federal district court to declare the Pennsylvania abortion law unconstitutional. In 1972 Marilou Theunissen, by then state coordinator for the Pennsylvania CCS, served on an all-female commission appointed by Gov. Milton J. Shapp to make a recommendation on reforming the state abortion law (the sharply divided commission recommended legalizing abortion up to twenty weeks into pregnancy).[104]

The clergy were influential pro-reform witnesses at legislative hearings, in part because they were generally white men, listened to and respected by mostly male lawmakers; doors opened to them in a way they did not for women. For that very reason, the male clergy who testified were rightfully resented by women who had to fight to make their own voices heard in the legislative process. At a 1969 judicial committee hearing in the Connecticut legislature on a reform bill, the testimony of women was put off until the very end of the day, and the official stenographer did not even record it. Amy Kesselman quotes one of the women, Ann Hill, who recalled that it was "infuriating" to listen to doctors, priests, and progressive clergy expound on the issue. "We were at the hearings— but we were invisible. We were not 'experts' or 'professionals.' We had no credentials, no degrees, and the lawmakers did not want to hear us."[105] The radical feminist group Redstockings broke up a committee hearing on abortion at the New York legislature in 1969; one woman's voice was heard shouting, "Why are 14 men and only one woman on your list of speakers—and she a nun?"[106] The inclination of male lawmakers to consult other men preferentially in hearings regarding the reproductive health of women continued well into the twenty-first century.[107]

A Medical Consumers' Union

While the clergy worked to reform the law, they realized that making abortion accessible meant making it available to all women. Larry Lader, the writer and activist who had worked with the CCS as it formed, wrote in his book *Abortion II* that in the early days fewer women than expected came to the New York clergy from low-income neighborhoods. "Red tape and travel costs to Pennsylvania and other states limited most black and Puerto Rican women to neighborhood abortionists despite low medical standards," he wrote.[108] Before 1969, the group sent many women to Puerto Rico. Soon the doctors there raised their prices to $500 and $600, matching typical U.S. fees. It was then that the clergy realized that their referrals were valuable — and powerful. Lader wrote, "Moody found he could control prices at $400 or less by sending most cases to one clinic, which maintained superior medical and pricing standards."[109] Other CCS chapters used their referrals as leverage to lower prices. The group found a doctor in Pennsylvania and one in New Orleans who charged $300 per case and occasionally would take a hardship case for free. By late 1969, Lader said, Dr. Bernard N. Nathanson — then an OB-GYN who provided abortions, later a vocal opponent of abortion — had persuaded St. Luke's Hospital in New York to read the existing abortion law liberally and take most of the CCS's referrals of poor women, whose abortions were paid for through social services.[110]

When the CCS began its work in New York, the cost of an abortion was quite high — around $600 in 1967 (more than $4,000 in 2017 dollars).[111] Arlene Carmen said, "We were really serving the needs of white, middle-class, college-educated people, who probably would have gotten an abortion anyway, some other way, perhaps, not as good an abortion. They might not have wound up in the hands of a doctor who was as qualified as the one we finally sent her to see. We never deluded ourselves that we were really providing a service for the women who most needed it, and that was the poor woman who could not afford the $600, plus transportation."[112]

For the purposes of advocating legal change, that middle-class clientele was perfect. Recalling the clergy's testimony before the New York legislature's joint committee on public health as it considered reforming the state's abortion law, Moody said, "We were the only ones doing anything about abortion, the clergy. . . . We would report to the health committee our findings. That was very impressive to them, that it was mothers and daughters and wives of middle-class people. I'm telling you, it's the middle-class thing that really changed it. I don't believe for a moment — if it had only been poor people we were serving, [a change in New York state law] wouldn't have happened."[113]

In Chicago, Parsons referred some poor women locally to Dr. T. R. M. Howard, who would reduce or waive his fee in a percentage of cases.[114] The New York CCS also negotiated some free and very low-cost abortions for poor women, but it never provided actual funds for the procedure. Asked in 1976 why they had not done so, Carmen said, "We thought about it, and people encouraged us to set up what everybody calls a slush fund, but we had a real problem with how you play God in that situation. I mean, there's limited financing, and who we give to, and who we don't give to becomes a very difficult issue, and one that I don't think we felt we wanted to undertake. There just wasn't enough money. There would not have been enough money that any philanthropist could have given that would have subsidized the number of abortions that women could not pay for."[115]

A few services around the country did find funds to help women. In the case that became public and controversial in 1972, the Chicago CCS paid all expenses for a suicidal girl and her grandmother to travel from Chicago to New York City for an abortion (see chapter 6).[116] In Atlanta, Rev. J. Emmett Herndon, then a Presbyterian campus minister at Emory University, was part of a group administering a $50,000 grant from a Presbyterian donor to the church to help implement the national General Assembly's 1970 statement on abortion, which called on clergy to provide pastoral care for women with problem pregnancies. Herndon said in a phone interview that some of that money was used to give women throughout the South loans and grants. "Most tried to pay it back," he recalled. "Some were very poor, and they'd send one dollar a week. It was kind of pitiful and made you feel sad to open an envelope with a dollar in change in it." He approved one $600 grant for a woman to go from Kentucky to New York City for an abortion. He recalled, "She couldn't read or write, so someone had to go with her. She already had twelve children. She didn't go—her husband didn't let her go—so I guess she had a thirteenth child." Herndon arranged another grant of $275 to enable Florida's State Welfare Division of Family Services to send a young girl to New York City for a successful abortion.[117] In Kalamazoo, Rev. Wayne Conner remembered one couple that borrowed money for an abortion and came back to him afterward to return at least some of it. Conner said the money hadn't come from his church and thought the CCS—either local or state—must have provided the loan.[118] Some clergy counselors also offered financial assistance on an individual basis. In Chicago, Rev. Donna Schaper sometimes helped women with her own personal funds.[119]

Carmen was instrumental in creating a true medical consumers' union out of the CCS by negotiating with doctors over price and insisting on high standards of practice. Doctors who used the "packing" method—packing the cervix with gauze to induce abortion—were ruled out. In the late 1960s, the standard for abortion procedures became vacuum or suction aspiration, which had a lower complication rate than the dilation and curettage (D&C) that had been the best available method up to that time. One of Carmen's "negative" lists, undated but probably from 1968 or 1969, with many entries underlined for emphasis, names practitioners in seven states and territories with notations such as, "Too old, bad news . . . Butcher; avoid at all costs . . . Filthy dirty; expensive; avoid . . . Old; careless; under surveillance . . . On probation for 3 years; slum area; filthy; bad procedure packing and DC; 2 visits req.; avoid . . . Bad news; avoid . . . Not licensed Dr."[120] A member of the Philadelphia CCS said in 1969 that they had a national negative list that included about 500 unsafe abortionists.[121]

The group found a New Orleans doctor, Hale Harvey, through a New York University graduate student, Barbara Pyle, who had studied with Harvey at Tulane University.[122] Carmen made a trip to New Orleans, and found, Lader wrote, that "the doctor and his staff laid special stress on supportive counseling before and after abortion, and taught each patient the fundamentals of contraception. 'He made women feel they were good people—a positive experience we had rarely developed elsewhere,' Carmen noted. 'He quickly became our prime source.'"[123] Harvey also set a high standard for care, one that he and others instituted later at the Women's Services clinic. The CCS was able to insist on their requirements—safe and clean surroundings, a set price, competent medical care, no "packing" procedures or general anesthesia, and respectful treatment—because they had power. They brought doctors many referrals, but they offered more than that. Carmen and Moody wrote,

> The clergy were able to do for them something which had not been done before, namely, refer to them a steady volume of patients who had been examined, screened, and counseled in advance. This meant that only patients without medical contraindications were referred; also these patients arrived with a certain sophistication about and understanding of what was in store for them, having had their fears allayed and a detailed explanation of the medical procedure provided by their clergy-counselor. . . . Having gone through the CCS meant there was less risk that the woman was a police operative and this factor made the doctors feel more secure. Under these circumstances we had no hesitation about dropping a doctor who blatantly violated our understanding.[124]

The CCS gradually became aware of the economic power they held over the physicians to whom they referred hundreds of women, but the doctors were well aware of that power from the beginning. Rev. John Wightman, chair of the New Jersey CCS at the time, recalled, "We used a doctor, maybe in Puerto Rico, who started giving me gifts. That got me very nervous. Shortly after that we stopped using him."[125]

The numbers of women referred by the CCS also provided valuable—and previously unavailable—statistics about the safety of abortion as an outpatient procedure. Even where legal abortions were available under medical restrictions—with the approval of hospital committees, for example—they were performed in hospitals, and women were admitted as inpatients, usually for a few days. The thousands of women referred by the CCS, however, were nearly all treated as outpatients, often making a long trip home on the same day as the procedure, with very few serious complications reported. In at least some cases of complications, the doctors who had performed the abortions covered the patients' expenses for treatment, apparently at the insistence of the CCS.[126] Most of the CCS chapters could refer women who returned with complications to local doctors and hospitals where they would receive knowledgeable care and sympathetic treatment.

When abortion was made legal in New York state in 1970, the CCS's experience with many thousands of successful abortions done on an outpatient basis plus their wish to make abortion available and affordable to all women caused the group to take the most radical step yet: opening an outpatient abortion clinic in New York City.

8

Available and Affordable

State Abortion Law Reform

From the time New York state's reform bill was defeated in March 1967 through 1970, thirteen states passed liberalized abortion laws, and four—Alaska, Hawaii, Washington, New York (in 1970)—practically repealed theirs.

It is important to recall, looking back through years of polarization of the political parties on the subject of abortion, that in the 1960s and early 1970s, abortion law reform was a bipartisan issue. In fact, many leaders of the fights to liberalize state laws at that time were Republicans—legislators Constance Cook in New York and Lorraine Beebe in Michigan, for instance—and there were Democrats who—usually on the basis of their Catholic faith—opposed legalizing abortion. Many Republicans saw abortion law reform as promoting the ability of doctors to practice their profession as well as the rights of women to make their own choices about reproduction without government regulation. Abortion did not appear as an issue in either party's national platform until 1976, when Republicans merely recognized it as an issue on which the party was divided, and Democrats acknowledged concerns about abortion but called any attempt to overturn *Roe v. Wade* "undesirable." After that the divergence became more pronounced. In 1980 the Democratic platform again affirmed *Roe* while Republicans added a call for "the right to life for unborn children." Republican antiabortion rhetoric grew in vehemence in the 1990s.[1]

In Colorado, Republican governor John Love signed a law in April 1967 permitting abortions in hospitals only with unanimous approval by a committee of three doctors. North Carolina passed a similar bill (also requiring three doctors' approval, though they didn't have to be part of a committee) in May that year. In June, California governor Ronald Reagan, a Republican, signed into law a reform bill permitting abortion with physicians' approval when the woman's physical or mental health was in jeopardy.[2] The sudden spate of successes in liberalizing state laws energized activists on both sides of the issue: the Roman Catholic Church was determined to fight liberalization; abortion rights supporters turned their attention to repeal, rather than reform. The politics of abortion became more highly charged, and organizations—the CCS and NARAL among them on the repeal side—prepared for what looked like a protracted struggle.

Not much progress had been made in the courts until September 1969, when the California Supreme Court struck down the vague provisions of that state's abortion law in the case of *People v. Leon P. Belous*, a doctor who had performed abortions for many years and was accused of accepting a kickback from another doctor. Even though Belous was charged under the old, pre-1967 abortion law, the 1967 reform contained some of the same problematic language—permitting a woman to get an abortion "when necessary to preserve her life," which the court ruled had "no clear meaning"—and put its interpretation up for question.[3] The Belous case sparked the interest of Charles Munger, the California attorney, investor, and philanthropist who also supported Rev. Huw Anwyl, the Los Angeles CCS, and Los Angeles Planned Parenthood, and who campaigned to force Los Angeles hospitals to liberalize their abortion policies. He and his high-powered law firm worked on the Belous case pro bono. The victory for Belous renewed court challenges to abortion laws around the country. In California, many more abortions began to be approved. With Munger's support, Anwyl and the Los Angeles CCS, which was referring a tremendous number of women, pushed the hospitals to accept more patients, lower fees, and provide better care (see chapter 4).[4]

Although California had not passed a law that was any more liberal than a number of other state laws, the *Belous* decision and CCS efforts to work with hospitals meant that abortions were easier to obtain there. Several CCS chapters in the West and Midwest referred women to Los Angeles for abortions. For example, in spite of their own state abortion law reform, many Colorado women went to Los Angeles.

In Washington, DC, the autumn of 1969 also saw an important court decision. Dr. Milan Vuitch had been arrested in 1968 for performing abortions at his office. He had been operating quite openly, contending that the district's abortion law, unlike laws elsewhere, permitted abortion for the "preservation of the woman's life and health"—not just in life-threatening situations—and he read that as including a woman's mental health. In November 1969, the Federal District Court struck down the DC law as unconstitutional, making abortion legal in the district. Exonerated, Vuitch was back in business and opened a new clinic where he received as many as 100 patients a week.[5] The CCS referred women to his clinic, where early term abortions cost $300 in 1970. Vuitch and NARAL, under the leadership of Larry Lader, pressed the DC Health Department to comply with the court's decision and offer free abortion services, but in fact DC hospitals and physicians mostly did not change their practices: hospital approval committees continued to refuse most applicants, and physicians were not interested in signing on to NARAL's proposed clinic.[6] It took more than a year for two more abortion clinics to open: an outpatient clinic at Washington Hospital Center and the nonprofit Preterm Clinic.[7]

Meanwhile, in March 1970, Hawaii passed a law permitting abortion up to twenty-four weeks. It was important for Hawaiians, but did not help women elsewhere, as the law applied only to residents—defined as those who had lived in Hawaii at least ninety days—and the procedure had to be done in a hospital. In Alaska, thanks to advocacy by clergy across the state, the legislature overrode (barely) the governor's veto to repeal the state's abortion law. Under the new law, abortions could be done only in hospitals and required a thirty-day residency.[8]

In New York state, where NARAL, the CCS, the National Organization for Women, and other large pro-repeal organizations were based but where the Roman Catholic influence was also very strong, the battle was close and hard-fought. Upstate Republican Constance Cook—"the only mother in the legislature," as she called herself—and Franz Leichter, a New York City Democrat, introduced a repeal bill in 1970.[9] The bill passed in the state Senate after an emotional five-hour debate. In the Assembly, the dramatic vote came to a tie; but before the speaker had cast his tie-breaking vote, Assemblyman George M. Michaels, a Jewish Democrat from a largely Catholic district upstate, stood up and, taking the microphone with shaking hands, said, "I realize, Mr. Speaker, that I am terminating my political career, but I cannot in good conscience sit here and allow my vote to be the one that defeats this bill. I ask that my vote be changed from 'no' to 'yes.'"[10] The bill passed, and on April 10, 1970, Governor Nelson Rockefeller signed the law, setting off a frenzy of activity. As of July 1, 1970, it would be legal in New York for physicians to perform abortions on women up to twenty-four weeks' gestation, and thereafter to save the woman's life. There was no hospital requirement, so outpatient procedures could presumably take place at clinics and physicians' offices. Beyond that, New York was now the only state with a broadly permissive law that did not impose a residency requirement. New York hospitals, physicians, family planning clinics, social service departments, and insurance companies scrambled to prepare for an unknown—but predictably high—demand for the procedure. Hospitals purchased equipment and hired and trained extra staff.[11] Few physicians had much experience. Doctors who had been performing abortions, legally or illegally—including Dr. T. R. M. Howard from Chicago—were brought to New York to teach the procedure.[12] Planned Parenthood and the New York City Health and Hospital Corporation set up special phone lines to answer questions and refer women for abortions. Blue Cross and Blue Shield of Greater New York announced they would pay up to $300 for an inpatient abortion.[13] Many doctors and private clinic operators—including some very shady ones—saw the opportunity to set up in the abortion business and make a lot of money.[14]

The New York CCS after State Legalization

The New York Clergy Consultation Service was preparing to shut down its referral work on July 1—although the National CCS would continue to be coordinated from Judson Church. Howard Moody and Chicago CCS administrator Ron Hammerle made efforts to get Planned Parenthood to take up the referral role played by CCS, and in New York Planned Parenthood agreed to open phone lines to help women find abortions. Hammerle thought that if the clergy network could continue and apply itself to medical care generally, they could have been a powerful force for health care consumers, but Moody wanted to shut down the CCS and get out of the counseling business wherever abortion was legal.[15] Moody prevailed, but in 1976 Judson Church did sponsor a health care advocacy group called the Center for Medical Consumers, which operated until 2014. Moody formed another group to address problems with the health care system as the New York abortion law took effect.[16]

The clergy of the CCS had good reason to know how very high the demand would be, and they had no confidence that New York hospitals—especially the public hospitals—would be able to meet the need. Linda Greenhouse wrote in the *New York Times* just as the law was about to take effect, "Last year [1969], there were an estimated 1.2 million abortions performed in the United States. All but 30,000 or 40,000 of them were illegal. In addition, an estimated 800,000 women carried their pregnancies to term only because they could not get legal abortions and could not bring themselves to go to an illegal abortionist. Thus there is a potential national demand for abortions of about two million a year." She continued, "With New York the only place for most of these women to go, what would happen if they all came here? Indeed, what would happen to the estimated 50,000 to 100,000 New York City women alone who would seek abortions?"[17]

The New York City Health Department, hospital administrations, and physicians were all eager to keep abortion a hospital-based procedure, but as the effective date of the new law drew near, even they conceded that women seeking abortions were likely to encounter delays at first. New York state, the city, and the Medical Society of the State of New York issued differing recommendations to limit where and how late in pregnancy abortions should be permitted. Unless adopted as law, these recommendations created a "standard of practice" but were not legally binding. The eighteen municipal hospitals would have to abide by the city's guidelines requiring that abortions be done in hospitals and that recipients be local residents. No law prevented physicians from performing office procedures or the establishment of outpatient clinics.[18]

The CCS knew that hospitals would be overwhelmed and that poor women in particular would have difficulty finding affordable care. A reformed law was of no practical use if abortions were still unavailable. Who would monitor the availability of services, especially at city hospitals? At a joint press conference with Planned Parenthood of New York City in June 1970, Howard Moody announced the formation of Clergy and Lay Advocates for Hospital Abortion Performance, a watchdog group that would track complaints from callers to the city's and Planned Parenthood's phone lines and could intercede when necessary to help callers schedule procedures more speedily.[19] A member of Judson Memorial Church who had helped start the CCS in Pennsylvania, Barbara Krasner, would run the program from the CCS side. Moody recalled that after that press conference, the city backed down on its recommendation that abortions be performed in hospitals only.[20] That summer, CCS members were shocked and dismayed when Dr. Robert E. Hall, the professor of obstetrics and gynecology at Columbia University and director of the birth control clinic at Presbyterian Hospital who had been an early champion of reforming the state abortion law, argued that abortions should be performed only in hospitals. In Chicago, Ron Hammerle complained that Hall was ignoring statistics showing that that first-trimester abortions performed in clinics were safer than second-trimester abortions in hospitals. The comparison was fair, given that public hospitals had waiting lists up to six weeks long, and those women would have to wait until later in their pregnancies for hospital abortions.[21]

An Outpatient Clinic

The CCS had also been preparing for a much more radical action: setting up its own outpatient abortion clinic. As early as 1968, Arlene Carmen and Moody wrote later, the CCS "fantasized about setting up an 'abortion ship' just outside the three-mile limit under a foreign (Japanese) flag." They checked with a maritime lawyer, who told them the project was possible but subject to U.S. government pressure on the country whose flag the ship flew. They tried to raise funds, but with little success. The final blow to the idea came when the group's medical advisors expressed concern about how safe shipboard procedures would be.[22] Some thirty years later, in 1999, Dutch physician Rebecca Gomperts put just such an idea into action with Women on Waves, taking a clinic ship to countries where abortion was highly restricted. Women boarded the ship, which then sailed to international waters. There, under Dutch law, the women received medical abortions via mifepristone (RU-486), which had none of the risks associated with surgery at sea.[23] The drug was not available at the time the CCS was operating.

Still, the dream of a CCS clinic persisted. In 1969, when progress in the New York legislature had stalled, the group discussed opening its own abortion clinic, even in violation of the law as it then stood. The goals, Carmen and Moody wrote, would be to demonstrate the safety of outpatient abortions and "to expose the hypocrisy of a law which allowed 'therapeutic' abortions for the rich but denied them to the poor." They were surprised when their lawyer, Ephraim London, and NYCLU director Aryeh Neier supported the idea of a setting up an outpatient abortion clinic, as long as it operated openly and didn't profit anyone.[24] The old law on therapeutic abortion did not require that the procedure be done in a hospital; that was just accepted practice. The CCS clinic could have its own Therapeutic Abortion Committee that, unlike those at hospitals, would approve *all* requests, as long as they came with the legally required letters from two psychiatrists stating that a woman's life would be in jeopardy if her pregnancy continued. A small group from the New York CCS began meeting regularly to discuss this proposal.

The group approached physicians and found a number of obstetrician/gynecologists who would be willing to take the risk; one, Dr. Bernard Nathanson, made a full commitment to the project. Psychiatrists would be important to the enterprise, and this was a stumbling block. The psychiatrists the group approached were reluctant, because, as Carmen and Moody wrote, their "plans called for psychiatrists simply to provide 'rubber stamp' approval to a woman's request for an abortion, not a terribly attractive role for a professional."[25]

Nonetheless, the planning continued. The group wrote up a "confidential prospectus," which said, in part, that the facility was to be completely nonprofit, seeking "to establish the feasibility of providing medical services to women with problem pregnancies at a minimum cost without refusing service to anyone because she lacks funds"; that except for clergy counselors staff would be paid salaries that would match those of professionals working elsewhere; and that an accountant would prepare quarterly reports that would be open to public scrutiny.[26]

The small group invited selected abortion activists to a series of larger meetings to let them in on the plan and get their support. Dr. Alan Guttmacher had been the chief of obstetrics and gynecology at Mt. Sinai Hospital and in 1969 was a leader of the International Planned Parenthood Federation; Dr. Robert Hall, the OB-GYN who was president of the Association for the Study of Abortion, the group that had advocated for hospitals to perform more abortions; and attorney Harriet Pilpel, general counsel for the Planned Parenthood Federation of America and special counsel for Planned Parenthood of New York City. It soon became clear that the newer additions to the group were more cautious than the original nucleus, and the expanded committee could not reach consensus. But the original organizers felt that "the women who needed abortions might not be able to wait until a 'perfect' plan was developed," so they determined to go ahead, with or without the support of their activist friends.[27] Moody later wrote, "I often thought that if we had done a plebiscite among the liberal reformers before we started the CCS, there would have been the same reluctance to take the risk of breaking the law."[28]

The clinic committee discussed renting offices. They feared entering into a long-term lease in case they were shut down early, but on the open market they could find nothing that involved a lease shorter than a year. Judson Church came to the rescue again. The church owned an adjacent three-story brownstone known as Judson House, and it had just become empty. At various times, it had housed the associate minister of the church, visiting artists and writers, the Judson Health Center, and, most recently, an experimental residence for runaway youth. Moody proposed that the second floor be used as—in the words of the church board's minutes—an "abortorium," at a set-up cost of about $40,000, which the organizers intended to raise through donations, grants, and perhaps a loan. On March 24, 1970, the Judson board approved the use of Judson House for that purpose, whether or not the abortion repeal bill then under consideration in the state legislature passed.[29]

Just a little over two weeks later, when the abortion repeal bill became law, the clergy group was ready to act. Dr. Hale Harvey, the New Orleans doctor to whom the group had referred women for more than a year, phoned Moody immediately after the New York bill passed, offering to set up a clinic, to be housed in its own premises rather than at Judson, and be ready to go by July 1, when the new law took effect. Their experience with Harvey had been so positive that they agreed immediately. Carmen and Moody wrote that as an "illegal" abortionist, Harvey provided many imaginative amenities that other providers had not. "For example, he put colorful potholders on the stirrups of the operating table for both the comfort and pleasure of patients; he told patients calling for appointments to bring along their knitting or magazines or something else to occupy them while waiting; he had cokes and cookies available post-operatively for patients who had not eaten for twelve hours; and he mimeographed a sheet of things to do for patients with free time before catching their return flight. This combination of extras, plus excellent medical skill, made women feel good about the doctor, themselves, and the experience."[30] In addition, Harvey had been willing to accept the price assigned to each woman by the clergy counselors based on her situation, whether the top price of $300 or as little as $100.

Barbara Pyle, a New York University graduate student who had introduced the New York CCS to Harvey in early 1969, worked with Harvey to create the Center for Reproductive and Sexual Health (CRASH)—which quickly came to be known as Women's Services.

Pyle grew up south of Oklahoma City and went to Tulane University in New Orleans. After graduation, she spent a summer in London, researching sex education, abortion clinics, and referral groups. After graduating from Tulane Phi Beta Kappa in 1969, she entered graduate school in philosophy at New York University. There she brought the results of her British research to the CCS—and put them in touch, in early 1969, with her mentor, Dr. Harvey.[31]

Horace Hale Harvey III was a practicing physician who, at the time Pyle was at Tulane, was working on a Ph.D. in philosophy and teaching philosophy and ethics there. His dissertation, submitted to Tulane in 1969, was titled "Decision Theory in the Good Life: Mathematical, Logical, Ethical and Other Tools and Techniques as Aids for Making Ethical-Moral Decisions." Pyle told the New York CCS that Harvey had determined to perform abortions in Louisiana even though doing so was a violation of state law. Moody and Carmen invited Harvey to New York to talk with them—the only time the New York clergy met with a doctor to whom they referred—and Carmen visited him in New Orleans. Moody and Carmen described Harvey as "curiously impersonal but totally dedicated," and very much on the same wavelength as the CCS. And he was willing to take CCS referrals. Moody and Carmen wrote, "Impressed by his sincerity, we forced ourselves to beware that beneath a surface of concern and conviction, hidden from view, must lie some form of self-interest. But during the year that we referred patients to him, we never detected any secret motive, only genuine compassion and concern for the welfare of women."[32] Harvey's illegal but exemplary practice—based at a New Orleans hotel—became a model for the later clinics.

"When abortion became legal here [in New York], I wrote to Hale and said, 'Why don't we start a clinic?' I knew all about it from the research I'd done in England," Pyle told the *New York Times* in 1971.[33] When Harvey offered to come to New York and set up a clinic, the clergy of the CCS felt that it couldn't be in better hands. They hoped that Harvey would create a clinic that would be a model for others, demonstrating the safety of outpatient abortions and setting new standards in quality of care and in affordability for poor women. Although the CCS was supportive and would refer women, the clinic would operate quite separately from the CCS. Pyle became the administrator of Women's Services, and she and Harvey set up the clinic as an independent entity, using Harvey's own money. Pyle told the *New York Times* in 1971, "He sent me $30,000 and that's what it took—two months' supplies and everything, drugs, medications, pumps and everything. I figured we would make Hale's money back in six weeks and we did."[34]

They quickly found a suite of about a dozen offices in a medical building on East 73rd Street at Lexington Avenue. Each procedure room contained an operating table, a vacuum aspirator, and a sterilizer and had its own small waiting room. The offices were painted in bright colors, with posters on the walls and even on the ceilings of the procedure rooms; Harvey insisted that the atmosphere be friendly and warm, not hospital-like, so that women felt more comfortable and calm. He and Pyle converted the small waiting rooms into counseling offices, and hired as counselors young women who had had abortions themselves. The counselors would explain the procedure and what to expect. Harvey viewed the counselors' academic and work credentials as much less important than their compassion and people skills. A counselor would stay with the woman throughout her procedure and recovery, and she might even assist the physician, although most of the counselors were not registered nurses. This shocked many other physicians and hospital administrators but set a new standard for compassionate abortion care that is followed by many clinics to this day.[35] In addition, Carmen insisted that the head counselor, a woman, would have the power to call the physicians to account if their treatment of or attitude toward a woman was abusive in any way.[36]

Carmen and Moody's book recounts their first visit to the clinic on June 30, 1970—the day before it was to open. As they drove uptown, Harvey asked what they should charge women for abortions. Carmen and Moody knew that $300 was about the lowest cost then available and suggested charging $200. Harvey readily agreed. "He also suggested that Clergy Service counselors should, at their own discretion, be able to reduce the fee to $100 or even to nothing. In the belief that no woman should receive a free abortion, that both her dignity and self-respect would be damaged by such charity, we persuaded a very reluctant Harvey to agree that poor women would have to pay a token fee of $25," Carmen and Moody wrote.[37]

Harvey had also made an offer to his patients when he had his private—and illegal—abortion practice in Louisiana: he personally would pay their medical expenses for any complication that arose as a result of the abortion. He followed through on that promise to his private patients, and he instituted the same practice at Women's Services: the clinic would reimburse any patient for the medical expenses of complications. The CCS was able to press some physicians to whom they referred elsewhere to do the same.[38]

Women's Services

When July 1 arrived, the waiting list for hospital abortions in New York City had the names of 717 women on it. Women were arriving from all over the country, suitcases in hand, without appointments, hoping to find a hospital or clinic that could see them immediately.[39] The Center for Reproductive and Sexual Health—Women's Services—opened on July 1, and by the end of the month was performing abortions for 100 women a day, nearly all referred by CCS chapters outside the state.[40] The clinic was open sixteen hours a day, seven days a week, except for legal holidays. A young staff doctor in those early days recalled in her interview with Carole Joffe, "The clinic was just inundated. There were lines of patients around the block every single morning we opened. From 7:00 a.m. to 11:00 p.m., we did two eight-hour shifts of all the staff and personnel." Some of the clinic space was rented for only part of the day, and the doctor recalled "a big board that told us which hours we could use which rooms," though there were consistent areas for recovery and storage. Harvey had hired some doctors who had experience performing illegal abortions, but other physicians had no experience. The doctor told Joffe she taught the procedure to a Columbia Medical School faculty member who worked at Women's Services part-time. He worked under a false name to protect his position at the medical school.[41]

Six months later, Women's Services was performing as many first-trimester abortions as all of the New York City hospitals combined, at a lower price, and with exemplary conditions and results.[42] Patients were asked for their feedback. Clergy counselors were asked to keep records of any problems reported by the women they referred. And the Women's Services counselors were asked to report any problems, mistakes, or omissions by the clergy who had counseled their patients.[43] Harvey worked to accommodate the demand by women, but Moody cautioned Harvey not to expand Women's Services beyond its ability to provide accurate research—which would be crucial to establishing the clinic as a model and in advocating for legal abortion in other states.[44] The *New York Times* reported that a U.S. Public Health Service officer had reviewed the clinic's data and found a satisfactorily low complication rate of 23.6 per 1,000 abortions—no other New York abortion facility had undergone such an independent review.[45]

In November 1970, Ron Hammerle joined the administration team at Women's Services. Hammerle had completed his Ph.D. at the medical school and his D.Min. at the divinity school of the University of Chicago in 1969 with his dissertation, "The Abortion Situation at the End of the Sixties," based on statistics from and his work with the Chicago CCS. He continued as full-time administrator of the Chicago service, employed for one year thanks to a grant from the Playboy Foundation. At the end of that year, Hammerle and Spencer Parsons did not want to reapply to the Playboy Foundation for funding. Hammerle visited Women's Services during its first summer of operation, hoping to take its methods to doctors and clinics in the Midwest, perhaps to Kansas, whose abortion law had been liberalized about the same time as New York's.[46]

When Hammerle arrived in November 1970 to work at Women's Services, the clinic had been open for four months and was running at high speed—but it was not yet officially licensed. As Hammerle worked to gather the paperwork for the license, he discovered that Harvey was not licensed to practice medicine in New York—nor in any state in the country. Accused of performing illegal abortions in Louisiana, Harvey's license had been revoked by that state's medical board in 1969, a fact of which the clergy of the CCS was unaware. Hammerle recalled that he informed Moody of the crisis: the clinic was performing 700 abortions a week, running seven days a week, and employed twenty-two physicians. But there were no payroll records; $20,000 to $30,000 in cash was carried to the bank each week down the streets of New York City. No taxes were withheld, and there was no insurance. The city and state of New York required licensure, but the law was brand new and ambulatory abortion clinics unheard of, so there was no precedent for the licensing requirements; existing regulations would require the clinic to provide all the services a hospital would. Both city and state said they wanted the clinic to have a written transfer agreement with a receiving hospital to take patients who suffered complications; but hospitals would naturally be reluctant to serve a clinic that was taking business away from them. Women's Services had no credentials on file for its physicians, and to top it all off, the clinic was owned and operated by an unlicensed physician. If Women's Services were shut down, the National CCS would be hard-pressed to find alternatives that were as accessible, reliable, and inexpensive.[47]

The clinic operated illegally for six months. As Moody, Carmen, and Hammerle saw it, the only answer was to transform Women's Services into a nonprofit organization with a proper board of directors. Most of all, the clinic needed a licensed medical director, and quickly. Howard Moody called Dr. Bernard Nathanson, then the chief of gynecology at the Hospital for Joint Diseases (in fact, it was a general hospital). Nathanson arrived about the time that Hammerle left to become a consultant for Planned Parenthood in Chicago and then executive director of Planned Parenthood of Iowa.[48]

Nathanson had been part of the original planning committee for NARAL and had been instrumental and successful in pressuring New York City hospitals to perform more abortions for poor women, even under the old law.[49] He was an outspoken man and an able physician who also knew the politics of abortion, and Moody knew that if he could persuade Nathanson to take over Women's Services, he would throw himself into the fray wholeheartedly. (In later years, Nathanson became as vehement an opponent of abortion as he had been a proponent of abortion rights. He first publicly expressed doubts in a 1974 article in the *New England Journal of Medicine*, writing that he had become "deeply troubled" that he had presided over more than 60,000 abortions at Women's Services.[50] He wrote in a later book, *The Hand of God*, that he never performed an abortion himself at Women's Services, although he had performed many elsewhere.[51] When he wrote the 1974 article, he did not advocate outlawing abortion, but called for "an end to blind polarity" in the debate of the issue.[52] He said his doubts about abortion increased as technology such as ultrasound revealed the developing fetus more clearly—though he had seen many fetuses before—and he stopped performing abortions completely in the late 1970s. He narrated the 1985 antiabortion film "The Silent Scream" and remained a strong antiabortion activist and speaker until his death in 2011.[53])

In 1971, Nathanson fully supported abortion rights and took on the leadership of Women's Services while continuing his hospital and private practice. He met with Pyle, who described the problems the clinic and now Nathanson faced: Harvey was still running the clinic, in spite of legal warnings; Women's Services had no formal affiliation with a hospital that could receive patients with complications, as regulations now required; and whereas Harvey and Pyle had been running the business themselves and setting the financial proceeds aside, Moody was insisting that the clinic become a proper nonprofit corporation with a board of directors. Nathanson's description of his first visit to Women's Services—written in 1979, after his conversion to the pro-life cause—paints a cartoonish picture of "incomprehensible bedlam" peopled by "young women in the most prodigal variety of dress—and undress . . . bawling at each other, brandishing sheaves of papers and fistfuls of instruments," and at least a couple of "vicious, even sadistic" doctors on staff—a picture that does not mesh with reports from patients.[54] A Chicago-area woman wrote to her CCS counselor in November 1970 that her visit to Women's Services "has been one of the most positive experiences that has ever occurred in my life. The total environment and atmosphere was warm and most conducive to the over all well being of the individual, both physically and psychologically." She described her experience in detail, including a meeting with a counselor who described the procedure and answered her questions, which, she said, "certainly alleviated many of the fears I had." She was given medication to help her relax, and once that had taken effect, the doctor and his assistant came into the procedure room, and the doctor again explained the procedure and answered her questions. She received a local anesthetic, the procedure took about five to seven minutes, and "except for two or three menstrual type cramps the procedure is almost painless. The doctor explains each step of the procedure as he goes along," the woman reported. She was observed as she recovered for about forty-five minutes, then she dressed and returned to the waiting room, where there was coffee, soda, and juice, and she rested for about twenty minutes until she felt ready to leave. She was given prescriptions for antibiotics and medication to prevent excessive bleeding, filled them at a pharmacy in the same building, and took a cab to the airport. She concluded, "The procedure started at 10:30 a.m.—I was back in Chicago at 1:40 p.m. the same day. Thanking you for your kind assistance."[55] Women's Services became a model for what physician Richard U. Hausknecht called the counselor-oriented clinic—one in which women counselors provide education, comfort, and assistance in decision making—as opposed to the physician-oriented clinic, which focuses on "the mechanical termination of pregnancy and are founded for the convenience of the physicians who perform those procedures."[56] Women's Services' emphasis on counseling and patient advocacy was a visionary innovation in medical care and should be credited to the CCS as well as Harvey and Pyle.

Nathanson struck a middle position. He quickly took control at the clinic, removing posters from walls and potholders from stirrups to create the more traditional professional medical atmosphere that Harvey had avoided. Although women counselors continued their work, he fired some of the staff and doctors and hired nurses and doctors with whom he had worked before, and he enforced stringent rules about referring at-risk patients to a hospital and limiting abortions to pregnancies of twelve weeks or less. He arranged for Lenox Hill Hospital to admit any cases of emergency complications. The clinic passed its state inspection.[57]

According to Nathanson's account, the reorganized Women's Services paid Harvey a settlement of $75,000 in back salary and to repay his start-up investment, and he quietly left the country to live in England.[58] The newly formed board of Women's Services was chaired by Dr. Allan Barnes, who had been head of the department of obstetrics and gynecology at Case Western Reserve University and Johns Hopkins University and was now at the Rockefeller Foundation. The board also included Rev. Jesse Lyons of Riverside Church, who had been a part of the CCS until 1968 and had since been active with NARAL; author and activist Betty Friedan; Rabbi Edward E. Klein, who

had headed the Clergy Advisory Board at Planned Parenthood in New York;
lawyer Ivan Shapiro; and, as treasurer, Arthur Levin, who was associated with
Judson Church and later headed Judson's Center for Medical Consumers.
Marchieta Young Ceppos took on the role of patient advocate at Women's
Services, concerned with patient care and answerable directly to the board.[59]

Under pressure from Moody and Carmen, by November 1971 Women's
Services—now in new offices on East 62nd Street—also lowered its standard
fee for first-trimester abortions to $125, the lowest price in the country. Even
with that lower standard fee, the clinic committed to being able to provide abortions at the token price of $25 to a substantial number (one quarter, according
to Carmen and Moody, one fifth according to Nathanson) of the patients sent
by the National CCS and other referring groups.[60]

The Legacy of Women's Services

Other abortion facilities, including private, for-profit clinics, were forced to
compete with Women's Services in both price and amenities. Although most of
Women's Services patients came from CCS referrals, CCS counselors sent
women to other clinics and hospitals in New York as well. While the National
CCS coordinated its referrals so that overall 75–80 percent of the women it
referred to Women's Services could pay the full $125, other referral services
around the country—both nonprofit and commercial—did not take the big
picture at Women's Services into account and tended to send women who could
pay to commercial clinics and only the poorest women to Women's Services.
As Moody and Carmen later wrote, the CCS knew "the power of corporate
action. . . . If a person only cares that *one* woman with a financial problem gets
helped and has no perspective on *all* the women in the other parts of the country
who have the same problem, what is forfeited is the united action that could
make available a lot more help for many more women."[61] If all the referral
services had sent women from the full range of economic situations to Women's
Services, the enterprise would have been more easily self-sustaining financially.
Nathanson wrote in 1974, it was "the first—and the largest—abortion clinic in
the Western world."[62] He continued as director of the clinic until the end of
August 1972.[63]

In 1973, Women's Services, by then a million-dollar enterprise—was ceded
(given as a gift, really) to Judson Church, and its board taken over by staff and
lay members of Judson. With a grant from Planned Parenthood, the clinic paid
off old debts and expanded its services. In 1974 it took on pioneering work in
outpatient breast biopsies—a new idea that was soon adopted by other clinics
and hospitals. Their success in providing in a clinic setting procedures and
services that had been limited to hospitals led Nathanson to write to Moody in

1974, "Arlene and I felt that ambulatory child birth is a very important next step in the ob/gyn field." Having heard that a pilot project was already under way in New York City, Nathanson continued, "Wish we'd gotten to it first but I'm glad that someone is going to do it."[64]

In 1975, Women's Services added health services for and outreach to sex workers, whom Carmen called "working women." This last project did not attract the foundation funding it needed. Competition from other abortion clinics—including one opened by Planned Parenthood—led to a smaller patient load. The clinic ran for several years on the very edge of solvency. Carmen and Moody were finding that the clinic took too much of their time and attention. Financial setbacks continued until the clinic's board decided in 1978 to end the experiment. Women's Services carried on as a nonprofit under the joint owner-ship of a physician and the group that had provided laboratory services to the clinic, and it closed at last in 1988.[65]

In February 1972 Nathanson published an article in the *New England Journal of Medicine*, based on statistics from Women's Services, "Ambulatory Abortion: Experience with 26,000 cases (July 1, 1970, to August 1, 1971)."[66] He described the clergy referral system, the innovative patient counseling and advocacy at the clinic, the paracervical block anesthesia and vacuum curettage method used for the procedure, and the twenty-four-hour phone service for reporting complications. He described another protocol pioneered by Women's Services: the requirement that the physician carefully examine the tissues removed imme-diately after the procedure, so that if the abortion was incomplete, a repeat curettage could be performed at once. Of the 26,000 abortions performed, none resulted in death; there were only 36 perforations of the uterus; 90 proce-dures were incomplete and required a repeat curettage; and 391 infections were reported—all well within an acceptable range for complications. Nathanson wrote that the clinic's policy of reimbursing women for medical expenses result-ing from complications encouraged them to report any problems. He suggested the possibility of designating an OB-GYN doctor in the urban home areas from which most of the patients came who would perform a follow-up exam two weeks after the procedure. The visit would be subsidized by the clinic. Nathanson concluded that "the use of hospital facilities for abortion is probably unnecessary except for a relatively small number of women who have coexisting medical, surgical, gynecologic or psychiatric abnormalities." In the same issue of the *New England Journal of Medicine*, biostatistician Christopher Tietze wrote an opinion piece recognizing outpatient abortion as safe and holding up Women's Services as a model for organization and procedures.[67] Former Chicago CCS coordinator Ronald L. Hammerle attributed today's wide success of outpatient surgical centers generally to the proof that outpatient abortion procedures were so safe and effective.[68] In the early 1970s, outpatient clinics provided the best combination of medical safety, accessibility, and affordability, and those benefits have not changed.

Direct protests, sit-ins, harassment, and violent attacks on abortion providers and clinics did not arise until the late 1970s and gained momentum in the 1980s when some individuals and antiabortion groups—notably the Pro-Life Action League and Operation Rescue—became impatient with the slow progress of legislative and judicial efforts to turn back the effects of *Roe v. Wade.*[69] Deceptive crisis pregnancy centers (CPCs), which pose as neutral medical clinics but in reality do not offer medical services beyond pregnancy tests and ultrasounds, predated outpatient abortion clinics. They exist merely to dissuade women from getting abortions, often by giving incorrect information. The first of the CPCs was founded in Hawaii in 1967; funded by antiabortion foundations and religious groups, they spread quickly around the rest of the country under such names as Birthright. As outpatient abortion clinics were established, CPCs more easily confused women by building or moving to similar-looking buildings, sometimes very close to real clinics; such a ploy would have been difficult if most abortions took place in hospital clinics. CPCs proliferated in the 1980s and 1990s at the same time protests against abortion clinics increased in ferocity.[70]

Another genuine drawback to outpatient abortion clinics, then and now, and foreseen by Dr. Robert Hall, is that migrating abortion care to these clinics allowed hospitals to evade responsibility for providing the service themselves. Isolating abortion care from other ordinary gynecological care has encouraged a continuing tendency for private and hospital-based physicians to stigmatize abortion providers. When hospitals avoid doing abortions, medical students and residents often cannot get training in abortion in teaching hospitals but must seek out special rotations in outside clinics.[71] Physician Richard U. Hausknecht now seems prescient, writing in 1971,

> If I were to be permitted the luxury of creating the best possible facility for termination of pregnancy, I should choose an area that was adjacent to or part of a hospital and I should create a separate facility staffed by sympathetic women—women physicians if possible—and those well-motivated male obstetricians and gynecologists that might be needed. While the need for the facilities of a major hospital are rare, it does occur. . . . It is also important to recognize that the creation of a friendly, warm, nonthreatening environment, such as has been established in several of the larger abortion clinics in this city [New York], represents a breakthrough in medical care. The establishment of ambulatory abortion facilities appended to our major institutions should be encouraged.[72]

The free-for-all that resulted from the patchwork of different laws in different states was a good argument for a national law on abortion. The legalization of abortion in New York brought many competing clinics in the state—most of them commercial enterprises—and many referral services around the country. Some of the referral services were nonprofit groups, but many were themselves commercial enterprises that advertised heavily—especially in college newspapers—charged a fee for referral, and sometimes took fees from or were otherwise tied to particular abortion clinics in New York. The CCS had to instruct women carefully about where to go and how to get there, because drivers for one clinic would "steal" the patients of others right from the airport. Nathanson told of a clinic whose offices were in the same building, and even in the lobby women on their way to Women's Services were likely to be intercepted and misdirected to the other clinic.[73]

The CCS itself was not immune from the temptation to benefit from the burgeoning referral-for-profit business. In his memoir, Moody wrote that the Detroit chapter of the CCS asked him to arrange for Women's Services to give them a kickback from the fees of women they had counseled. Even if the money would go to office staff and services and not to the clergy themselves, Moody absolutely opposed any such arrangement. In his letter to the Detroit group, he said, "I do not believe that any counseling that's part of the ministry of the church ought to be paid for by the recipient except voluntarily. This I feel on general principles, but more particularly in regard to the field of abortion counseling. In this instance women were somewhat forced to go to clergymen who had some corner on the information which they needed and couldn't get any place else. To place a price on this service may not be the 'sale of indulgences' but for a lot of people outside the church it could have the flavor of that."[74] The Detroit CCS backed down on its request.

In 1971, Alden Hathaway, then the CCS state coordinator for Michigan, told the Associated Press that the CCS had referred 15,000 Michigan women in the preceding year, all free of charge. He said that the CCS would continue to make free referrals "until this state provides protection for pregnant women from the handful of hustlers who are capitalizing on their problems. . . . Michigan law doesn't say that a woman may not have an abortion. It says only that she can't have it in Michigan, in a medical facility close to her home, performed by a physician she knows and trusts. The law thus has created a situation whereby women with unwanted pregnancies become innocent prey to the handful of entrepreneurs who have found in this gap the most lucrative new business of the year."[75] The CCS continued to fight against for-profit referral services, eventually winning a legal ban on them in New York in 1971.[76]

The travel from other states to New York for abortions and then home again immediately afterward was itself a risk that the CCS took pains to mitigate. The Pennsylvania CCS included nurses from the Harrisburg area who rode the bus to Women's Services in New York City without eating after midnight, so that they could better understand the circumstances of the women they referred.[77] Missouri women flying to New York City for abortions took a specific flight from St. Louis first thing in the morning. Judy Widdicombe, a nurse who co-founded the St. Louis CCS, flew with them about once a month to make sure that everything went smoothly, that drivers from the right clinics picked the women up, and that counselors had up-to-date information. On the trip back to Missouri, she asked the flight attendants to watch for abortion patients and instructed them in first aid for women who were hemorrhaging. Georgie Gatch, director of the Columbia, Missouri, CCS chapter, recalled that the women wore yellow ribbons so the flight attendants would recognize them.[78]

Other CCS-Related Clinics

The need for more low-cost resources was clear, and the CCS was instrumental in the establishment of other outpatient abortion clinics around the country. In fact, in St. Louis, Widdicombe founded the nonprofit Reproductive Health Services clinic immediately after *Roe v. Wade*—the decision came down in January 1973, and the clinic opened in May. Widdicombe had seen Women's Services and other clinics at work, and she copied the parts of each that she liked best. She set out to create a nonprofit clinic, offering low fees and an emphasis on counseling, with an atmosphere that was neither too homey nor too cold and antiseptic, but appropriate for the seriousness of a medical procedure. The clinic was run by women; male physicians were employees, not in charge. For many years, Reproductive Health Services clinics were the only places in eastern Missouri where women could obtain outpatient abortions. Widdicombe ran it until 1986, and the organization merged with Planned Parenthood in the 1990s. Widdicombe also started Adoption Associates, an agency that promoted adoption, and she herself fostered nine children.[79]

The Jacksonville, Florida, CCS incorporated as a nonprofit in September 1971, and when in 1972 a ruling by the state attorney general cleared the way for outpatient abortion clinics, the Jacksonville CCS made plans to open its own clinic. Rev. Marvin Lutz, a Presbyterian minister and co-founder of the Jacksonville CCS, modeled the new clinic on Women's Services in New York. Even after the *Roe v. Wade* decision, the CCS found that it was less expensive for women to fly to New York and go to Women's Services than to obtain abortions locally, so the group went ahead to open a low-cost, nonprofit outpatient abortion clinic—one of the first in Florida. They secured a bank loan of $12,000 with twelve co-signers—both clergy and laypersons, including a physician, a lawyer, and a financial adviser. Area clergy, including the local Presbytery (the Presbyterian Church's regional administrative body), wrote letters of support. By June 1973 the Jacksonville Women's Center for Reproductive Health opened, prepared to perform eight to ten abortions a day at a cost of $125. Like Women's Services, they planned to take up to a quarter of their patients for a reduced fee of $25. By November they had retired their loan. Lutz later wrote, "In addition to abortion, the center eventually provided well woman care, family planning and, at one time, tubal ligation. Women seeking abortions were never turned away for financial reasons." The clinic also did public education and legislative advocacy. Lutz continued as director of the clinic for twenty years.[80] The Jacksonville clinic was the model for a feminist health clinic in Gainesville, Florida, started in 1974 by Byllye Avery and others; Avery went on to found the National Black Women's Health Project and the Avery Institute for Social Change.[81]

Of the Southern states, Alabama had one of the most liberal abortion laws, and the CCS directors in the region, meeting in Atlanta in 1972, agreed to work to open a nonprofit outpatient abortion clinic on the model of Women's Services. We were unable to learn if such a clinic opened before the *Roe* decision. A clinic "patterned after Women's Services and encouraged by the CCS" had already opened in Philadelphia by May 1972.[82]

As the Chicago CCS administrator, Ron Hammerle worked to improve resources for the Midwest. Kansas law had been liberalized at the same time as New York's, and Hammerle was frustrated that there were so few accessible resources there. He pressed for lower fees and quality improvements at Douglass Hospital in Kansas City, but continuing problems had prompted him to pursue the idea of opening a new clinic in Kansas, perhaps in cooperation with Planned Parenthood. That plan didn't work out. After an interlude in New York working out the crisis at Women's Services and then at Planned Parenthood in Chicago, Hammerle moved on to become executive director of Iowa Planned Parenthood. He brought his knowledge from the CCS and Women's Services and worked to make Iowa a model for other Planned Parenthood affiliates.[83] Diana March, a lay member of the Chicago CCS, opened Crossroads Clinic in Palatine, Illinois, in 1973, and eventually added abortion to the services it offered.

We heard of at least a couple of CCS clergy who helped reliable doctors set up illegal local abortion practices. Rev. Carl Bielby recalled in an interview that in 1968 or 1969 while he was still the chair of the Michigan CCS he helped a physician establish a private (illegal) abortion practice in Detroit. The doctor, head of gynecology at a medical school and a Catholic, learned abortion technique from Bielby—who had no medical training outside his CCS experience. Bielby recalled, "I helped him set up a clinic. We identified a luxury high-rise building in downtown Detroit, in Lafayette Park. . . . It had a garage on the lower level where you could push a button and up comes the door and out you go, and out go the women up into the doctor's office." They turned one bedroom into an operating room, another became a recovery room, and the living room was the waiting room. Bielby said, "He took a desk and turned it into an operating table, with stirrups and the whole thing. It unfolded so when he was not using it, it looked like a desk, and if anybody ever came into the apartment, they'd never know that he had a clinic there. . . . I remember saying to myself, if I have to go to jail, there's nobody I'd rather to jail with than Dr. [——]. He had the credentials that would stand up in any place. Between the two of us, I didn't think anybody would touch us."[84] The doctor was not added to the general CCS referral list but Bielby sometimes referred women to him.

Another illegal abortion practice was set up by Rev. Hayes Fletcher, pastor of the First United Methodist church in Oak Park, Illinois, who had been active in social justice issues such as race, equal housing, and the Vietnam War. He joined the Chicago CCS after contacting Spencer Parsons to find out where a couple from his church could go for a safe abortion. Fletcher educated himself through reading and by visiting Cook County Hospital. He visited out-of-state resources, including Dr. Jesse Ketchum in Detroit and Dr. Lynn Weller in Kansas City, to vet them for CCS referrals, and he helped negotiate conditions and fees. Then, knowing that long-distance travel was too difficult and expensive for many women, Fletcher helped a Chicago doctor set up a facility in a apartment building in the suburbs. They hired a nurse and set up a phone line to take only clergy referrals from the Chicago area. Fletcher took the doctor to Detroit to be trained by Ketchum. Fletcher later wrote, "The doctor worked three nights a week and the results were very satisfactory. We were lucky that someone didn't expose the operation or one of the apartment dwellers did not get suspicious. This lasted for about ten months and was ended in the spring of 1971."[85]

Since Women's Services in New York handled early abortions only, the CCS referred women to other facilities for later abortions. Fletcher had visited a facility in New York to which the Chicago CCS had been referring women for abortions up to twenty-four weeks. He recalled later, "The doctor was very abrupt, rude, inconsiderate, and at times hostile toward the women. The operating facility was not clean and the procedure for disposal of the fetal matter was unbelievably crude." Fletcher recommended that Chicago CCS and Planned Parenthood stop referring women there, and he told the clinic owners why. The owners listened to his advice and soon moved to Royal Hospital in the Bronx, where they could use an operating room and a certified anesthesiologist. They found an acceptable doctor, brought in a counselor to work with patients, and changed their business name to Sutton Medical Group. Women were picked up by a driver at the airport, stayed one night in the hospital, and flew home the next morning. Sutton later opened another site at Williamsburg Hospital in Brooklyn.[86] Fletcher visited both locations and approved them.

In June 1971, exhausted by divisions over race and war within his congregation, Fletcher decided to leave the ministry. That fall he became the administrator of Sutton Medical Group in New York. He recalled that when he arrived, he hired an additional counselor and set up a new counseling space.

> Since we were accepting women who could not pay the full fee (and sometimes paid nothing), I had to deal with the doctors' occasional complaints about having too many "freebies." I feared that if the doctors knew which ones were reduced fee patients they might treat them differently. I worked out a system with codes on the forms the doctors received whereby they could not determine how much the patient was paying. This worked very well and I did not have to deal with the problem again. From the $280 fee, we paid the anesthesiologist $20 and the hospital $60. The rest went to pay office rent, staff salaries, "limo" services, and accountants. If the patient had insurance, we filed the forms for them so they could be reimbursed.[87]

Fletcher also ensured that Sutton would accept welfare recipients, even from out of state. Under his leadership, Sutton switched from Williamsburg to Whitestone Hospital in Queens. In 1972, the doctors in the Sutton Medical Group bought out the original owners and were able to lower prices further. Once *Roe v. Wade* enabled most women to find safe abortions in their home states, Sutton wound down its operation and closed in May 1973. Fletcher served as a consultant to a new clinic in Chicago, worked for a Stamford, Connecticut, business association, and eventually returned to his home state of Tennessee to become development and external affairs director at his alma mater, Lambuth College.[88]

Another Chicago clergy counselor left the group to work elsewhere. Starting in early 1971, Chicago Area Planned Parenthood and the Chicago CCS worked together to start a nonprofit counseling and referral service. Rev. W. L. Gustin, minister at Edison Park United Methodist Church, left the CCS for a (probably part-time) job at Planned Parenthood as "consultant director," setting up and running the new service. On July 6, 1971, the two groups announced the launch of the service, called CARES (Cooperative Abortion Referral and Evaluation

Services), which expected to be able to handle 250 calls a week and planned to refer women out of state, since abortion was still illegal in Illinois. Planned Parenthood bore the cost of the service. The CARES phone number was added to the Chicago Area CCS answering machine message, along with the number of at least one CCS clergy counselor. The Chicago CCS had the same concern that National CCS had when its Los Angeles chapter merged with Planned Parenthood: Planned Parenthood generally charged a sliding fee for services. Reassured that the abortion referral counseling would be free, the CCS continued its relationship with Planned Parenthood and CARES.[89]

Gustin, however, left Planned Parenthood less than a month after CARES opened. He began working with a referral service, Choice, Inc., which opened in Chicago in August 1971 and sent women to New York for legal abortions. Reports vary on whether Choice was a nonprofit or for-profit enterprise, but women paid for their abortions through the agency and it seems clear that Choice would have taken a referral fee out of the $200–300 they charged. In November 1971 Choice announced that it had made arrangements to send women needing early abortions to two doctors in Milwaukee, Wisconsin. A ruling striking down Wisconsin's abortion law was still under consideration by the courts, but one clinic was operating openly in Madison. The new clinic in Milwaukee was apparently arranged by Choice. CARES and the Chicago CCS were not sending women to Wisconsin because New York was less expensive, even with travel costs. Immediately after the *Roe v. Wade* decision, Choice opened the Chicago Reproductive Health Center to offer outpatient abortions. Now that Gustin was involved in operating a clinic, the Chicago CCS officially removed him from their roster.[90]

Another Chicago clinic was at the ready when the *Roe v. Wade* decision was announced: Friendship Medical Center, run by Dr. T. R. M. Howard, the doctor who had provided so many abortions to women referred by the CCS. Howard announced that Friendship was ready immediately to perform 60–100 abortions a day. Twenty-five women were already waiting in line on January 22, 1973, and Howard performed a legal abortion just one hour after the *Roe* decision was handed down. One of his first patients that day was just fourteen years old. Photographs of Howard in the operating room performing an abortion appeared on the front page of the nationally influential black-owned *Chicago Daily Defender* and on the cover of *Jet* magazine. The unfortunate effect of this publicity was to change the reputation of Howard's medical center from that of a fine general medical facility serving an underserved population to that of an abortion mill. The clinic lost some of its best medical staff and ran into other management problems that eventually led to its financial demise.[91]

Advocacy and Cooperation

In many places, even after abortion was legalized, CCS members continued to advocate to make abortion available and affordable. Abortion was now legal, but many doctors and hospitals resisted offering the procedure. Some clergy turned their efforts to importuning hospitals directly. Rev. Margaret E. (Peggy) Howland, a Presbyterian minister in Troy, New York, and a member of the CCS, said in an interview, "Then what we found was that the doctors in town wanted us to keep going on having the Clergy Consultation Service because they didn't want to do abortions. And so we got together and we decided that our job then . . . was to go to the hospitals and talk with the hospitals about doing abortions. I went to Leonard Hospital in north Troy and spoke with them, and Leonard became the only hospital in Troy that did abortions at that time." Progress was slow, she recalled. "There were clinics that began to open, but you know, all that had to start—and the start-up meant that people had to realize that it needed to be done, and that they had to be willing to do it rather than sending people away somewhere."[92] Howland and many other New York clergy continued to press hospitals, doctors, and Planned Parenthood affiliates to offer abortion services.

In Chicago, immediately after the *Roe v. Wade* decision, the CCS met with Planned Parenthood and other agencies to form the Abortion Information and Evaluation Service (AIES) to continue some of the work that the CCS and CARES had been doing—evaluating medical services, counseling, educating, pressing for lower fees, and providing legal information in the event of harassment of clients or doctors. The CCS recommended that counseling be offered where abortions were performed and that the standards and prices set by Dr. T.R.M. Howard be used to negotiate with other physicians and hospitals.[93]

The CCS continued to work on monitoring the safety of legal abortion. In the early 1970s, the CCS worked with the Centers for Disease Control and Prevention in Atlanta on a program to monitor the safety of abortions performed in legal facilities—at the time, those in New York, Washington, DC, and California.[94] The CCS provided a model for nonprofit abortion providers that has lasted to the present, prioritizing excellent medical care, compassionate and empowering counseling, affordability, and accessibility. The group fought the medical establishment's insistence that abortion could only be provided in a hospital setting, demonstrating that outpatient abortion was safe and publishing proof in the *New England Journal of Medicine*.[95]

Dr. Bernard Nathanson believed the Supreme Court's decision in *Roe v. Wade* itself rested on the evidence that early abortion was a safe procedure, as demonstrated in New York and documented at Women's Services. In March

1973, speaking with the *New York Times*, he said, "In its ban on regulating first-trimester abortion, the court cited 'the now-established medical fact' of safety during this period." He continued, "Everybody knows this 'medical fact' was 'established' here and that the court relied on the data, experience and abortion-safety record of New York City—which, ironically, was based on strict regulation."[96] We don't really know whether the Supreme Court decision weighed the statistics from Women's Services itself in their decision; but Justice Harry A. Blackmun, who had been resident counsel for the Mayo Clinic in the 1950s, worked in Mayo's medical library in July 1972 as he wrote the court's opinion, and Nathanson's *New England Journal* article had just come out in February.[97] The clergy may not have testified in the case themselves, but the clinic they set up, the procedures they insisted on, and the documentation of their system may well have provided background for the landmark *Roe v. Wade* decision.

9

Roe v. Wade and Beyond

The 1960s was a time of activism in many arenas—civil rights, peace, poverty—and more radical members of the clergy felt called to speak out, demonstrate, commit acts of civil disobedience, organize, preach, prophesy, and lead.[1] The Clergy Consultation Service on Abortion was formed by those who had spoken out on abortion, in the pulpit and in political forums, and felt the strong call to act. They were inspired by the suffering of women they had counseled, and challenged by the loud and public opposing voices of the Catholic Church. Howard Moody expressed the need to atone in a practical way for the oppression that he felt that organized religion had visited upon women.[2] Clergy who joined the CCS, even if they hadn't had previous experience with abortion counseling, nonetheless saw women's lack of access to safe abortion services as an injustice that called for their action very much the same way that racism, war, and poverty did. Nearly all of the clergy we interviewed had already been involved in combatting one or more of those problems before they joined the CCS—and, in fact, most of the clergy organizers in the various regions identified potential recruits by their social justice activism. It was a generation of radical clergy inspired by Protestant theologians including Paul Tillich, Reinhold Niebuhr, and Dietrich Bonhoeffer. Huw Anwyl said he was influenced by and worked with Joseph Fletcher, the founder of the theory of situational ethics, which consider the context of an action, rather than setting down moral absolutes.[3]

The next generation of activist clergy faced a changed situation. The *Roe v. Wade* Supreme Court decision made abortion legal throughout the United States. It also galvanized antiabortion activists, including clergy. The fact that legalization of abortion had been a judicial rather than a legislative decision had taken away the arena where the opposition could be heard. Moody told us,

> I'm convinced that since we never had the national debate in 1967 or 1970, etc., because in 1973 the judiciary made it—that was it. And so the national debate never took place. The statewide debate took place in 1970 with the New York state law changing, but not in the public. That's what made our opposition so angry, is that somebody else decided that, and they didn't get to put forth their reason for feeling the way they did about the fetus, etc. So some people make the [argument]—and they made the argument with us at that point—it should be a legislative change, not a judiciary change, because then you get to argue the positions.[4]

The antiabortion side felt unheard and disenfranchised by the court's decision.

When the law changed—starting with the liberalization in New York in 1970—the clergy's role changed, too. When the clergy were free to take their convictions to their logical conclusion by opening a clinic, the opposition's reaction was strong. Moody and Carmen commented on the founding of Women's Services in their 1973 book: "With the changing of the law so that abortion up to the twenty-fourth week was permissible, the task of the clergy shifted from the pastoral to the prophetic. Now anyone who knows anything about the history of church/world relations knows that pastors are indulged but prophets are stoned."[5] Religious groups that had remained silent on the subject of illegal abortion and the pastoral counseling of the CCS were angered—and perhaps frightened—by the clergy's prophetic stand in favor of legal abortion.

The Roman Catholic Church reacted strongly to the legalization of abortion in New York in 1970. Moody later wrote, "Catholic schools in New York City were closed and children were bussed to Albany to roam the legislative halls of the state capitol with signs proclaiming, 'abortion is murder.'"[6] If the only strong religious speakers against abortion up to that point had been the Catholic clergy, the *Roe v. Wade* decision added the support of evangelical Christians. The National Conference of Catholic Bishops had founded the Right to Life League in 1967, and until 1973 it was run as a Catholic organization. But in 1973, the group incorporated independently as the National Right to Life Committee and embraced the conservative Protestants and others who had been motivated by changes in state laws and then *Roe* to take action.[7] Conversely, with the law of the nation now on the side of legal abortion, the clergy who supported reproductive rights saw less need to speak and act publicly. The generation of clergy that followed the CCS seemed less inclined to activism, and the public mainly heard the voices of those who were against abortion. Antiabortion clergy spoke up strongly in favor of more restrictive state laws—nearly 200 such bills were introduced in 1973 alone, with 62 passing—and pro-life campaigns chipped away steadily and successfully at the availability and affordability of abortion.[8] In the following years, the Roman Catholic Church stepped up its antiabortion rhetoric and organization, establishing a hierarchy of pro-life committees and resources down to the parish level.[9] The net effect was that by the beginning of the twenty-first century, the general U.S. public didn't remember the clergy's activism on reproductive rights, much less the work of the CCS. In 1998, Tom Davis, a CCS alumnus who was by then chair of Planned Parenthood's national Clergy Advisory Board, said, "I think this piece of history has been lost and most Americans think most clergy are anti-abortion."[10] Therese Wilson, a spokesperson for Planned Parenthood Golden Gate in California said in 2005, "I think that in the media, [the abortion debate] is religious vs. nonreligious."[11]

The public impression that clergy were against abortion was not true, of course. Pro-choice clergy groups still existed, either founded by or taking inspiration from members of the now disbanded CCS.

Legacies of the CCS: Advocacy Groups

In 1973, after *Roe v. Wade*, the Roman Catholic Church pledged to overturn the decision. In response, pro-choice Protestant and Jewish leaders gathered at the United Methodist Building in Washington, DC, at the invitation of the United Methodist Board of Church and Society, to discuss what they could do. This was the founding meeting of the education and advocacy group Religious Coalition for Abortion Rights (RCAR). Its members were religious denominations and organizations as well as individual clergy and lay people, and it was funded mainly through donations from member organizations and individuals. Around the country, many former CCS counselors joined the state chapters of RCAR and spoke up—specifically as a counterweight to the religious voices on the other side—against state laws that would further restrict abortion. The national group provided pro-choice clergy to speak at the federal level—former CCS member Rabbi Balfour Brickner spoke against a constitutional ban on abortion before a U.S. Senate subcommittee in 1974, and many clergy testified against the Hyde Amendment, which severely limited Medicaid funding for abortion. In 1993, the group broadened its scope and became the Religious Coalition for Reproductive Choice (RCRC); five years later it formed a Clergy Advisory Committee to coordinate a nationwide Clergy for Choice Network.[12] In 2007, in honor of the CCS and Howard Moody, Clergy for Choice set up the Rev. Moody Clergy Consultation Fund to support training clergy counselors.[13]

Since the time of Margaret Sanger, Planned Parenthood made use of clergy spokespersons in favor of access to contraception. The organization knew the value of clergy support. But the relationship between Planned Parenthood—both the national group and its big-city affiliates—and the CCS—both the national group and its chapters—had been fraught. Although there were examples of cooperation between the groups—notably in Los Angeles and Chicago—the CCS generally found little practical support from Planned Parenthood and viewed the organization as too conservative and unwilling to speak up, much less act, on the issue of abortion. Moody later pointed out that when the CCS announced itself in 1967, the reaction of Planned Parenthood of New York was the same as that of the Roman Catholic Church: silence.[14] In fact, that same month, Planned Parenthood's national body was still debating whether all affiliates should offer contraceptive services to unmarried women—some did, but many served only married women.[15] Planned Parenthood had concerns about the legality of what the CCS was doing and perhaps could not fully trust the big personalities and outspoken approach of the CCS clergy. Ultimately, as Tom Davis points out in his book *Sacred Work*, they shared a common goal and common adversaries. In July 1970, when abortion became legal in New York, the Planned Parenthood Federation of America (PPFA) formed a Religious Affairs Committee. Unlike Planned Parenthood's past Clergymen's Advisory Council, the new committee included women and nonclergy members. The committee's charge was to formulate an answer to the criticism that Planned Parenthood was not doing anything about abortion and specifically to reach out to the CCS to improve communications and, if possible, work together.[16] However, the Women's Services clinic—and by extension the National CCS—were irritated with Planned Parenthood affiliates for referring large numbers of poor women to Women's Services for low-cost abortions and sending women of means to private clinics. For the sake of the survival of Women's Services, the CCS had imposed on its own counselors a 20–25 percent limit on reduced-fee cases. The National CCS charged its counselors to meet with their local Planned Parenthood officials and urge them to keep the big picture in mind, spread the financial burden more widely, and develop their own low-cost resources, "if for no other reason than that when the Clergy Services go out of business Planned Parenthood will need to carry the whole load."[17] Regional services apparently were already cooperating with Planned Parenthood affiliates; the Cleveland CCS, for instance, in 1971 had started a cooperative counseling project with Planned Parenthood and the free clinic there, receiving a $14,000 grant from a local fund to launch the program.[18]

In 1972 Planned Parenthood's Religious Affairs Committee issued a pamphlet defending a woman's right to choose abortion, but about a year after the *Roe v. Wade* decision, that particular committee ceased to exist, perhaps under the impression that once abortion had been legalized, there was no longer such a pressing need for people of faith to speak up in support of abortion rights.[19] However, the 1970s and 1980s brought intensified attacks on abortion from religious groups—groups that, as Davis pointed out, in the past had not tried to stop illegal abortion.[20] In response, clergy supporters of Planned Parenthood in several parts of the country formed local associations, in some cases as committees within affiliates. In upstate New York, Tom and Betsy Davis, both UCC ministers who had been CCS participants, and other clergy started the Adirondack Religious Coalition for Choice. Rev. Dr. Robert Meneilley, a Presbyterian minister, formed a Religious Affairs Committee for Planned Parenthood of Greater Kansas City. At some Planned Parenthood affiliates, the clergy also took on a counseling role based on the CCS model. In the 1990s, violence—much of it inspired by religious rhetoric—against abortion providers and clinics increased, and pro-choice clergy were further moved to speak out. In 1994, the PPFA formed a new national group, the Clergy Advisory Board, to theologically defend the work of Planned Parenthood, including abortion. Davis was a longtime chair of the group. In 1994, the PPFA appointed its first national chaplain, a Methodist, Rev. Ignacio Castuera.[21]

Other organizations have also acknowledged a debt to the CCS. The National Abortion Federation is an association of abortion providers that has carried on the efforts of the CCS to offer accurate and supportive medical, legal, and financial information and referrals to safe, qualified practitioners. It established a national telephone hotline that has been in operation since 1979.[22] Faith Aloud had its origins in the CCS chapter founded in St. Louis and became part of the RCRC. The group became independent in 2008 and offered all-options counseling training to clergy and free phone counseling by clergy to women. In 2015, Faith Aloud and its phone counseling service became a part of Backline, a nonprofit that "promotes unconditional and judgment-free support for people in all their decisions, feelings and experiences with pregnancy, parenting, adoption and abortion."[23] The work of the CCS also continues in the work of the National Advocates for Pregnant Women to protect the rights of pregnant women, particularly low-income women, women of color, and drug-using women.[24] The CCS showed clergy—and the country—the power of its advocacy, and that legacy lives on.

Legacies of the CCS: Counseling

The CCS also revived an interest in pastoral counseling. Ron Hammerle, speaking in a 2005 interview, pointed out that the role of counseling in the churches had languished for some years before 1967. During the civil rights struggle, he said, the clergy were "externally focused"; but all members of the CCS had to be on call to counsel, and they did counsel large numbers of people. For many, "abortion counseling was satisfying because one could see immediate resolution in a short time, which is rare in most counseling," Hammerle said.[25]

One result that surprised some of the clergy was how the counseling, and even the abortion procedure itself, empowered women when the atmosphere was supportive and the doctors nonjudgmental. Rev. Gregory Dell said in a 2004 interview that women found it helpful to understand their options with a problem pregnancy. "As soon as a pregnancy is defined as a problem, that it's not a matter of having one option, it's a matter of being able to choose. Adoption is a possibility, carrying the baby to term and adoption. Making other kinds of legal arrangements is a possibility. These are possibilities. Abortion is a possibility. Every option can be weighed. You get to make that decision. That's what's empowering," Dell said. "So even if a woman came in saying, 'I'm clear,' or saying, at least, 'I guess I need to have an abortion,' to be able to have some conversation with her as she explored the other possibilities, she could then decide, 'That option is not an option for me, but it is an option out there, so I get to make a choice about it.' And I think that's what becomes empowering, is when people feel they can choose. It's when people feel they have no choice that I think that the tragedy gets multiplied."[26]

Rev. Mark Rutledge was a UCC minister at Iowa State University, running an ecumenical campus ministry that worked with antiwar activists during the time he was also a counselor with the CCS. He later earned a master's degree in counseling and went on to complete a doctorate in clinical psychology. His doctoral research, inspired by his experience with the CCS, showed empirically that patients who received counseling, whether from a female or male counselor, experienced decreased anxiety, greater sense of personal control over life events, and increased positive self-concept.[27] Glenna Halvorson-Boyd, co-director of women's clinics in Albuquerque and Dallas with her husband, Dr. Curtis Boyd, said in a 2002 documentary about their work that "abortion counseling as it is now done" can be attributed to the CCS and the feminist health movement. The clergy saw the importance of addressing the spiritual needs of a woman seeking abortion, and its meaning to herself and her family, while the feminist movement emphasized the open sharing of information to make the procedure less mysterious.[28]

Together, the counseling and public advocacy work of the CCS also empowered the clergy who participated. Asked about the influence and importance of the CCS, Rabbi Balfour Brickner said,

Well, it wasn't the effect that they had on the women so much as the effect they had on themselves. They found out that they could be enablers, and that you could stand up, you could bring your truth to their power, and you could make a difference, and you didn't get killed for it. You were all right. It gave 'em strength. That's the beauty of the whole Clergy Consultation Service. I mean, sure, it helped some women. But way beyond help that it gave to the few women that it helped—I think of the hundreds of thousands that it helped, and millions needed help—is that it empowered the clergy. They saw what they could do. They never knew that about themselves. A lot of them, anyway. And they began to feel good. They walked a little straighter.[29]

Moody had seen and heard the same thing. "A lot of ministers that I knew, that came on board—and partly because I asked them to, we were really colleagues and friends—some of them told me that it was the most meaningful part of ministry they ever had. I mean, no ministry they ever had was that meaningful. . . . And probably, for a lot of them who were into the church business for the most part, and weren't concerned about the world in which we live, that that might have been quite a change for them."[30]

As we talked with dozens of CCS members some forty years after their participation, most were still moved—some to tears—with feeling at some particular memory of a woman or young girl who had come to them in distress. It was a powerful experience for all of them. They had agreed to join the CCS for a variety of reasons—compassion, conscience, politics, feminism, respect for the clergy person issuing the invitation, a history of involvement in progressive causes—but the act of counseling individual women left a deep personal and professional impression on each of them. Indeed, a number of the CCS clergy went on to make counseling or therapy their primary careers, in or outside the ministry.

After the CCS

The majority of the clergy we interviewed continued as passionate, outspoken activists at the time we spoke with them, when the youngest of them was about sixty years of age and the oldest in their eighties. We interviewed Gregory Dell in 2004 at the rainbow-festooned Broadway United Methodist Church in Chicago, where he was an outspoken supporter of lesbian, gay, bisexual, transgender, and queer (LGBTQ) civil rights. In 1998, he had conducted a service of holy union for a gay couple and was charged, tried by the United Methodist Church, and found guilty of "disobedience of the Order and Discipline" of the church. He was suspended, then reinstated after a year at Broadway, where he continued his outspoken support for LGBTQ rights. In 2008, he was inducted into the Chicago Gay and Lesbian Hall of Fame.[31]

Huw Anwyl, director of the Los Angeles CCS and founder of many of the western chapters, spoke with us in 2006. He was still the active minister of Shepherd of the Hills, a combined Disciples of Christ and UCC church in Laguna Niguel, California, where his projects had included a housing renovation project in Watts, Compton, and Long Beach; a child care center for working families; an ecumenical group to discuss science and religion; and the idea of establishing a museum—or chain of museums—of world religions. He served a three-year term as chair of the Resources and Development Committee of Church World Service, which serves refugees around the world. When we spoke with him, he had just returned from Saudi Arabia, and his exhausting itinerary in the first decade of the twenty-first century also included Bosnia, Nigeria, East Timor, Sudan, Iran—and Iraq in 2003. He was energetic and optimistic that people around the world could find commonality even in the diversity of religion.[32] Anwyl retired from Shepherd of the Hills in 2015.

Liz Canfield, co-founder of the Los Angeles CCS, went on to work at student health centers at the University of California, Northridge, and then University of Southern California, providing sex education and birth control. She was also an advocate for LGBTQ civil rights, chairing a group to fight a California amendment that would have outlawed gay teachers. Canfield moved to Albuquerque, where she worked for twenty-three years as a birth control and options counselor at Planned Parenthood. In Albuquerque, she created an emergency fund to assist people with HIV/AIDS; the fund continued twenty-six years later, under a new director.[33]

Spencer Parsons, who headed the Chicago CCS, retired as dean of Rockefeller Chapel at the University of Chicago in 1979. He moved back to Massachusetts, taught as adjunct faculty at Andover Newton Theological Seminary, and remained a powerful progressive voice and active in the American Baptist denomination. He passed away in 2013.[34] Ron Hammerle, who ably administered the Chicago CCS, helped bring Women's Services into legal compliance and then went on to become head of Planned Parenthood of Iowa (now part of Planned Parenthood of the Heartland). He continued his career in health care, working with corporations and health care systems on strategic planning and management. Most recently he was chairman and CEO of Health Resources, an organization devoted to helping implement medical aid in dying—a movement that is opposed by some of the same groups that have opposed abortion and with progress so far measured in state-by-state legal reform.[35]

Finley Schaef, a founding member of the New York CCS when he was at Washington Square United Methodist Church, moved on to Park Slope

United Methodist in 1972 and led that church in activism against apartheid and in support of Central American liberation movements, LGBTQ civil rights, low-cost housing, environmental awareness, and a host of other issues. After retiring in 1997, Schaef continued to preach as a visiting minister and speak out on social justice issues.[36]

Arlene Carmen, the administrator of the National CCS, did pioneering work with sex workers, artists, and prisoners and worked with the People With AIDS Health Group to provide education, support, and access to experimental treatments for people with HIV/AIDS. She died in 1994.[37]

Howard Moody's prophetic leadership of Judson Memorial Church and its support of the arts continued. He was on the forefront of fights for free speech, health care, LGBTQ civil rights, and reproductive rights. After his retirement from Judson in 1992, he continued to speak out and organize. Moody, feeling that current drug laws were racist, unjustly applied, and ineffective, founded Religious Leaders for a More Just and Compassionate Drug Policy. In 2004, he was a founder of the Coalition for Baptist Principles, an organization devoted to the Baptist tradition of freedom for local churches, with "no hierarchy that dictates to Baptists what they must believe or how their ministries will be carried out," valuing nonconformity and theological diversity within the denomination. His memoir about his time at Judson, *A Voice in the Village: A Journey of a Pastor and a People*, was published in 2009. He died in 2012 at the age of ninety-one.[38]

Nearly all the participants in the CCS whom we contacted were glad to talk with us. Few of them had been asked about their work with the service since 1973. Many said that even at their current age, if the *Roe v. Wade* decision were overturned or abortion became otherwise illegal nationally, they would do the same again. Except for the large chapter organizers like Moody, Parsons, and Anwyl, most of the clergy worked locally and did not see the big picture of the CCS network and the legacies it left. Many became aware of the national organizations that followed in the footsteps of the CCS—RCRC and Planned Parenthood's Clergy Advisory Board—and joined affiliated state and local groups. Most knew about the Women's Services clinic because they had referred women there; few realized what importance it had as a pioneer in outpatient surgical services, a revolution in health care that took off in the years after the CCS disbanded. The clinic, founded by clergy on compassionate principles, was a model for today's abortion and reproductive health clinics and outpatient surgery in general. Moreover, it was a model for all kinds of medical care where the patient's natural anxiety is alleviated by medical staff in colorful attire instead of white; comfortable, welcoming surroundings; and patient advocates who explain procedures and deal with problems.

Lessons for Activists

The CCS also left an important legacy in the lessons it offers to today's activists. The service demonstrated the value of allyship. The mainline clergy of the 1960s, predominantly privileged white men, might have seemed the least likely group to stand up effectively for women's reproductive rights—especially poor women's rights. Indeed, they were not welcomed as allies by all feminists. Not all of them were perfect speakers for a feminist revolution, steeped as they were in old-school thinking. Feminist writer and activist Susan Brownmiller wrote that one of the male clergy she interviewed for her 1969 article for *New York Magazine* "preened with self-importance, which did not sit well with my growing militance."[39] But the clergy used their privilege, their voice, and their power to help change individual lives, laws, and the system of reproductive health care.

They discerned the need, but before they took action, they educated themselves. They invited doctors, lawyers, and women who had had abortions to teach them what they would need to know. They became so expert that, for example, Rev. Carl Bielby of the Michigan CCS was able to teach a gynecologist how to perform an abortion.[40] The group recruited ministers and rabbis who had had no previous experience with abortion and provided the information they needed to counsel and refer women. Learning as they went along, they were willing to change and adapt procedures as problems or opportunities arose.

The Metropolitan Associates of Philadelphia and the CCS there demonstrated that taking the time to educate those inside a power structure—in their case, doctors who worked in hospitals—could be a successful way to recruit allies. Applying pressure from outside the power structure meant that those allies did not have to shoulder all responsibility for the change they were promoting, since they did not appear to be the initiators of that change.

Most of all, the clergy of the CCS were a model for bold direct action. Speaking the word *abortion* was daring enough in 1967. The New York clergy set up and publicized an abortion referral service without knowing whether they would find themselves in police custody—or out of a job—the next day. They gave up many hours a week to their counseling work. And they are willing to do it all over again if need be.

Outlook for the Future

If anyone thought that the struggle for access to legal, safe, affordable abortion was over after *Roe v. Wade*, they know better now. State restrictions on abortion have steadily—and then with increasing speed—eroded access. A study conducted by the Guttmacher Institute found that of the 1,074 state abortion restrictions enacted after *Roe* (1973) through 2015, more than a quarter had been passed in just the most recent five years. In the first quarter of 2016, state legislators introduced 411 provisions seeking to limit women's access to abortion.[41] Some clinics have been regulated out of existence. Many seeking abortions must travel farther, stay longer, and make repeat visits. The Hyde Amendment, still in effect, means that Medicaid assists very few poor women in paying for abortion procedures. Attacks on Planned Parenthood specifically have made their work more difficult. In September 2015, GOP members of the House Oversight and Government Reform Committee lambasted Cecile Richards, the President of Planned Parenthood, for five hours leading up to a vote on defunding Planned Parenthood in the House of Representatives.[42]

Where were the prophetic clergy voices in these rounds of attacks on reproductive justice? In 2015 the Planned Parenthood Clergy Advocacy Board, which includes members from the United Church of Christ, American Baptist Churches, Episcopal Church, Unitarian Universalist, and Reformed Jewish clergy, did issue a statement in support of Planned Parenthood, which read in part, "Our religious traditions call us to offer compassion, not judgment. People who work for Planned Parenthood give care and respect to those in need, doing God's work. For this we are grateful."[43] Rev. Tom Davis, a former CCS member, has been a longtime member of the Planned Parenthood Clergy Advocacy Board, and in this advocacy work, the legacy of the CCS lives on. Other faith-based organizations, such as RCRC, do speak at the national level, and there are supportive clergy members working with local chapters of Planned Parenthood and other groups.

However times have changed since the days of the CCS. In 1967, it was possible to call a network of activist clergy to direct action because there was an existing clergy network forged by the civil rights movement and protests against the Vietnam War. There has been no issue in recent years that has brought progressive clergy together nationally in the same way. In addition, mainline Protestant denominations do not command the nearly universal respect, cultural influence, and even political power that they did in the 1960s; from a peak membership of about 40 million around 1965, they have shrunk to around 15 million in recent years.[44] In 2014, only 14.7 percent of Americans belonged to a mainline Protestant denomination—and they were older than members of other major religions, with a median age of fifty-two. Meanwhile, evangelical Protestant churches have been on the rise, accounting for 25.4 percent of the population.[45] As many evangelical churches joined the Catholic Church to oppose abortion after *Roe*, clergy advocates of reproductive rights have found themselves no longer in authority and very much on the defensive. If access to abortion continues to erode, or if *Roe* is overturned all together, reconstituting or replicating the CCS would be very difficult.

What is the path forward, then, for people of faith? Abortion providers sometimes speak of themselves as conscientious practitioners who are called by conscience or religion, as the CCS was, to ensure that safe abortion care is accessible. This parallels the argument of providers who claim a religious right to except themselves from providing certain reproductive health services and suggests constitutional protection. Meanwhile, journalist Ruth Graham speculates that liberal Christianity is lying dormant and that there could be a resurgence; she points to clergy like Lutheran pastor Nadia Bolz-Weber, whose Denver congregation is one-third LGBTQ identified.[46] There is hope in the broader reframing of the abortion rights movement as an element of reproductive justice. In that way people of faith can find intersections with racial justice, economic justice, and gender equality and build coalitions with communities of color, the poor, LGBTQ activists, and religious communities that were not represented in the CCS. Many of the visionary members of the CCS were already finding those intersections in the 1960s and 1970s and continued to do so throughout their careers. Their willingness to take risks, speak up, and take direct action out of compassion for people—including people who were not necessarily just like themselves—continued in their work and can inspire those who follow.

Appendix A

Clergy Statement on Abortion Law Reform and Consultation Service on Abortion, Spring 1967

The present abortion laws require over a million women in the United States each year to seek illegal abortions which often cause severe mental anguish, physical suffering, and unnecessary death of women. These laws also compel the birth of unwanted, unloved, and often deformed children; yet a truly human society is one in which the birth of a child is an occasion for genuine celebration, not the imposition of a penalty or punishment upon the mother. These laws brand as criminals wives and mothers who are often driven as helpless victims to desperate acts. The largest percentage of abortion deaths are found among the 35–39-year-old married women who have five or six children. The present abortion law in New York is most oppressive of the poor and minority groups. A 1965 report shows that 94 percenet of abortion deaths in New York City occurred among Negroes and Puerto Ricans.

We are deeply distressed that recent attempts to suggest even a conservative change in the New York State abortion law, affecting only extreme cases of rape, incest, and deformity of the child, have met with such immediate and hostile reaction in some quarters, including the charge that all abortion is "murder." We affirm that there is a period during gestation when, although there may be *embryo* life in the fetus, there is no living *child* upon whom the crime of murder can be committed.

From Arlene Carmen and Howard Moody, *Abortion Counseling and Social Change, from Illegal Act to Medical Practice: The Story of the Clergy Consultation Services on Abortion* (Valley Forge, PA: Judson Press, 1973), 30–31.

Therefore we pledge ourselves as clergymen to a continuing effort to educate and inform the public to the end that a more liberal abortion law in this state and throughout the nation be enacted.

In the meantime women are being driven alone and afraid into the under-world of criminality or the dangerous practice of self-induced abortion. Confronted with a difficult decision and the means of implementing it, women today are forced by ignorance, misinformation, and desperation into courses of action that require humane concern on the part of religious leaders. Belief in the sanctity of human life certainly demands helpfulness and sympathy to women in trouble and concern for living children, many of whom today are deprived of their mothers, who die following self-induced abortions or those performed under sub-medical standards.

We are mindful that there are duly licensed and reputable physicians who in their wisdom perform therapeutic abortions which some may regard as illegal. When a doctor performs such an operation motivated by compassion and concern for the patient, and not simply for monetary gain, we do not regard him as a criminal, but as living by the highest standards of religion and of the Hippocratic oath.

Therefore believing as clergymen that there are higher laws and moral obligations transcending legal codes, we believe that it is our pastoral responsibility and religious duty to give aid and assistance to all women with problem pregnancies. To that end we are establishing a Clergymen's Consultation Service on Abortion which will include referral to the best available medical advice and aid to women in need.

Appendix B

Questionnaire Completed
by Chicago CCS Counselors
for Each Counselee, February 1970

Chicago CCS on Problem Pregnancies   2/70

Case number _____   Clergy number _____   Date _____

1. Source of finding Chicago CCS
   1. Another CCS
   2. Dr. or hosp.
   3. Planned Parenthood
   4. Friend
   5. Other (newspaper, etc.)

Number of inquiries before us:
Time spent in searching:

PROBLEM:

2. Woman's status
   1. Single
   2. Married
   3. Widowed
   4. Divorced

From folder 17, box 2, Chicago Clergy Consultation Service records, Special Collections and University Archives, University of Illinois at Chicago.

3. Age _____ and classification
    1. 17 or under
    2. 18–25
    3. 26–39
    4. 40 or over

4. Ethnic group
    1. Caucasian
    2. Negroid
    3. Other

5. Religion
    1. Protestant
    2. Catholic
    3. Jewish
    4. Other
    5. None or not reported

6. Accompanied by
    1. Husband
    2. Mate
    3. Parent(s)
    4. Relative
    5. Friend
    6. No one

7. Woman's occupation
    1. Student
    2. Housewife
    3. Professional _____
    4. Non-professional _____

8. Husband/mate's occupation
    1. Student
    2. Professional _____
    3. Non-Professional _____

9. No. of previous pregnancies
    1. None
    2. Other _____

10. Previous miscarriages
     1. None
     2. Other _____

11. Previous induced abortions
     1. None
     2. Other _____

12. No. of living children
     1. None
     2. Other _____

13. Contraception used
     1. None
     2. Condom
     3. Diaphragm
     4. Pill
     5. IUD (spiral, loop or bow—if known)
     6. Other (incl. rhythm) _____

FIRST DAY OF LAST MENSTRUAL PERIOD: _____

14. Weeks pregnant _____ and code
     1. 10 or under
     2. 11–12
     3. 13–15
     4. 16+

PREGNANCY TEST (chemical)? _____

INTERNAL EXAMINATION? _____

DATE _____

DISCUSSION OF ALL ALTERNATIVES

     • Continue preg. & raise child as a single parent
     • Marriage
     • Take preg. to term and place child for adoption
     • Terminate pregnancy

15. If termination is desired, what is the given reason? _____
    1. Medical
    2. Psychological
    3. Family/environmental

16. Desire of the husband _____, mate_____, or parent_____.
    1. Not informed.
    2. Does not consent.
    3. In agreement with consultee.
    4. Unknown, or not reported.

IN YOUR JUDGMENT, MIGHT THE CONSULTEE QUALIFY FOR TREATMENT AT A LOCAL HOSPITAL?

17. Consultee's decision
    1. Not indicated or not decided.
    2. Continue pregnancy for single parent_____, marriage_____, adoption_____
    3. Termination in state (through hospital).
    4. Termination out of state.
    5. Termination—foreign.

ANY PROBLEMS WITH OR REACTIONS TO
      • Antibiotics
      • Penicillin
      • Other

DISPOSITION:

      Adoption—Mother's Agency_____
      Psychiatrist _____
      Hospital _____
      Medical resource or code _____

      in

      Illinois _____
      Other state _____
      Foreign _____

CHECKBACK
　　　　Call or letter received _____
　　　　Any discrepancy in arrangements
　　　　　　　　　price, or
　　　　　　　　　service

18. Complications
　　　1. None reported
　　　2. Minor (specify) _____
　　　3. Major (specify) _____

Appendix C

Referral Guidelines
for Clergy Consultation Service
Chapters

After progress reports from each of the represented groups, the following guidelines were proposed for national adoption, recognizing highly diverse local conditions.

    1. Only physicians licensed to practice in the state in which they operate are to be used by CCS groups. (Some services wanted only OBGYN people.)

    2. Each Service should check with the others upon receiving negative information.

    3. Do not use resources in any state where there is a Clergy Service without first checking with that group.

    4. No doctor should be used without an adequate, prior checkout procedure. (Procedures may vary from group to group.)

    5. Extreme caution should be used in pregnancies after 12 weeks. (Some services wanted to propose a limit at 12 weeks.)

    6. Pelvic examinations prior to consultations are extremely important to both detect false or tubal pregnancies and to provide adequate medical information in cases with possible complications. (Some services wanted to rule out consultations without prior examinations and pregnancy certifications.)

As proposed, these guidelines are in keeping with our current practices.

From a report to Chicago CCS on the May 28, 1969, meeting of National CCS, folder 5, box 1, Chicago Clergy Consultation Service records, Special Collections and University Archives, University of Illinois at Chicago. E. Spencer Parsons or Ronald L. Hammerle must have been the author. Parenthetical notes are from the original report.

Appendix D

Statistics:
Sampling of 6,455 Women Seen by
New York Clergy Consultation Service

Age:

# under 16	107
# under 18	480
# over 18	3,269
# over 25	1,871
# over 35	728

Race:

# White	5,328
# Negro	786
# Puerto Rican	115
# Other	90

Length of Pregnancy:

# 4–8 weeks	3,203
# 8–10 weeks	1,258
# 10–12 weeks	559
# over 3 months	219
# over 4 months	102

Statistics from National CCS, undated, reprinted at the end of transcription of Arlene Carmen interview by Ellen Chesler, January, 1976, New York, NY, Schlesinger-Rockefeller Oral History Project, Radcliffe College.

Referred to CCS by:

# Psychiatrist	127
# M.D.	1,832
# Planned Parenthood or similar agency	695
# Friend	1,847
# Other	474

Marital Status:

# Married	1,618
# Single	4,141
# Divorced	280
# Separated	228

Religion:

# Protestant	2,208
# Catholic	2,174
# Jewish	1,497
# Other	104

Type of Contraception Used:

# Oral	612
# IUD	101
# Diaphragm	188
# Foam	353
# Rhythm	340
# Male Prophylactic	719
# None	3,053
# Other	18

[Section crossed out:]

Occupation:

Housewife

Student

Other

Notes

Introduction

1. Edward B. Fiske, "Clergymen Offer Abortion Advice," *New York Times*, May 22, 1967.

2. Fiske, "Clergymen Offer Abortion Advice"; Arlene Carmen and Howard Moody, *Abortion Counseling and Social Change: From Illegal Act to Medical Practice: The Story of the Clergy Consultation Service on Abortion* (Valley Forge, PA: Judson Press, 1973), 51.

3. Rosemary Nossiff, *Before* Roe*: Abortion Policy in the States* (Philadelphia: Temple University Press, 2001), 49.

4. For example, Moody had been arrested during a civil rights protest (Howard Moody, interview by the authors, April 25, 2005, New York; "200 Racial Pickets Seized at Building Projects Here," *New York Times*, July 23, 1963); and Rev. Charles H. (Chick) Straut, a founder of the New Jersey CCS, was arrested at a peace demonstration (Charles H. Straut, telephone interview by Relf, June 7, 2010); Paul L. Montgomery, "Peace Delegates Urge Strong U.N.," *New York Times*, February 21, 1965.

5. Fiske, "Clergymen Offer Abortion Advice."

6. *New York Times*, May 24, 1967, and Lewis "Buz" Bogage, email message to Patricia Relf, March 22, 2007.

7. Joshua D. Wolff, "Ministers of a Higher Law: The Story of the Clergy Consultation Service on Abortion," undergraduate thesis, Amherst College, April 10, 1998, 51. Only one negative letter from 1967 was found in the Judson Memorial Church archive at New York University Fales Library, and the same one was in Wolff's personal research papers.

8. Martha C. Ward, *Poor Women, Powerful Men: America's Great Experiment in Family Planning* (Boulder, CO: Westview Press, 1986), 58. Note that members of the CCS avoided the term *underground* as they did not want to sound clandestine.

9. One fatality in England was attributed to a problem with anesthesia, not the abortion itself. See chapter 6 for details of the case.

Chapter 1. How Can It Not Be Legal?

1. Robert Spike, farewell sermon at Judson Memorial Church, quoted in Howard Moody, *A Voice in the Village: A Journey of a Pastor and a People* (N.p.: Xlibris, 2009), 395.

2. Moody, *A Voice in the Village*, 18–19.

3. Jerry Tallmer, "Village Minister," *New York Post*, May 25, 1967.

4. Moody, *A Voice in the Village*, 19–26, 36–37; Howard Moody, conversation with Relf, July 5, 2007, Santa Barbara, CA; Tallmer, "Village Minister," *New York Post*, May 25, 1967.

5. Howard Moody, interview by the authors, April 25, 2005.

6. Moody, *A Voice in the Village*; "200 Racial Pickets Seized at Building Projects Here," *New York Times*, July 23, 1963.

7. Moody interview.

8. Daniel K. Williams, *Defenders of the Unborn: The Pro-Life Movement Before* Roe v. Wade (New York: Oxford University Press, 2016), 32, citing Samuel A. Cosgrove and Patricia A. Carter, "A Consideration of Therapeutic Abortion," *American Journal of Obstetrics and Gynecology* 48 (September 1944), 299–314.

9. Sharon Gold-Steinberg and Abigail J. Stewart, "Psychologies of Abortion: Implications of a Changing Context," in Rickie Solinger (ed.), *Abortion Wars: A Half Century of Struggle, 1950–2000* (Berkeley: University of California Press, 1998), 363.

10. Rickie Solinger, "Pregnancy and Power before *Roe v. Wade*, 1950–1970," in Rickie Solinger (ed.), *Abortion Wars: A Half Century of Struggle, 1950–2000* (Berkeley: University of California Press, 1998), 24; Nanette J. Davis, *From Crime to Choice: The Transformation of Abortion in America* (Westport, CT: Greenwood Press, 1985), 54.

11. Lawrence Lader, *Abortion* (Indianapolis: Bobbs-Merrill, 1966), 24; Lawrence Lader, *Abortion II: Making the Revolution* (Boston: Beacon Press, 1973), 21–22.

12. Lader, *Abortion II*, 22.

13. Leslie J. Reagan, *When Abortion Was a Crime: Women, Medicine, and Law in the United States, 1867–1973* (Berkeley: University of California Press, 1997), 198–200. For examples, see Ellen Messer and Kathryn E. May, *Back Rooms: Voices from the Illegal Abortion Era* (Buffalo, NY: Prometheus Books, 1994), especially the chapter "Back Alleys, Dark Streets."

14. Martha Ward, *Poor Women, Powerful Men: America's Great Experiment in Family Planning* (Boulder, CO: Westview Press, 1986), 14.

15. Lader, *Abortion*, 67–69; Loretta J. Ross, "African American Women and Abortion," in Rickie Solinger (ed.), *Abortion Wars: A Half Century of Struggle, 1950–2000* (Berkeley: University of California Press, 1998), 161, citing Robert Staples, *The Black Woman in America*.

16. As Rickie Solinger has written in *Wake Up Little Susie* (2nd ed.; New York: Routledge, 2010, 6–7, 199), adoption was an option more available to white women than to women of color for several reasons: white babies were seen as more adoptable, adoption agencies were slower to approve prospective adoptive parents who were black, maternity homes were generally for whites only, and black communities generally rallied to support a single mother and her child whereas white communities rejected them.

17. Huw Anwyl, interview by the authors, February 22, 2006, Laguna Niguel, CA.

18. Tom Davis, telephone interview by the authors, July 19, 2004.

19. Moody, *A Voice in the Village*, 386.

20. Defund Planned Parenthood Act of 2015, H.R. 3134, 114th Congress (2015–16), passed September 18, 2015; Sarah Klift, "In 2012 Campaign, Women's Health Plays a Role Like Never Before," *Washington Post*, September 5, 2012.

21. Adam Liptak, "Supreme Court Appears Sharply Divided as It Hears Texas Abortion Case," *New York Times*, March 2, 2016; MSNBC Town Hall with Donald

Trump Moderated by Chris Matthews, March 16, 2016, transcript at http://info
.msnbc.com/_news/2016/03/30/35330907-full-transcript-msnbc-town-hall-with-
donald-trump-moderated-by-chris-matthews?lite; Matt Flegenheimer and Maggie
Haberman, "Donald Trump, Abortion Foe, Eyes 'Punishment' for Women, Then
Recants," *New York Times*, March 30, 2016; Robert Draper, "Mr. Trump's Wild Ride,"
New York Times Magazine, May 18, 2016, http://www.nytimes.com/2016/05/22/magazine
/donald-trump-primary-win.html?_r=5.

Chapter 2. The Push for Change

1. Daniel Schiff discusses the complexities, interpretations, and translations of this
passage in *Abortion in Judaism* (Cambridge: Cambridge University Press, 2002), 1–26.

2. Carol Collier and Rachel Haliburton, *Bioethics in Canada: A Philosophical Introduction*
(Toronto: Canadian Scholars' Press, 2015), 263–264.

3. Collier and Haliburton, *Bioethics in Canada*, 264.

4. R. Sauer, "Attitudes to Abortion in America, 1800–1973," *Population Studies* 28,
no. 1 (1974), 53–67.

5. Patricia Knight, "Women and Abortion in Victorian and Edwardian England,"
History Workshop 4 (Autumn 1977), 52–68.

6. Suzanne M. Alford, "Is Self-Abortion a Fundamental Right?," *Duke Law Journal*
52, no. 5 (2003), 1011–1029.

7. Sauer, "Attitudes to Abortion in America," 54.

8. Sauer, "Attitudes to Abortion in America," 55.

9. Nicola Beisel and Tamara Kay, "Abortion, Race, and Gender in Nineteenth
Century America," *American Sociological Review* 69 (August 2004), 498–518.

10. Mary D. McConaghy, "School of Medicine: Historical Development, 1765–
1800," http://www.archives.upenn.edu/histy/features/1700s/medsch.html#1 (accessed
August 8, 2016).

11. Abraham Flexner, "Medical Education in America: Rethinking the Training
of American Doctors," *Atlantic*, June 1910, http://www.theatlantic.com/magazine
/archive/1910/06/medical-education-in-america/306088/ (accessed August 8, 2016).

12. Ludwig Edelstein, "The Hippocratic Oath: Text, Translation, and Interpretation," in Robert M. Veatch (ed.), *Cross-Cultural Perspectives in Medical Ethics* (Sudbury,
MA: Jones and Bartlett Publishers, 2000), 3.

13. Lisa R. Hasday, "The Hippocratic Oath as Literary Text: A Dialogue between
Law and Medicine," *Yale Journal of Health Policy, Law, and Ethics* 2, no. 2 (2002), 1–27.

14. Rosemary Nossiff, *Before* Roe*: Abortion Policy in the States* (Philadelphia: Temple
University Press, 2001), 31–34, 45; David J. Garrow, *Liberty and Sexuality: The Right to
Privacy and the Making of* Roe v. Wade, updated edition (Berkeley: University of California
Press, 1998), 271–275.

15. Statistic from the research of Frederick J. Taussig, cited by Garrow, *Liberty and
Sexuality*, 272.

16. Nanette J. Davis, *From Crime to Choice: The Transformation of Abortion in America*
(Westport, CT: Greenwood Press, 1985), 54.

17. Loretta J. Ross, "African-American Women and Abortion: A Neglected History," *Journal of Health Care for the Poor and Underserved* 3, no. 2 (1992), 278.

18. Ross, "African-American Women and Abortion," 278.

19. The states were California, Kentucky, Minnesota, Ohio, and Oregon. Daniel K. Williams, *Defenders of the Unborn: The Pro-Life Movement before* Roe v. Wade (New York: Oxford University Press), 40; United Nations, Declaration of the Rights of the Child, General Assembly Resolution 1386 (XIV), November 20, 1959, available online at http://www.unicef.org/malaysia/1959-Declaration-of-the-Rights-of-the-Child.pdf.

20. Mary Calderone (ed.), *Abortion in the United States* (New York: Harper and Bros., 1958).

21. Garrow, *Liberty and Sexuality*, 277.

22. Jerome Kummer and Zad Leavy, "Criminal Abortion—A Consideration of Ways to Reduce Incidence," *California Medicine* 95 (September 1961), 170–175, cited in Garrow, *Liberty and Sexuality*, 280.

23. Garrow, *Liberty and Sexuality*, 282.

24. Garrow, *Liberty and Sexuality*, 292.

25. Sherri Finkbine, interview, *From Danger to Dignity: The Fight for Safe Abortion*, video by Dorothy Fadiman, Beth Seltzer, and Daniel Meyers (San Jose, CA: KTEH-TV, 1995).

26. "Mrs. Finkbine Undergoes Abortion in Sweden," *New York Times*, August 19, 1962; Garrow, *Liberty and Sexuality*, 285–289.

27. College of Physicians of Philadelphia, "The History of Vaccines: Rubella," http://www.historyofvaccines.org/content/articles/rubella, last modified July 31, 2014.

28. Kristin Luker, *Abortion and the Politics of Motherhood* (Berkeley: University of California Press, 1984), 86–87.

29. Betty Friedan, *The Feminine Mystique* (New York: Norton, 1963).

30. Jo Freeman, "The Women's Liberation Movement: Its Origins, Structure, and Ideas," http://www.jofreeman.com/feminism/liberationmov.htm.

31. Lawrence Lader, *Abortion II: Making the Revolution* (Boston: Beacon Press, 1973), 35–37.

32. Jessie Daniels, "The Second Wave: Trouble with White Feminism," *Racism Review*, March 4, 2014, http://www.racismreview.com/blog/2014/03/04/second-wave-white-feminism/; Loretta Ross, "Understanding Reproductive Justice," March 2011, http://www.trustblackwomen.org/our-work/what-is-reproductive-justice/9-what-is-reproductive-justice; bell hooks, *Feminist Theory: From Margin to Center* (Cambridge, MA: South End Press, 1984).

33. Garrow, *Liberty and Sexuality*, 453.

34. Lader, *Abortion II*, 58.

35. Garrow, *Liberty and Sexuality*, 296–298; *New York Times*, February 13, 1965.

36. "Abortion and the Law," *CBS Reports*, April 5, 1965; *New York Times*, April 7, 1965; Lawrence Lader, "The Scandal of Abortion—Laws," *New York Times Magazine*, April 25, 1965.

37. Garrow, *Liberty and Sexuality*, 302.

38. Garrett Hardin, interview by Otis Graham, March 9, 1997, Santa Barbara, at http://www.garretthardinsociety.org/gh/gh_graham_interview.html; Garrow, *Liberty and Sexuality*, 293–295.

39. Garrow, *Liberty and Sexuality*, 302–303.

40. Frances Kissling, "How the Vatican Almost Embraced Birth Control," *Mother Jones*, May/June 2010, http://www.motherjones.com/politics/2010/05/catholic-church-vatican-bishops-birth-control.

41. Stephen D. Mumford, "Why Is the Vatican Obliged to Halt Legalized Abortion and Contraception Despite the Strong Wishes of Americans?," *Church and State*, August 2012, http://churchandstate.org.uk/2012/08/why-is-the-vatican-obliged-to-halt-legalized-abortion/.

42. Kissling, "How the Vatican Almost Embraced Birth Control."

43. It was only after feminist activism of the late 1960s that by the early 1970s lawyers began to argue for the rights of women to decide when to bear children. Williams, *Defenders of the Unborn*, 96; Amy Kesselman, "Women versus Connecticut: Conducting a Statewide Hearing," in Rickie Solinger (ed.), *Abortion Wars: A Half Century of Struggle, 1950–2000* (Berkeley: University of California Press, 1998), 42.

44. In 1966, for example, the National Catholic Welfare Conference published a booklet opposing liberalization of abortion laws (Russell B. Shaw, *Abortion and Public Policy* [Washington, DC: Family Life Bureau, NCWC, February 1966], cited by Garrow, *Liberty and Sexuality*, 303); a number of major Protestant denominations, in contrast, were issuing or considering statements supporting a liberal view, and antiabortion evangelical Protestants did not wish to ally themselves publicly with Catholics at the time (see chapter 7). Prominent Catholics were also the major antireform voices at hearings held by state legislatures around the country, including those in New York in 1966 and 1967.

45. Lader, *Abortion II*, 67–68; Elizabeth Canfield, telephone interview by Relf, January 8, 2015.

46. Carl E. Bielby, video interview by Relf, February 9, 2010.

47. Michigan Council for the Study of Abortion executive committee meeting minutes, March 6, 1968, folder 2, Jack M. Stack Papers, 1967–71, Bentley Historical Library, University of Michigan; Bielby, video interview by Relf, March 11, 2010.

48. Nossiff, *Before* Roe, 78–80; Lader, *Abortion II*, 57–60.

49. John Sibley, "Abortion Reform Urged in Albany," *New York Times*, March 8, 1966.

50. Nossiff, *Before* Roe, 79; Lader, *Abortion II*, 58–59. The coalition assembled by Lassoe was called the Organization for Abortion Law Reform.

51. Sydney H. Schanberg, "The Abortion Issue—Some Pros and Cons," *New York Times*, March 8, 1967.

52. "Abortion Change Killed in Albany by Vote of 15 to 3," *New York Times*, March 8, 1967.

53. Lawrence Lader, *The Margaret Sanger Story and the Fight for Birth Control* (Garden City, NY: Doubleday, 1955).

54. Lawrence Lader, 1991 interview, cited in Douglas Martin, "Lawrence Lader, Champion of Abortion Rights, Is Dead at 86," *New York Times*, May 10, 2006.

55. Lawrence Lader, *Abortion* (Indianapolis: Bobbs-Merrill, 1966); Lader, excerpts from *Abortion* published as "Let's Speak Out on Abortion," *Reader's Digest*, May 1966.

56. Lader, *Abortion II*, viii–ix.

57. Joan Summers Lader, interview by Relf, February 27, 2009, New York.

58. Joan Summers Lader interview.

59. Williams, *Defenders of the Unborn*, 105.

60. Richard D. Jackson, interview by the authors, December 9, 2002. Also present were Lorraine Beebe and Marcia Jackson.

61. Lader, *Abortion II*, ix–x.

62. Lader, *Abortion II*, x.

63. Joan Summers Lader interview.

64. Lader, *Abortion II*, 88; Joan Summers Lader interview.

65. Lader, *Abortion II*, 44. Lester Kinsolving later left the Episcopal Church but remained a minister within the conservative Anglican Communion and was best known as a political gadfly, radio talk show host, and unconventional White House correspondent for WorldNetDaily. John Krumm, who had been chaplain of Columbia University and was, in 1966, rector of the Church of the Ascension on West 11th Street in New York, later became bishop of southern Ohio.

66. Howard Moody, interview by the authors, April 25, 2005, New York; Lewis Bogage, interview by Relf, February 15, 2007, Denver, CO.

67. Finley Schaef, email to Relf and others, May 31, 2007; Lader, *Abortion II*, 44.

68. Lader, *Abortion II*, 44.

69. Moody interview.

70. Robert Pierce, interview by Relf, September 25, 2010, Babylon, NY.

71. James Ridgeway, "Birth and Non-Birth," review of *Abortion* by Lawrence Lader, *New Republic*, November 26, 1966, 38–39, cited in Joshua Wolff, "Ministers of a Higher Law: The Story of the Clergy Consultation Services on Abortion," undergraduate thesis, Amherst College, April 10, 1998, 41.

72. Moody interview.

73. Wolfgang Saxon, "Balfour Brickner, Activist Reform Rabbi, Dies at 78," *New York Times*, September 1, 2005.

74. Balfour Brickner, interview by the authors, June 12, 2003, New York.

75. Moody interview.

76. London first met Howard Moody when Moody offered Judson Church as a screening venue for the film of *Lady Chatterley's Lover* in 1962.

77. Moody interview; Arlene Carmen and Howard Moody, *Abortion Counseling and Social Change, from Illegal Act to Medical Practice: The Story of the Clergy Consultation Service on Abortion* (Valley Forge, PA: Judson Press, 1973), 25–27; Howard Moody, *A Voice in the Village: A Journey of a Pastor and a People* (N.p.: Xlibris, 2009), 248, 313; Lader, *Abortion II*, 45; Wolff, "Ministers of a Higher Law," 51.

78. Moody interview.

79. Carmen and Moody, *Abortion Counseling*, 26.

80. Moody interview.

81. Carmen and Moody, *Abortion Counseling*, 26.

82. Moody interview.

83. "Clergy Consultation Service on Abortion: Funds," list of donations, 1967, Wolff Personal Research Papers.

84. Wolff, "Ministers of a Higher Law," 63.

85. Pierce interview; Cynthia Clark Wedel to Moody, June 6, 1967, Wolff Personal Research Papers.

86. Schaef, email to Relf and others, May 31, 2007; Lader, *Abortion II*, 45.

87. Moody, quoted by Lader, *Abortion II*, 45.

88. Moody, address at fortieth anniversary celebration of the CCS, May 19, 2007, Judson Memorial Church, New York.

89. Soltau quoted by Diane Nottle, "Hospital Will Decide on Abortion Policies," *Daily Collegian* (Pennsylvania State University), February 1, 1973.

90. Carmen and Moody, *Abortion Counseling*, 30–31. The full statement is reproduced in Appendix A.

Chapter 3. To Offer Compassion

1. Arlene Carmen and Howard Moody, *Abortion Counseling and Social Change, from Illegal Act to Medical Practice: The Story of the Clergy Consultation Service on Abortion* (Valley Forge, PA: Judson Press, 1973), 19.

2. Carmen and Moody, *Abortion Counseling*, 33–35; Martin Tolchin, "Defiance Pledged on Abortion Law," *New York Times*, March 12, 1967.

3. Carmen and Moody, *Abortion Counseling*, 34.

4. Edward B. Fiske, "Clergymen Offer Abortion Advice," *New York Times*, May 22, 1967. The female minister and others may have been omitted from the original press release because they did not respond in time to Moody's request for permission to be listed publicly.

5. Carmen and Moody, *Abortion Counseling*, 34.

6. Carmen and Moody, *Abortion Counseling*, 29.

7. "35 Call Clergymen for Aid on Abortion," *New York Times*, May 24, 1967; Lewis E. (Buz) Bogage, email to Relf, March 22, 2007.

8. Carmen and Moody, *Abortion Counseling*, 39–40, includes quotes from letters; Wolff Personal Research Papers include copies of representative letters.

9. *New York Post*, May 23, 1967; Linda Charlton, "Clergy Differ on Abortion Unit Referrals," *New York Newsday*, May 23, 1967, cited by Joshua Wolff, "Ministers of a Higher Law: The Story of the Clergy Consultation Services on Abortion," undergraduate thesis, Amherst College, April 10, 1998, 55.

10. Fiske, "Clergymen Offer Abortion Advice," citing the original CCS statement.

11. Wolff, "Ministers of a Higher Law," 57–58.

12. Arlene Carmen, interview by Ellen Chesler, January, 1976, New York, Schlesinger-Rockefeller Oral History Project, Schlesinger Library, Radcliffe Institute, Harvard University.

13. Carmen interview.

14. Carmen interview.

15. Carmen interview.

16. All of the preceding quotes from Carmen come from the Carmen interview; text of letter to doctors, Carmen and Moody, *Abortion Counseling*, 37–38.

17. Robert E. Hall, "New York Abortion Law Survey," *American Journal of Obstetrics and Gynecology* 93 (December 15, 1965), 1182–1183, cited by David J. Garrow, *Liberty and Sexuality: The Right to Privacy and the Making of Roe v. Wade*, updated edition (Berkeley: University of California Press, 1998), 297–298.

18. Carmen and Moody, *Abortion Counseling*, 38.

19. T. Richard Snyder and Douglas W. Schoeninger, Metropolitan Associates of Philadelphia, "Analysis of an Abortion Task Force," July 27, 1970, 9, personal files of Allen J. Hinand.

20. "Abortion Symposium to Be Held in N.J.," *Bucks County Courier Times* (Levittown, PA), December 4, 1969.

21. Chicago CCS notice of January 16, 1970, meeting, folder 5, box 1, Chicago Clergy Consultation Service records, Special Collections and University Archives, University of Illinois at Chicago (UIC).

22. Timeline of Pregnancy Testing, "A Thin Blue Line: The History of the Pregnancy Test Kit," Office of NIH History, National Institutes of Health, https://history.nih.gov/exhibits/thinblueline/timeline.html (accessed May 20, 2016).

23. Notes from Chicago CCS meeting, November 8, 1969; and memo to Chicago CCS, December 22, 1969; both from folder 3, Papers of the Clergy Consultation Service 1967–1979, Manuscript Series CXXVIII, Charles Deering McCormick Library of Special Collections, Northwestern University Library.

24. Information sheet dated June 6, 1970; letter from [American minister, name redacted] in Japan to "fellow CCSPP counsellors," June 8, 1970; and postcard from [American minister, name redacted] to Ron Hammerle in Chicago, June 10, 1970; all from folder 9, box 1, Chicago CCS records, UIC.

25. Carole Joffe, *Doctors of Conscience: The Struggle to Provide Abortion Before and After* Roe v. Wade (Boston: Beacon Press, 1995), 95; David Van Arsdale, email to Relf, April 17, 2016, regarding his father William A. Van Arsdale's referrals to Canada from upstate New York in 1970.

26. "Instructions for Girls Going to Mexico City," March 1970, folder 16, box 2, Chicago CCS records, UIC.

27. The Protestant minister asked to remain anonymous.

28. Anonymous Protestant minister, female, interview by the authors, April 26, 2005, New York.

29. Carmen and Moody, *Abortion Counseling*, 48.

30. Carmen's presence as a strong administrator is found throughout the extant correspondence to and from the National CCS office (Judson Memorial Church Archive, Fales Library, NYU; Chicago CCS Records, UIC; and CCS Papers, Northwestern). She also seems to have written much of the material in the National CCS newsletters, which was published from the Judson Church office.

31. Wolff, "Ministers of a Higher Law," 49; Rosemary Nossiff, *Before* Roe*: Abortion Policy in the States* (Philadelphia: Temple University Press, 2001), 21–22.

32. Carmen's biographical information, except as otherwise noted, comes from her sister, Jewel Carmen DeRoy, interview by the authors, February 20, 2006, Los Angeles, CA; Howard Moody, *A Voice in the Village: A Journey of a Pastor and a People* (N.p.: Xlibris, 2009), 142; Wolfgang Saxon, "Arlene Carmen, Who Ministered to Society's Castoffs, Dies at 58," *New York Times*, October 14, 1994; and Carmen interview. The last is also the source of all direct quotations from Carmen in this section, unless they are otherwise identified.

33. Carmen interview.

34. Arlene Carmen and Howard Moody, *Working Women* (New York: Harper & Row, 1985).

35. Howard Moody, interview by the authors, April 25, 2005, New York.

36. Carmen, address given when she joined Judson Memorial Church, May 1, 1988, quoted in Moody, *A Voice in the Village*, 142–144.

37. Moody, *A Voice in the Village*, 138–141. Judson Memorial Church today is officially affiliated with the American Baptist and United Church of Christ denominations, but it draws and welcomes people of diverse faith backgrounds.

38. Anonymous Protestant minister interview; Buz Bogage, interview by Relf, February 15, 2007, Denver, CO.

39. Jewel Carmen DeRoy, interview by the authors, February 20, 2006, Los Angeles, CA; Abigail Hastings, "Arlene Carmen," in Elly Dickason and Jerry G. Dickason (eds.), *Remembering Judson House* (New York: Judson Memorial Church, 2000), 177.

40. Carmen interview.

41. Cynthia Gorney, "Abortion: Once Upon a Time in America," *Washington Post*, April 26, 1989.

42. Carmen interview.

43. Ronald L. Hammerle, "The Politics of Abortion: Reflections after 100,000 Cases," paper presented to Regional Family Planning Conference, Kansas City, MO, February 4, 1971, folder 19, box 2, Chicago CCS Records, UIC; Christopher Tietze and Sarah Lewit, "Legal Abortions: Early Medical Complications: An Interim Report on the Joint Program for the Study of Abortion," *Family Planning Perspectives* 3, no. 4 (October 1971), 6–14.

44. Lawrence Lader, *Abortion II: Making the Revolution* (Boston: Beacon Press, 1973), 45.

45. Arlene Carmen, memo on trip to London and the effects of the Abortion Act of 1968 in England, August 18, 1969, box B, folder 1, National CCS Mailings, CCS records, Judson Archive, NYU.

46. Joffe, *Doctors of Conscience*, 93–94.

47. Moody interview by the authors.

48. Carmen interview.

49. Carmen and Moody, *Abortion Counseling*, 54–55.

50. Moody interview.

Chapter 4. The Network Grows

1. Howard Moody, interview by the authors, April 25, 2005, New York.

2. Charles H. (Chick) Straut, telephone interview by Relf, June 7, 2010; Straut, email to Relf, June 7, 2010; Paul L. Montgomery, "Peace Delegates Urge Stronger U.N.," *New York Times*, February 21, 1965.

3. This and other direct quotes from Straut come from the telephone interview.

4. Straut telephone interview; John Wightman, telephone interview by Relf, December 8, 2014.

5. "Report on Clergy Consultation Services," undated but apparently from National CCS meeting held in New York City on May 28, 1969, National Mailings folder, box B, Judson Archive, NYU.

6. Straut telephone interview.

7. Straut telephone interview.

8. Orrin T. (Ted) Hardgrove, telephone interview by Relf, July 28, 2010.

9. "Report on Clergy Consultation Services."

10. Howard Moody, memo naming Wightman as NJ CCS chair as of November 1, October 22, 1969, Abortion Referral folder, box B, Judson Archive, NYU; Wightman telephone interview.

11. Philip Wechsler, "State's Abortion Rate Soaring," *New York Times*, November 25, 1973.

12. Allen J. Hinand, telephone interview by Joshua D. Wolff, February 16, 1998, quoted by Joshua Wolff, "Ministers of a Higher Law: The Story of the Clergy Consultation Services on Abortion," undergraduate thesis, Amherst College, April 10, 1998, 98.

13. Allen J. Hinand, telephone interview by Relf, July 16, 2010.

14. Hinand telephone interview by Relf.

15. Sue Gingrich, "Pastor Offers Abortion Counseling," *Today's Post* (King of Prussia, PA), February 22, 1971.

16. Peter H. Binzen, "Clerical Group Offers Counseling on Abortions," *Philadelphia Bulletin*, November 15, 1968.

17. Howard Moody, *A Voice in the Village: A Journey of a Pastor and a People* (N.p.: Xlibris, 2009), 140–141.

18. Hinand telephone interview by Relf.

19. Audrey Wennblom, "Abortion Counseling: New Form of Mission," *Crusader* (American Baptist publication), December 1969, 5, personal files of Allen J. Hinand.

20. Binzen, "Clerical Group Offers Counseling on Abortions."

21. E. Spencer Parsons or Ronald L. Hammerle (probable author), report to the Chicago CCS on the meeting of the National Clergy Consultation Services held in New York City on May 28, 1969, folder 3, CCS Papers, Northwestern.

22. Hinand telephone interview by Relf.

23. T. Richard Snyder and Douglas W. Schoeninger, Metropolitan Associates of Philadelphia, "Analysis of an Abortion Task Force," July 27, 1970, 12, 1–2, personal files of Allen J. Hinand.

24. Theodore Irwin, "The New Abortion Laws: How Are They Working?," *Today's Health*, March 1970, 80.

25. Robert Hall, "The Abortion Revolution," *Playboy*, September 1970, 276.

26. Snyder and Schoeninger, "Analysis of an Abortion Task Force."

27. Parsons or Hammerle, report to Chicago CCS.

28. Snyder and Schoeninger, "Analysis of an Abortion Task Force," 4.

29. CCS national newsletter, February 1970, Wolff Personal Research Papers.

30. Huw Anwyl, interview by the authors, February 22, 2006, Laguna Niguel, CA. This is the source for the information about and quotes by Anwyl, unless otherwise identified.

31. Anwyl interview.

32. Anwyl interview.

33. Anwyl interview; John Dart, "Mt. Hollywood to Vote on Removing Minister," *Los Angeles Times*, February 15, 1969.

34. Elizabeth Kanitz (Liz) Canfield, telephone interview by Relf, January 8, 2015. This is the source for the information about and quotes by Canfield, unless otherwise identified.

35. See, for example, "Puerto Rico: The Emko Program," *Studies in Family Planning* 1, no. 1 (July 1963), 7–9, http://www.jstor.org/stable/1965342. To some, the Emko Program, which was directed at poor women, especially Latina women in California and Puerto Rico, expressed a remnant of eugenics; see, for example, Laura Briggs, *Reproducing Empire: Race, Sex, Science, and U.S. Imperialism in Puerto Rico* (Berkeley: University of California Press, 2002), 126–128.

36. Canfield interview; Daniel K. Williams, *Defenders of the Unborn: The Pro-Life Movement before* Roe v. Wade (New York: Oxford University Press), 65.

37. "Pike Names Vicar to Be Lobbyist," *Pittsburgh Press*, June 28, 1966. Kinsolving later became a columnist and radio commentator.

38. Kristin Luker, *Abortion and the Politics of Motherhood* (Berkeley: University of California Press, 1984), 88.

39. Canfield interview; Susan Brownmiller, "Abortion Counseling: Service beyond Sermons," *New York*, August 4, 1969, 26–31.

40. John Dart, "Abortion Counseling Service Formed by Clergymen, Rabbis," *Los Angeles Times*, May 15, 1968.

41. Anwyl interview.

42. Canfield, letter to Moody, May 31, 1968, California folder, box A, Judson Archive, NYU.

43. Canadian abortion law was liberalized in 1969.

44. Anwyl interview.

45. San Diego and northern California referrals reported in Chicago CCS minutes, November 8, 1969, CCS Papers, Northwestern; Elizabeth Canfield confirmed that she was in communication with Maginnis and they shared information about resources in Mexico (telephone interview).

46. Dart, "Mt. Hollywood to Vote on Removing Minister."

47. Janet Lowe, *Damn Right! Behind the Scenes with Berkshire Hathaway Billionaire Charlie Munger* (New York: Wiley, 2000), 137–139.

48. Anwyl interview.

49. Lynn Lilliston, "New Law Liberal in Intent, but Is It in Practice?," *Los Angeles Times*, March 1, 1970.

50. Marjie Driscoll, "Clergymen Challenge Abortion Laws," *Los Angeles Times*, December 3, 1969; Ronald L. Hammerle, letter to Arlene Carmen re Anwyl's negotiations with hospitals, October 30, 1971, Iowa folder, box A, Judson Archive, NYU.

51. Jean Murphy, "Refuge for Problem Pregnancies Opened," *Los Angeles Times*, June 26, 1970.

52. Lawrence Lader, *Abortion II: Making the Revolution* (Boston: Beacon Press, 1973), 111.

53. Canfield interview; Anwyl, letter to Carmen re Canfield's departure, December 23, 1970, California folder, box A, Judson Archive, NYU.

54. Anwyl interview.

55. Roger Lowenstein, *Buffett: The Making of an American Capitalist* (New York: Random House, 1995), 168.

56. Metropolitan column, *Los Angeles Times*, April 20, 1971.

57. Charles Remsberg and Bonnie Remsberg, "Abortion: Two Views of One of the Most Perplexing Ethical and Practical Problems a Young Woman Can Face," *Seventeen*, September 1972, 140–141, 178–182.

58. Remsberg and Remsberg, "Abortion: Two Views," 140–141, 178–182.

59. The no-money rule was in place from the start (Arlene Carmen and Howard Moody, *Abortion Counseling and Social Change, from Illegal Act to Medical Practice: The Story of the Clergy Consultation Service on Abortion* [Valley Forge, PA: Judson Press, 1973], 29–30). Moody said the clergy were also deliberate in the decision not to be in contact directly with doctors; for the New York CCS, Carmen was the only contact (Moody interview). In fact, quite a few CCS clergy, notably Spencer Parsons in Chicago, did deal with doctors, usually to negotiate price or conditions, but they did not do so as the doctors' employers. When the New York CCS initiated Women's Services in 1970, the clinic ran as a nonprofit organization separate from the CCS, run by its medical director and administrator and eventually answerable to a board of directors (see chapter 8).

60. Jeanie Borba and Nancy Smith, "Abortions Yield Big Profits," *Evening Outlook* (Santa Monica, CA), October 6, 1972.

61. Lowell H. Fewster, co-chair of Wisconsin CCS, letter to Ben M. Peckham, M.D., University of Wisconsin School of Medicine, December 29, 1972, California folder, box A, Judson Archive, NYU; California did not appear on the list of chapters in the National Clergy Consultation Service Newsletter of May 1972 (folder 21, box 2, Chicago CCS records, UIC).

62. Wolff, "Ministers of a Higher Law," 100.

63. E. Spencer Parsons, interview by Relf, July 31, 2003, Worcester, MA. This was the source for nearly all of the biographical information about Parsons.

64. Abortion Rights Association of Illinois Records, biographical note, finding aids, Special Collections, Daley Library, UIC, http://www.uic.edu/depts/lib/specialcoll /services/rjd/findingaids/AbortionRightsf.html.

65. Playboy Enterprises, "The Playboy Foundation," http://www.playboyenterprises .com/home/content.cfm?content=t_title_as_division&ArtTypeID=0007687D-BB6E-1 C76-8FEA8304E50A010D&packet=FF3808D3-A129-F648-7FE2D1F85EF0DDFA&M menuFlag=foundation&viewMe=1 (accessed April 29, 2016).

66. Moody, correspondence with Chicago clergy, late 1967, Illinois folder, box A, Judson Archive, NYU.

67. "100 Plan U.C. Parley on Abortion," *Chicago Tribune*, April 28, 1968.

68. *Year Book of the American Baptist Convention, 1968–1969* (American Baptist Historical Society). The resolution passed—which, although it did not set official policy of the denomination, did express the majority opinion of that year's delegates.

69. Parsons interview.

70. Parsons, memo to Chicago CCS members on July 16, 1969, meeting, folder 5, box 1, Chicago CCS Records, UIC.

71. "How to Get Abortion? Group Offers Answers," *Chicago Tribune*, March 12, 1970.

72. Chicago CCS Accounts, 1970–1974, folder 31, box 2, Chicago CCS Records, UIC; Carmen and Moody, *Abortion Counseling*, 29–30.

73. Donna O. Schaper, interview by Relf, March 1, 2009, New York.

74. Schaper interview.

75. David T. Beito and Linda Royster Beito, *Black Maverick: T. R. M. Howard's Fight for Civil Rights and Economic Power* (Urbana: University of Illinois Press, 2009).

76. Parsons interview; Beito and Beito, *Black Maverick*, 204–205.

77. Carl E. Bielby, video interview by Relf, February 9, 2010.

78. Beito and Beito, *Black Maverick*, including citation of Ed Keemer from his memoir *Confessions of a Pro-Life Abortionist* (Detroit: Vinco Press, 1980), 204.

79. Ronald L. Hammerle, telephone interview by the authors, December 18, 2005. This interview and the archives at UIC and Northwestern are the sources for the following general discussion of the operation of the Chicago CCS.

80. Ronald L. Hammerle, "The Abortion Situation at the End of the Sixties," dissertation, University of Chicago, Divinity School and Department of Obstetrics and Gynecology, November 15, 1969.

81. Raymond A. Zwerin, telephone interview by Relf, February 16, 2007.

82. "262 Abortions Performed in Year," *Rocky Mountain News*, May 24, 1968.

83. Lewis E. "Buz" Bogage, interview by Relf, February 15, 2007, Denver, CO.

84. Olga Curtis, "Clergymen Who Offer Abortion Aid," *Denver Post, Empire* magazine, January 25, 1970, 26–29; handwritten summary for each state CCS, January 1, 1972, General Abortion Correspondence folder, box B, Judson Archive, NYU.

85. Hinand interview by Relf; Miriam Goodspeed, "Consultation for Problem Pregnancies New Clergy-Operated Service," *Greenville (SC) Piedmont*, November 7, 1970.

86. Brownmiller, "Abortion Counseling"; "A General Motors Heir Gives 9 Grants to Unusual Causes," *New York Times*, January 3, 1969; Douglas Martin, "Stewart R. Mott, 70, Offbeat Philanthropist, Dies," *New York Times*, June 14, 2008; Lowell Fewster, video interview by Relf, December 8, 2014.

87. National CCS Budget, September 1969, Foundations folder, box B, Judson Archive, NYU.

88. Obituary, Bennett Owens, TCPalm (Vero Beach, FL, *Press Journal*), http://www.legacy.com/obituaries/tcpalm/obituary.aspx?n=bennett-lee-owens&pid=141884216, posted April 17, 2010; Beth Owens, letter to Relf, April 11, 2015.

89. Bennett Owens, letter to Robert H. Iles, undated, almost certainly December 1968, California folder, box A, Judson Archive, NYU.

90. Parsons or Hammerle, probable author, report to Chicago CCS on the May 28, 1969, meeting of National CCS, folder 5, box 1, Chicago CCS Records, UIC.

91. "Protestant Clerics Set Up Abortion Advice Service," *Bridgeport* (CT) *Post*, October 30, 1969; National CCS lists, November 1970 and December 1972, both from box 2, folder 21, Chicago CCS Records, UIC.

92. Arlene Carmen, interview by Ellen Chesler, January 1976, New York, Schlesinger-Rockefeller Oral History Project, Radcliffe Institute, Harvard University; Wolff, "Ministers of a Higher Law," 110, citing records of the 1971 National CCS conference. The number of counselors is an estimate. In July 1971 the National CCS Newsletter (vol. 2, no. 1, cited by Wolff, 110) reported the number at 2,000, but as Wolff points out, by the time the CCS wound down in 1973, it is quite possible that 3,000 counselors had been part of the group at some time. The estimates for the number of referrals are much higher than the figure Carmen and Moody gave in their book about the CCS (*Abortion Counseling*); there they wrote, "In three years [up to July 1, 1970] CCS nationally had referred perhaps 100,000 women for office abortions without a single fatality." Some later writers (e.g., Carole Joffe, *Doctors of Conscience: The Struggle to Provide Abortion Before and After* Roe v. Wade [Boston: Beacon Press, 1995], 89) apparently picked up that three-year number erroneously as a total for the group's entire existence; we suspect that it was low even for a three-year total. Ron Hammerle also gave a low number—25,000 referred by all the services in the first two and a half years—in his 1969 dissertation ("The Abortion Situation at the End of the Sixties," 104). Even that low figure meant, by Hammerle's calculation, that the clergy had brokered about $13 million in fees to abortion providers. In 1967 and 1968, as chapters in states beyond New York were just forming, the numbers may well have been lower than they were once the full network was in operation. But in 1968 and 1969, the California CCS alone had referred 50,000 women—an average of 25,000 a year in its first two years of existence, according to figures that Huw Anwyl gave to the *Los Angeles Times* (Jack Birkinshaw, "Minister Predicts Ultimate OK by High Court for All Abortions," *Los Angeles Times*, May 6, 1970, C7). A July 7, 1971, *Chicago Tribune* article (Sheila Wolfe, "Agencies Combine Abortion Referrals," D4) gave an estimate of 7,500 women referred out of state in the past year by just the Chicago service. It is possible, too, that the numbers given to the press were somewhat inflated. So extrapolating a specific total from these isolated numbers is difficult, but at the very least they indicate that the scale of referrals was tremendous and that the higher estimates for the total given by Arlene Carmen, who had the best national overview, are not unreasonable.

93. Wolff, "Ministers of a Higher Law," took a similar route to an estimate of 350,000 to 450,000 total referrals (110).

94. Hammerle, "The Abortion Situation at the End of the Sixties," 104.

Chapter 5. The Women

1. [Author redacted], letter to Hayes Fletcher, January 3, 1969, folder 16, box 2, Chicago CCS Records, UIC.

2. Based on estimates from Joshua Wolff, "Ministers of a Higher Law: The Story of the Clergy Consultation Services on Abortion," undergraduate thesis, Amherst College, April 10, 1998, 166; and statistics in Arlene Carmen, interview by Ellen Chesler, January, 1976, New York, Schlesinger-Rockefeller Oral History Project, Schlesinger Library, Radcliffe Institute, Harvard University, 21, 24, and Appendix D.

3. Carmen interview, 21, 24; see Appendix D for the full set of statistics.

4. Chicago statistics from "A Summary of Consultation Reports and Data," April 7, 1970, and summary of questionnaire results, folder 13, box 1, Chicago CCS Records, UIC.

5. Ronald L. Hammerle, "Planning Pregnancy Termination Services in the United States," paper presented at the 75th Anniversary Symposium, University of Chicago Lying-In Hospital, June 19, 1970, folder 19, box 2, Chicago CCS Records, UIC.

6. Charles Remsberg and Bonnie Remsberg, "Abortion? Two Views of One of the Most Perplexing Ethical and Practical Problems a Young Woman Can Face," *Seventeen*, September 1972, 140–141, 178–182; Susan Brownmiller, "Abortion Counseling: Service beyond Sermons," *New York*, August 4, 1969, 26–31.

7. Shirley Chisholm, *Unbought and Unbossed*, 40th anniversary ed. (Washington, DC: Take Root Media, 2010), 132–133.

8. Haywood D. Holderness Jr., telephone interview by Relf, December 20, 2014.

9. Gregory Dell, interview by the authors, March 2, 2004, Chicago.

10. The Iowa Clergy Consultation Service on Problem Pregnancy, Adoption and Abortion, "Counselling Policies and Procedures," adopted November 17, 1969, folder 17, box 2, Chicago CCS Records, UIC. The same set of guidelines required the counselee, at the first session, "to sign an acknowledgment of her understanding of the services to be rendered, on a form approved by the service." The form itself asks the counselee to "be prepared to show your driver's license with date of birth." We know of no other chapter that imposed such requirements, and we don't know how closely the Iowa counselors observed them.

11. "Proposal: Milwaukee Area Clergy Consultation Service on P[roblem] Pregnancy," undated, folder 25, box 2, Chicago CCS records, UIC.

12. Dell interview. Dell said that in the three years he was active with the CCS, only two women he counseled, including this young woman, decided not to have an abortion.

13. Orrin D. Judd, telephone interview by Relf, September 10, 2010.

14. Robert Pierce, interview by Relf, September 25, 2010, Babylon, NY.

15. Anonymous Conservative rabbi, male, email to a grandson, October 2010, and telephone interview by Relf, October 18, 2010.

16. Desmond Ryan, "Hundreds Get Abortion Facts from Ministers," *Philadelphia Inquirer*, August 17, 1969.

17. Tom Davis, telephone interview by the authors, July 19, 2004.

18. Tom Davis, *Sacred Work: Planned Parenthood and Its Clergy Alliances* (New Brunswick, NJ: Rutgers University Press, 2005).

19. Davis telephone interview.

20. Janice Fialka, interviewed for *Back Alley Detroit: Abortion Before* Roe v. Wade, Daniel Friedman and Sharon Grimberg, Filmmakers Library, 1992.

21. [Author's name redacted], letter to E. Spencer Parsons, undated, folder 10, CCS Papers, Northwestern.

22. [Author's name redacted], letter to Chicago clergy counselor number 31, April 7, 1970, folder 16, box 2, Chicago CCS Records, UIC.

23. [Author's name redacted], letter to John Mendelsohn, August 27, 1970, folder 16, box 2, Chicago CCS Records, UIC.

24. Arlene Carmen and Howard Moody, *Abortion Counseling and Social Change, from Illegal Act to Medical Practice: The Story of the Clergy Consultation Service on Abortion* (Valley Forge, PA: Judson Press, 1973), 44.

25. [Author's name redacted], letter to E. Spencer Parsons, February 8, 1971, folder 10, CCS Papers, Northwestern.

26. [Author's name redacted], letter to E. Spencer Parsons, March 23, 1969, folder 10, CCS Papers, Northwestern.

Chapter 6. Brushes with the Law

1. Howard Moody, interview by the authors, April 25, 2005, New York.

2. Carl E. Bielby, video interview by Relf, February 9, 2010; "Religion: Clergy and Abortions," *Time*, November 28, 1969, http://www.time.com/time/magazine/article /0,9171,840433,00.html.

3. Ronald L. Hammerle, "The Abortion Situation at the End of the Sixties," dissertation, University of Chicago, Divinity School and Department of Obstetrics and Gynecology, November 15, 1969, 110.

4. Balfour Brickner, interview by the authors, June 12, 2003, New York.

5. Moody interview; Charles H. (Chick) Straut, telephone interview by Relf, June 7, 2010; Rev. Finley Schaef, telephone interview by Relf, June 1, 2007; Rev. Robert L. Pierce, interview by Relf, September 25, 2010, Babylon, NY.

6. Moody interview.

7. Arlene Carmen and Howard Moody, *Abortion Counseling and Social Change, from Illegal Act to Medical Practice: The Story of the Clergy Consultation Service on Abortion* (Valley Forge, PA: Judson Press, 1973]), 34–35.

8. James MacGregor, "Clergymen Stir Debate by Helping Women End Unwanted Pregnancies," *Wall Street Journal*, June 23, 1969, 1.

9. A. Keith Thompson, *Religious Confession Privilege and the Common Law: A Historical Analysis* (Leiden: M. Nijhoff, 2011), 266–267.

10. Carmen and Moody, *Abortion Counseling*, 35; Moody interview; Schaef telephone interview.

11. Moody interview. A search of the *New York Times* during the years the CCS was in operation did not reveal any comments on its legality by Hogan.

12. MacGregor, "Clergymen Stir Debate," 1.

13. Hammerle, "The Abortion Situation at the End of the Sixties," 109.

14. Arlene Carmen, interview by Ellen Chesler, January 1976, New York, Schlesinger-Rockefeller Oral History Project, Schlesinger Library, Radcliffe Institute, Harvard University.

15. Moody interview.

16. Carmen and Moody, *Abortion Counseling*, 36.

17. Judy Widdicombe in Angela Bonavoglia (ed.), *The Choices We Made: Twenty-five Women and Men Speak Out about Abortion* (New York: Four Walls Eight Windows, 2001), 126–127.

18. "Religion: Clergy and Abortions."

19. E. Spencer Parsons, interview by Relf, July 31, 2003, Worcester, MA.

20. Howard Moody, *A Voice in the Village: A Journey of a Pastor and a People* (N.p.: Xlibris, 2009), 321.

21. MacGregor, "Clergymen Stir Debate."

22. Chicago CCS, "Report on the Meeting of the National Clergy Consultation Services, in New York, May 28, 1969," folder 3, CCS Papers, Northwestern.

23. Cleveland *Plain Dealer*, May 23 and 24, 1969.

24. Henry Maule, "She Sought Abortion Abroad, Found Death," *New York Daily News*, May 23, 1969.

25. Howard Moody, memo to CCS counselors, May 23, 1969. Moody enclosed the *New York Daily News* article from May 23. Arlene Carmen and other CCS members had visited Sopher's clinic and found that Sopher provided excellent treatment for women who had the means to travel to London.

26. Farley W. Wheelwright, email to Relf, June 15, 2007.

27. Anthony Hordern, *Legal Abortion: The English Experience* (Oxford: Pergamon Press, 1971); American Embassy, London, Report of the Death of an American Citizen: Jo Ann Marie Michael, July 9, 1969, Ancestry.com (accessed January 4, 2015). Because this one known death of a CCS-related patient was not the result of the abortion procedure but from a reaction to anesthesia, the CCS considered the service's abortion referrals to have been without fatalities.

28. Robert Hare, interview by the authors, April 23, 2005, Croton-on-Hudson, NY.

29. Hare interview.

30. Hare interview.

31. Wheelwright email.

32. Gerald A. Messerman, "Abortion Counselling: Shall Women Be Permitted to Know?," in David F. Walbert and J. Douglas Butler (eds.), *Abortion, Society, and the Law* (Cleveland: Press of Case Western Reserve University, 1973), 253. The article was originally published under the same title in *Case Western Reserve Law Review* 810 (1973), 822. In addition to sources cited below, supportive information for the following account of the Hare case came from Robert Hare interview by Ellen Messer and Kathryn E. May in *Back Rooms: Voices from the Illegal Abortion Era* (Buffalo, NY: Prometheus Books, 1994); and Robert Hare, "The Case against Counseling," National Council of Churches *Bulletin*, May 4, 1970, Lawrence Lader papers, Manuscripts and Archives Division, New York Public Library, Astor, Lenox, and Tilden Foundations.

33. Carmen and Moody, *Abortion Counseling*, 55.

34. Edward P. Whelan, "Clergyman Indicted in Abortion Case," Cleveland *Plain Dealer*, June 12, 1969.

35. Hare interview. At the time, teachers were often forced to take unpaid maternity leave starting from the time a pregnancy became apparent. It wasn't until 1974 that *Cleveland Board of Education v. LaFleur* established that this requirement violated teachers' right to due process under the Fifth Amendment.

36. Hare interview.

37. Hare interview.

38. Carmen and Moody, *Abortion Counseling*, 55.

39. Hare interview.

40. Shelley Cohen, "Coed Testifies in Chelmsford Abortion Case," *Lowell* (MA) *Sun*, December 2, 1970; Elissa Papirno, "Dr. Brunelle, Released after 16 Months in Prison, Says He'd Perform Abortions Again," *Lowell Sun*, April 3, 1972.

41. James L. Grazier and John H. Burt, fund-raising letter for Committee for Bob Hare's Defense, undated, legal folder, box B, Judson Archive, NYU.

42. Ann Hellmuth, "Cleric Wins Test of Abortion Law," Cleveland *Plain Dealer*, March 28, 1970.

43. Lawrence Lader, *Abortion II: Making the Revolution* (Boston: Beacon Press, 1973), 75–76. The committee's statement, including the quotation given, is from "Summary: Motion Regarding the Case of the Commonwealth of Massachusetts vs. Robert Hare" and background information presented by the committee is in "State of the Hare Case," both found in Lader Papers, New York Public Library.

44. Messerman, "Abortion Counselling."

45. Hare interview; quote from Hellmuth, "Cleric Wins Test of Abortion Law."

46. Hare interview.

47. Hare interview.

48. Hare interview.

49. Max Ticktin, interview by Relf, March 31, 2006, Washington, DC; John Allen, "Hillel [Encapsulated]," *On Wisconsin*, winter 2009.

50. E. Spencer Parsons, letter to John W. Stiny, April 11, 1972, CCS Papers, Northwestern. The recipient was a legal assistant with a law firm in Buffalo, New York, so Parsons's statement must have been relevant to one of the cases brought against Ketchum.

51. Parsons letter to Stiny, April 11, 1972.

52. Ticktin interview.

53. Max Ticktin, statement, January 14, 1970, folder 16, Lader Papers, New York Public Library.

54. Ticktin statement.

55. Ticktin statement.

56. Ticktin interview.

57. John Camper, "Rabbi Here Charged in Abortions," *Chicago Daily News*, January 7, 1970; William Schmidt, "MD, Rabbi Linked to Abortion Ring," *Detroit Free Press*, January 7, 1970.

58. Cook County, Illinois, search warrant, January 6, 1970, personal files of Max Ticktin.

59. Ticktin interview.

60. Ticktin interview.

61. Camper, "Rabbi Here Charged in Abortions."

62. Ticktin interview.

63. For instance, Camper, "Rabbi Here Charged in Abortions," 1; Schmidt, "MD, Rabbi Linked to Abortion Ring," 1.

64. Chicago Clergy Consultation Service on Problem Pregnancies meeting notes, November 8, 1969, folder 5, Chicago CCS Records, UIC. Notes include detailed instructions to give women traveling to London and Detroit, the only two resources used at the time. The Detroit instructions say, "Patient will be given Detroit number only after a personal interview with CCS. . . . All procedures done in hotel," and names five hotels and motels where women could choose to stay. Parsons, Ticktin, Leifer, and twelve others were present at the meeting. Parsons later confirmed in a letter that he had left the location to Ketchum's discretion (Parsons letter to Stiny). Ron Hammerle's dissertation ("The Abortion Situation at the End of the Sixties," dissertation, University of Chicago, Divinity School and Department of Obstetrics and Gynecology, November 15, 1969, 107) used—in quotes—the term "house call" for procedures done in hotels as an interim measure where office or clinic resources were as yet unavailable.

65. One article that referred to the "international" link said, "A Chicago rabbi has been charged with participating in an abortion ring which authorities say may be international in scope" (Camper, "Rabbi Here Charged in Abortions"). We did not find the headline to which Ticktin referred, but newspapers that picked up any of the stories would have written their own headlines.

66. Schmidt, "MD, Rabbi Linked to Abortion Ring."

67. Ketchum was referred to as "Dr. K." in Chicago CCS meeting notes and by women who wrote letters about their experience with him.

68. Liette Gidlow, "The Michigan Women's Commission and the Struggle Against Sex Discrimination in the 1970s," in Paul Finkelman and Martin Hershock (eds.), *The History of Michigan Law*, Law Society and Politics in the Midwest (Athens: Ohio University Press, 2006), 248.

69. Ticktin interview.

70. Jean Sprain Wilson, "Campus Rallies behind 'Little Rabbi,'" *Detroit Free Press*, January 25, 1970.

71. Ticktin interview.

72. Outcome of the various Ketchum cases: "Michigan Test Nears," *New York Times*, April 1, 1970; Henry D. Locke Jr., "Ketchum Paroled in Abortion Death," Buffalo *Courier-Express*, March 19, 1976; and "Dr. Quaalude," editorial, *Lakeland* (FL) *Ledger*, April 4, 1979.

73. Robert Wallace, telephone interview by Relf, May 14, 2012.

74. Allen J. Hinand, telephone interview by Relf, July 16, 2010.

75. Wallace telephone interview. Wallace's arrest is also mentioned by Lader, *Abortion II*, 78 note.

76. "3 Pittsburgh Doctors Charged for Performing Abortions," *Warren* (PA) *Times-Mirror and Observer*, October 6, 1970.

77. Wallace telephone interview.

78. Wallace telephone interview.

79. "Two More Judges Rule Abortion Law Unconstitutional," *Clearfield* (PA) *Progress*, January 7, 1971.

80. Urgent memo to Iowa CCS members, July 27, 1971, Illinois folder, box A, Judson Archive, NYU. This particular stop must have been part of the investigation by the Kansas attorney general, State Board of Health, State Board of Healing Arts, and the Wyandotte County attorney's office into the legality of abortions performed at

Douglass Hospital; see David Redmon, "Query Abortion Legality," *Kansas City* (MO) *Times*, July 24, 1971—published the very day that the woman referred by the CCS was stopped. The article reported that Wyandotte County attorney Frank D. Menghini "confirmed that he had received complaints from at least two women who underwent therapeutic abortions at Douglass Hospital and who were dissatisfied with the professional treatment they had received there."

81. Urgent memo to Iowa CCS members.

82. "Douglass Hospital Told to Cease Abortions," *Kansas City* (MO) *Times*, July 28, 1971.

83. Summary of Illinois CCS meeting, October 27, 1971, Normal, IL, Illinois folder, box A, Judson Archive, NYU, at which time Weller was practicing in Washington, DC; Illinois CCS meeting, March 29, 1972, Illinois folder, box A, Judson Archive, NYU, by which time Weller had won his lawsuit in Kansas and was practicing there again.

84. Associated Press, "KC Man Arrested in Murder Case," *Lawrence Daily Journal-World*, September 19, 1973; "Carlos Once Convicted as Abortionist," *Kansas City* (MO) *Times*, March 5, 1974; "Jury Asks Carlos Get Life Term," *Leavenworth* (KS) *Times*, August 23, 1974.

85. "Violence Statistics and History," National Abortion Federation, http://prochoice.org/education-and-advocacy/violence/violence-statistics-and-history/ (accessed May 1, 2016). The first abortion provider killed for his work was Dr. David Gunn.

86. Rev. Donna Osterhoudt Schaper, interview by Relf, March 1, 2009, New York.

87. Anonymous Protestant minister, female, interview by the authors, April 26, 2005, New York. This interview was the source of the entire story that follows. Schaef did not remember the specifics, but said in a telephone interview that it sounded "probable."

88. Edith Evans Asbury, "Four Seized Here in Abortion Raid," *New York Times*, May 25, 1969; Lader, *Abortion II*, 101–107.

89. Lader, *Abortion II*, 101–107.

90. Asbury, "Four Seized Here in Abortion Raid."

91. Lader, *Abortion II*, 103.

92. Lader, *Abortion II*, 101–107.

93. Schaef telephone interview.

94. Will Lissner, "6 Indicted on Charges of Performing 3,000 Abortions in Riverdale," *New York Times*, October 17, 1969; Lader, *Abortion II*, 107.

95. Memorandum of Law, Lyons vs Lefkowitz et al. and Tisdall et al., U.S. District Court for the Southern District of NY 69 Civil 4285, copy in Harriet Pilpel Papers, box 22, folder 5, Sophia Smith Collection, Smith College; Fred P. Graham, "Court Fight for Legal Abortions Spurred by Washington Ruling," *New York Times*, November 11, 1969; Jennifer Nelson, *Women of Color and the Reproductive Rights Movement* (New York: New York University Press, 2003), 38–39; Linda Greenhouse, "Constitutional Question: Is There a Right to Abortion?," *New York Times Magazine*, January 25, 1970; David J. Garrow, *Liberty and Sexuality: The Right to Privacy and the Making of Roe v. Wade*, updated ed. (Berkeley: University of California Press, 1998), 379–381.

96. Michael Killian, "Abortion Measure Is Killed," *Chicago Tribune*, March 17, 1971; Parsons interview.

97. Mary B. Good, "Opponents Win Latest Round," *Elk Grove* (IL) *Herald*, March 23, 1971.

98. Parsons interview; this is also the source for Parsons's recollections and quotes that follow.

99. Mrs. Malcolm N. Smith, president YWCA of Metropolitan Chicago, telegram to E. Spencer Parsons, April 23, 1971, CCS Papers, Northwestern.

100. Brown's involvement in Parsons's grand jury preparation is confirmed by Jack G. Stein and Ralph E. Brown, Memorandum of Law, undated, summarizing abortion rulings and medical studies up to 1971, among Parsons's papers in the CCS Papers, Northwestern.

101. "Coalition Assails Abortion Clinic Raid," *Edwardsville* (IL) *Intelligencer*, May 5, 1972; Laura Kaplan, *The Story of Jane: The Legendary Underground Feminist Abortion Service* (New York: Pantheon Books, 1995), 218–221.

102. Edward Lee, "Judge Orders Stay of Girl's Abortion," *Chicago Tribune*, January 23, 1972.

103. "High Court Bars Abortion for Girl, 15," *Chicago Tribune*, January 27, 1972; "Way Cleared for Girl, 15, to Get Abortion Out of State," *Chicago Tribune*, February 1, 1972.

104. Harold Quigley, memo, undated, folder 31, box 3, Chicago CCS Records, UIC; Sheila Wolfe, "One Girl's Abortion: Many Views Heard, Pro and Con," *Chicago Tribune*, February 7, 1972.

105. Quigley memo, March 10, 1972, folder 31, box 3, Chicago CCS Records, UIC.

106. Charles N. Landreth, letter to Howard Moody, May 19, 1970, Florida folder, box A, Judson Archive, NYU.

107. "Deeb Says FSU Provides Illegal Abortion Counsel," *Tampa Tribune*, May 19, 1971. Deeb's investigation and the reaction to it are elaborated further in "Minister Denounces Attack; Abortion Service Defended," *Evening Independent* (St. Petersburg, FL), May 20, 1971; and "State Senator, Regent, Charge Open Sex in FSU Dormitories," *Playground Daily News* (Fort Walton Beach, FL), May 31, 1971.

108. "Investigation into Abortion under Fire," *St. Petersburg Times*, September 8, 1971.

109. "Abortion Counseling Charged of 2 Tallahassee Ministers," *Sarasota Herald-Tribune*, August 27, 1971.

110. Rich Oppel, "Abortion Law Challenge Tossed Out," *Daytona Beach Morning Journal*, September 22, 1971; Landreth v. Hopkins, 331 F.Supp. 920 (N.D. Fla. 1971), at Justia.com.

111. Robert Haywood, letter to Moody, October 22, 1971, Florida folder, box A, Judson Archive, NYU.

112. State of Florida v. Luis Bulas Barquet et al., 41600, 262 So.2d 441 (1972), at Leagle.com.

113. "Abortion Law Goes to Askew," *Panama City* (FL) *News-Herald*, April 8, 1972.

114. Ryan v. Specter, 321 F.Supp. 1109 (D. Pa. 1971); Linda Greenhouse and Reva B. Siegel (eds.), *Before* Roe v. Wade: *Voices That Shaped the Abortion Debate before the Supreme Court's Ruling* (New York: Kaplan, 2010), 167–196, 321.

Chapter 7. A Different Kind of Radical Group

1. This number was reported in "Legal Abortion: How Safe? How Available? How Costly?," *Consumer Reports* 37, no. 7 (July 1972), 470, and in CCS internal correspondence from the same period, Judson Archive, NYU. See further discussion of this number in the notes to the last paragraph of chapter 4.

2. "Religious Sexism: When Faith Groups Started (and Two Stopped) Ordaining

Women," ReligiousTolerance.org, http://www.religioustolerance.org/femclrg13.htm, updated March 29, 2011.

3. Marguerite (Peg) Beissert, interview by the authors, February 22, 2006, Rancho Palos Verdes, CA.

4. Allen J. Hinand, telephone interview by Relf, July 16, 2010; undated CCS brochure, personal files of Allen J. Hinand.

5. Carole Joffe, *Doctors of Conscience: The Struggle to Provide Abortion Before and After Roe v. Wade* (Boston: Beacon Press, 1995), 136.

6. Ione G. W. (Georgie) Gatch, video interview by Relf, May 12, 2011.

7. Elizabeth Canfield, telephone interview by Relf, January 8, 2015.

8. Charles Remsberg and Bonnie Remsberg, "Abortion: Two Views of One of the Most Perplexing Ethical and Practical Problems a Young Woman Can Face," *Seventeen*, September 1972, 140–141, 178–182.

9. Diana March, telephone interview by Relf, February 12, 2004.

10. March telephone interview.

11. March telephone interview.

12. Rev. Donna Osterhoudt Schaper, interview by Relf, March 1, 2009, New York.

13. Lauretta (Lauri) Talayco Holmes, telephone interview by Relf, June 30, 2014. Rickie Solinger, "Pregnancy and Power before *Roe v. Wade*, 1950–1970," in Rickie Solinger (ed.), *Abortion Wars: A Half Century of Struggle, 1950–2000* (Berkeley: University of California Press, 1998), 27. Many more black single women than white ones had kept their babies in the 1950s and 1960s, in part because the push for adoption focused on white families and babies, with maternity homes open to white women only and adoption agencies slow to approve adoptive black families; also, black communities supported single mothers with babies better than white communities. Meanwhile, the white power structure stigmatized single mothers of color as welfare abusers. See Rickie Solinger, *Wake Up Little Susie*, 2nd ed. (New York: Routledge, 2000), 6–7, 199, 219, 234.

14. Sharon Gold-Steinberg and Abigail J. Stewart, "Psychologies of Abortion," in Solinger (ed.), *Abortion Wars*, 361.

15. Solinger, *Wake Up Little Susie*, 236.

16. Lena Williams, "Pregnant Teen-Agers Are Outcasts No Longer," *New York Times*, December 2, 1993; George A. Akerlof and Janet L. Yellen, "An Analysis of Out-of-Wedlock Births in the United States," Brookings Policy Brief Series 4 (August 1996), http://www.brookings.edu/research/papers/1996/08/childrenfamilies-akerlof (accessed October 25, 2015).

17. Gretchen Tucker, Michigan CCS, letter to Arlene Carmen, July 13, 1971, Michigan folder, box A, Judson Archive, NYU, names Lauretta Talayco as a recently trained lay counselor at Family & Children's Services of Lenawee County, Adrian, MI; Holmes telephone interview.

18. Cynthia Gorney, *Articles of Faith: A Frontline History of the Abortion Wars* (New York: Simon & Schuster, 1998), 35.

19. Canfield telephone interview.

20. Laura Kaplan, *The Story of Jane: The Legendary Underground Feminist Abortion Service* (New York: Pantheon, 1995), 46.

21. Parsons, letter setting Chicago CCS organizational meeting for March 13, 1969, dated March 8, 1969, folder 3, CCS Papers, Northwestern; Parsons, letter to Carmen saying an initial Chicago group "will continue to function quietly for the next

month"; CCS ad in *Chicago Sun-Times*, December 14, 1969, per Lawrence Lader, *Abortion II: Making the Revolution* (Boston: Beacon Press, 1973), 76.

22. E. Spencer Parsons, interview by Relf, July 31, 2003.

23. Kaplan, *The Story of Jane*, 62–63.

24. Kaplan, *The Story of Jane*, 63.

25. Kaplan, *The Story of Jane*, 64.

26. Susan Brownmiller, *In Our Time: Memoir of a Revolution* (New York: Delta, 1999), 124.

27. Howard Moody, "Man's Vengeance on Woman: Some Reflections on Abortion Laws as Religious Retribution and Legal Punishment of the Feminine Species," *Renewal* (February 1967).

28. Moody, "Man's Vengeance on Woman."

29. Howard Moody, interview by the authors, April 25, 2005.

30. Moody interview.

31. Howard Moody, *A Voice in the Village: A Journey of a Pastor and a People* (N.p.: Xlibris, 2009), 350.

32. Moody, *A Voice in the Village*, 331–332.

33. Rev. Huw S. Anwyl, interview by the authors, February 22, 2006.

34. Ontario Consultants on Religious Tolerance, "Roman Catholicism and Abortion Access: Pagan and Christian Beliefs 400 BCE–1983 CE," http://www.religious tolerance.org/abo_hist.htm. See further discussion in chapter 2.

35. Martin Luther King Jr. Research and Education Institute at Stanford University, http://kingencyclopedia.stanford.edu/encyclopedia/encyclopedia/enc_tillich_paul_1886_1965/.

36. Lyle Guttu, interview by the authors, April 26, 2005, New York.

37. E. Spencer Parsons, "Abortion: A Private and Public Concern," January 26, 1971, lecture published in *Criterion* 10, vol. 2 (winter 1971).

38. Israel R. Margolies, "A Reform Rabbi's View," in Robert E. Hall (ed.), *Abortion in a Changing World: The Proceedings of an International Conference Convened in Hot Springs, Virginia, November 17–20, 1968, by the Association for the Study of Abortion* (New York: Columbia University Press, 1970), vol. 1, 33.

39. Kit Snedaker, "Abortion," California Living, *Los Angeles Herald-Examiner*, January 18, 1970, 15–25.

40. Balfour Brickner, interview by the authors, June 12, 2003, New York.

41. Balfour Brickner in Angela Bonavoglia (ed.), *The Choices We Made: Twenty-five Women and Men Speak Out about Abortion* (New York: Four Walls Eight Windows, 2001), 192.

42. Brickner interview.

43. Anonymous Conservative rabbi, male, telephone interview by Relf, October 18, 2010.

44. Arlene Carmen, interview by Ellen Chesler, January, 1976, New York, Schlesinger-Rockefeller Oral History Project, Schlesinger Library, Radcliffe Institute, Harvard University.

45. Stephen Forstein, interview by the authors, June 18, 2003, Kalamazoo, MI; master list of Kansas CCS members, December 19, 1972, Kansas folder, box A, Judson Archive, NYU.

46. Loretta J. Ross, "African-American Women and Abortion: A Neglected History," *Journal of Health Care for the Poor and Underserved* 3, no. 2 (1992), 279–281.

47. Ross, "African-American Women and Abortion," 171, citing Carole R. McCann, *Birth Control Politics in the United States, 1916–1945* (Ithaca, NY: Cornell University Press, 1994), 100.

48. Mary Ziegler, "Eugenic Feminism: Mental Hygiene, the Women's Movement, and the Campaign for Eugenic Legal Reform, 1900–1930," *Harvard Journal of Law and Gender* 31 (2008), 111.

49. Martha C. Ward, *Poor Women, Powerful Men: America's Great Experiment in Family Planning* (Boulder, CO: Westview Press, 1986), 92.

50. Harriet A. Washington, *Medical Apartheid: The Dark History of Medical Experimentation on Black Americans from Colonial Times to the Present* (New York: Harlem Moon, 2006), 2 (Sims), 158 (Tuskegee), 192–193 (eugenics), 196–199 (Sanger, Black Power Conference).

51. Ross, "African-American Women and Abortion," 282.

52. Shirley Chisholm, *Unbought and Unbossed*, 40th anniversary ed. (Washington, DC: Take Root Media, 2010), 130.

53. Amy Kesselman notes that other black women activists also spoke out on behalf of abortion at the time, including Frances Beale, Patricia Robinson, Florynce Kennedy ("Women versus Connecticut: Conducting a Statewide Hearing on Abortion," in Rickie Solinger [ed.], *Abortion Wars: A Half Century of Struggle, 1950–2000* [Berkeley: University of California Press, 1998], 66n36), and Dr. Dorothy Brown, a Tennessee state legislator (Ross, "African-American Women and Abortion," 183; Jael Silliman, Marlene Gerber Fried, Loretta Ross, and Elena R. Gutiérrez, *Undivided Rights: Women of Color Organize for Reproductive Justice* [Cambridge, MA: South End Press, 2004], 55). The authors note that the Young Lords, a Puerto Rican nationalist organization, supported abortion rights as the Black Panthers did, but a similar Chicano organization in Los Angeles, the Brown Berets, saw birth control and abortion as genocide (223–224).

54. C. Eric Lincoln, *The Black Church since Frazier* (New York: Schocken Books, 1974), 127.

55. Lincoln, *The Black Church since Frazier*, 129.

56. Robert F. Drinan, "The Right of the Foetus to Be Born," *Dublin Review* 241 (Winter 1967–1968), 365–381, quoted in David J. Garrow, *Liberty and Sexuality: The Right to Privacy and the Making of Roe v. Wade*, updated ed. (Berkeley: University of California Press, 1998), 342–343.

57. David McFarlane, interview by Relf, July 18, 2003, Sewickley, PA. Also present was Emily R. Hanavan.

58. Keith Spore, "Abortion Hearing Bares Emotions, *Milwaukee Sentinel*, April 14, 1972; Dorothy Austin, "A New Kind of Nun in a New Kind of Ministry," *Milwaukee Sentinel*, April 21, 1972.

59. Parsons interview.

60. Moody interview.

61. Kavanaugh named in John Dart, "Mt. Hollywood to Vote on Removing Minister," *Los Angeles Times*, February 15, 1969; Kavanaugh's website, www.jkavanaugh.com.

62. Shirley Jacks, "Human Need Was Catalyst for Clergy Abortion Group," *Main Line Times*, August 28, 1969.

63. Gatch interview.

64. Wayne Conner, interview by Relf, May 30, 2013, Kalamazoo, MI.

65. Report to the Chicago CCS on the meeting of the National CCS in New York, NY, on May 28, 1969, folder 5, box 1, Chicago CCS Records, UIC.

66. Spreadsheet, folder 13, box 1, Chicago CCS Records, UIC.

67. Jacksonville CCS statistics for 247 women, January 1–August 31, 1972, Florida folder, box A, Judson Archive, NYU.

68. Parsons interview.

69. Benjamin Bohnsack, telephone interview by Relf, April 7, 2010.

70. Daniel K. Williams, *Defenders of the Unborn: The Pro-Life Movement before* Roe v. Wade (New York: Oxford University Press, 2016), 28, 41; Lambeth Conference, Resolution 16, "The Life and Witness of the Christian Community—Marriage and Sex" (1930), http://www.anglicancommunion.org/media/127734/1930.pdf.

71. Pew Research Center, "Religious Groups' Official Positions on Abortion," January 16, 2013, http://www.pewforum.org/2013/01/16/religious-groups-official-positions-on-abortion/ (accessed January 29, 2015).

72. *Year Book of the American Baptist Convention 1968–1969* (Valley Forge: American Baptist Board of Education and Publication), 52–53, 125.

73. Minutes of the 110th General Assembly of the Presbyterian Church in the United States, June 1970, 124 ff., cited by Charles N. Landreth, "The Sexual Revolution: A Challenge to the Christian Community: Part II: Abortion," sermon text, Florida folder, box A, Judson Archive, NYU.

74. Rosemary Nossiff, *Before* Roe*: Abortion Policy in the States* (Philadelphia: Temple University Press, 2001), 54–55n84; Linda Greenhouse and Reva B. Siegel, *Before* Roe v. Wade: *Voices That Shaped the Abortion Debate before the Supreme Court's Ruling* (New York: Kaplan, 2010), 69–70.

75. Gorney, *Articles of Faith*, 188. The Southern Baptist Convention did not rescind its approval of moderate abortion law reform until 1980, according to Williams, *Defenders of the Unborn*, 237.

76. Matthew Avery Sutton, *American Apocalypse: A History of Modern Evangelicalism* (Cambridge, MA: Belknap Press of Harvard University Press, 2014), 145–146.

77. Sutton, *American Apocalypse*, 303, 307.

78. Williams, *Defenders of the Unborn*, 67.

79. Greenhouse and Siegel, *Before* Roe v. Wade, 73.

80. Greenhouse and Siegel, *Before* Roe v. Wade, 99–100; Williams, *Defenders of the Unborn*, 141–144.

81. Williams, *Defenders of the Unborn*, 67.

82. Moody interview.

83. Rev. Finley Schaef, telephone interview by Relf, June 1, 2007.

84. Brownmiller, *In Our Time*, 107–109.

85. Janette Pierce, "Protestant Ministers to Counsel on Abortions," *Suburban and Wayne Times*, November 21, 1968.

86. McFarlane interview.

87. Anwyl interview.

88. John Dart, "Abortion Counseling Service Formed by Clergymen, Rabbis," *Los Angeles Times*, May 15, 1968.

89. Dart, "Mt. Hollywood to Vote on Removing Minister."

90. Rabbi Lewis E. Bogage, interview by Relf, February 15, 2007.

91. Rev. Dr. Charles H. Straut Jr., telephone interview by Relf, June 7, 2010.

92. Bernard O. Brown, interview by the authors, March 2, 2004, Chicago.

93. Brown interview.

94. Conner interview.

95. Bohnsack telephone interview.

96. Nossiff, *Before* Roe, 45–47.

97. Lader, *Abortion II*, 60.

98. Moody, address at fortieth anniversary celebration of the CCS, Judson Memorial Church, May 19, 2007, New York.

99. Nossiff, *Before* Roe, 81. Neier had served as a legal adviser at the founding of the CCS; in 1978 he co-founded Human Rights Watch.

100. Lader, *Abortion II*, 61; Canfield telephone interview.

101. Michigan Clergy for Problem Pregnancy Counceling, "Report to Michigan State Senate Legislative Hearing on Abortion," December 6, 1969, Jack M. Stack Papers, 1967–71, Bentley Historical Library, University of Michigan.

102. John Wightman, telephone interview by Relf, December 8, 2014.

103. "Abortion Bills Stir Up Conflict," *Bridgeport* (CT) *Post*, March 26, 1971.

104. Jeff Becker, "Abortion Decision Stirs Controversy," *Daily Collegian* (Pennsylvania State University), September 20, 1970; "Abortion Panel Is Divided," *Lock Haven* (PA) *Express*, June 6, 1972.

105. Ann Hill, "Abortion, Self-Determination and the Political Process," paper dated May 22, 1971, quoted by Kesselman, "Women versus Connecticut," 45.

106. Edith Evans Asbury, "Women Break Up Abortion Hearing," *New York Times*, February 14, 1969, 42.

107. For example, a 2012 hearing by the U.S. House Oversight and Government Reform Committee on mandatory insurance coverage for birth control did not include a single woman on its initial witness list. "The five-person, all-male panel consists of a Roman Catholic Bishop, a Lutheran Reverend, a rabbi and two professors," wrote George Zornick for *The Nation* ("Republican Hearing on Contraception: No Women Allowed," February 16, 2012, http://www.thenation.com/article/republican-hearing-contraception-no-women-allowed/).

108. Lader, *Abortion II*, 46.

109. Lader, *Abortion II*, 46.

110. Lader, *Abortion II*, 46.

111. Arlene Carmen and Howard Moody, *Abortion Counseling and Social Change, from Illegal Act to Medical Practice: The Story of the Clergy Consultation Service on Abortion* (Valley Forge, PA: Judson Press, 1973), 42.

112. Carmen interview.

113. Moody interview.

114. Parsons interview.

115. Carmen interview.

116. Sheila Wolfe, "One Girl's Abortion: Many Views Heard, Pro and Con," *Chicago Tribune*, February 7, 1972; also see chapter 6 for further detail.

117. J. Emmett Herndon, telephone interview by Relf, October 10, 2014; [name redacted], letter to Herndon, August 11, 1971, Wolff Personal Research Papers.

118. Conner interview.

119. Schaper interview.

120. "Negative List," undated, Michigan folder, box A, Judson Archive, NYU.

121. Audrey Wennblom, "Abortion Counseling: New Form of Mission," *Crusader* (American Baptist publication), December 1969, 5, personal files of Allen J. Hinand.

122. Carmen and Moody, *Abortion Counseling*, 72–73; Barbara Pyle interviewed by Susan Edmiston, "A Report on the Abortion Capital of the Country," *New York Times*, April 11, 1971. Their accounts are at odds with Lader, who wrote that the CCS had been referred to Harvey by a patient of his (*Abortion II*, 46).

123. Lader, *Abortion II*, 46, including quotation of Carmen.

124. Carmen and Moody, *Abortion Counseling*, 42–43.

125. Wightman telephone interview.

126. Ronald A. Hammerle, letter to Carmen, March 17, 1970, Illinois folder, box A, Judson Archive, NYU.

Chapter 8. Available and Affordable

1. Shikha Dalmia, "The Death of Pro-Choice Republicans," Reason.com, August 19, 2015, http://reason.com/archives/2015/08/19/the-death-of-pro-choice-republicans. Even at a time of especially strong Republican opposition to abortion in 2015, however, a poll found that 40 percent of Republicans favored legal abortion (Nancy Benac and Emily Swanson, "AP-GfK Poll: Support for Legal Abortion at Highest in 2 Years," AP-GfK, December 22, 2015, http://ap-gfkpoll.com/featured/ap-gfk-poll-support-for-legal-abortion-at-highest-level-in-2-years; "Democratic Party Platform of 1976," *Political Party Platforms*, American Presidency Project, http://www.presidency.ucsb.edu/ws/?pid =29606 [accessed May 7, 2016]).

2. Reviews of changes in states' abortion laws found in Ruth Roemer, "Abortion Law Reform and Repeal: Legislative and Judicial Developments," *American Journal of Public Health* 61, no. 3 (March 1971), 500–509; Lawrence Lader, *Abortion II: Making the Revolution* (Boston: Beacon Press, 1973), chs. 5 and 9; and "Abortion and the Changing Law," *Newsweek*, April 13, 1970, 53–61.

3. Lader, *Abortion II*, 109–110.

4. Janet Lowe, *Damn Right! Behind the Scenes with Berkshire Hathaway Billionaire Charlie Munger* (New York: John Wiley & Sons, 2000), 137–140.

5. Roemer, "Abortion Law Reform and Repeal," 502; Lader, *Abortion II*, 1–2, 111–114.

6. Lader, *Abortion II*, 1–2, 111–114; Chicago referral information, January 16, 1970, folder 5, box 1, Chicago CCS Records, UIC.

7. Lader, *Abortion II*, 114.

8. Roemer, "Abortion Law Reform and Repeal," 501; Lader, *Abortion II*, 115–117.

9. Lader, *Abortion II*, 126; Dennis Hevesi, "Constance E. Cook, 89, Who Wrote Abortion Law, Is Dead," *New York Times*, January 24, 2009.

10. Bill Kovach, "Abortion Reform Is Voted by the Assembly, 76 to 73; Final Approval Expected," *New York Times*, April 10, 1970.

11. Jane E. Brody, "State's Liberal Abortion Law Takes Effect Today amid Prospects for Initial Delays," *New York Times*, July 1, 1970; Linda Greenhouse, "After July 1, an Abortion Should Be as Simple to Have as a Tonsillectomy, But—," *New York Times*, June 28, 1970.

12. David T. Beito and Linda Royster Beito, *Black Maverick: T. R. M. Howard's Fight for Civil Rights and Economic Power* (Urbana: University of Illinois Press, 2009), 210.

13. Brody, "State's Liberal Abortion Law Takes Effect Today."

14. Arlene Carmen and Howard Moody, *Abortion Counseling and Social Change, from Illegal Act to Medical Practice: The Story of the Clergy Consultation Service on Abortion* (Valley Forge, PA: Judson Press, 1973), 88–89.

15. Ronald L. Hammerle, telephone interview by the authors, December 18, 2005; "Abortion Service Starting July 1 to Offer Advice," *New York Times*, June 20, 1970.

16. "About Us," Center for Medical Consumers, https://medicalconsumers.org /about/ (accessed May 26, 2016); Howard Moody, interview by the authors, April 25, 2005.

17. Greenhouse, "After July 1."

18. Greenhouse, "After July 1."

19. "Abortion Service Starting July 1 to Offer Advice."

20. Carmen and Moody, *Abortion Counseling*, 84; Moody interview.

21. Ronald L. Hammerle, letter to Arlene Carmen, June 30, 1970, Illinois folder, box A, Judson Archive, NYU; Ronald L. Hammerle, "A Reply to Robert Hall," folder 23, box 2, Chicago CCS records, UIC. Statistics showing the safety of early outpatient abortions and in-hospital abortions were later published in Christopher Tietze and Sarah Lewit, "Legal Abortions: Early Medical Complications: An Interim Report of the Joint Program for the Study of Abortion," *Family Planning Perspectives* 3, no. 4 (October 1971), 6–14.

22. Carmen and Moody, *Abortion Counseling*, 67.

23. Julie Ferry, "The Abortion Ship's Doctor," *Guardian*, November 14, 2007, www .theguardian.com/world/2007/nov/14/gender.uk.

24. Carmen and Moody, *Abortion Counseling*, 67–68.

25. Carmen and Moody, *Abortion Counseling*, 68.

26. Carmen and Moody, *Abortion Counseling*, 69.

27. Carmen and Moody, *Abortion Counseling*, 70.

28. Howard Moody, *A Voice in the Village: A Journey of a Pastor and a People* (N.p.: Xlibris, 2009), 322.

29. Moody, *A Voice in the Village*, 322–323.

30. Carmen and Moody, *Abortion Counseling*, 73–74.

31. Barbara Pyle, interviewed by Susan Edmiston in "A Report on the Abortion Capital of the Country," *New York Times*, April 11, 1971.

32. Carmen and Moody, *Abortion Counseling*, 72–73.

33. Pyle quoted by Edmiston, "A Report on the Abortion Capital of the Country."

34. Pyle quoted by Edmiston, "A Report on the Abortion Capital of the Country."

35. Carmen and Moody, *Abortion Counseling*, 75–76.

36. Moody interview.

37. Carmen and Moody, *Abortion Counseling*, 77.

38. Ronald L. Hammerle, telephone interview by the authors, December 18, 2005; Bernard N. Nathanson with Richard N. Ostling, *Aborting America* (New York: Pinnacle Books, 1979), 122.

39. Howard Moody, address at fortieth anniversary celebration of the CCS, Judson Memorial Church, May 19, 2007, New York; Carmen and Moody, *Abortion Counseling*, 84.

40. Hammerle telephone interview.

41. Carole Joffe, *Doctors of Conscience: The Struggle to Provide Abortion before and after Roe v. Wade* (Boston: Beacon Press, 1995), 136.

42. Lader, *Abortion II*, 156.

43. Carmen and Moody, *Abortion Counseling*, 77.

44. Moody to Harvey, August 25, 1970, Wolff Personal Research Papers.

45. Edmiston, "A Report on the Abortion Capital of the Country."

46. Hammerle telephone interview.

47. Hammerle telephone interview.

48. Lader, *Abortion II*, 156; Hammerle telephone interview.

49. Lader, *Abortion II*, 46, 95; Nathanson with Ostling, *Aborting America*, 94–95.

50. Bernard N. Nathanson, "Deeper into Abortion," *New England Journal of Medicine* 291, no. 22 (1974), 1189–1190.

51. Bernard N. Nathanson, *The Hand of God: A Journey from Death to Life by the Abortion Doctor Who Changed His Mind* (Washington, DC: Regnery Publishing, 1996), 105.

52. Nathanson with Ostling, *Aborting America*, 162–168; William Grimes, "B. N. Nathanson, 84, Dies; Changed Sides on Abortion," *New York Times*, February 22, 2011.

53. Grimes, "B. N. Nathanson, 84, Dies."

54. Nathanson with Ostling, *Aborting America*, 101–102, 110.

55. [Author redacted], letter to Chicago CCS counselor, November 10, 1970, folder 16, box 2, Chicago CCS Records, UIC.

56. Richard U. Hausknecht, "Free Standing Abortion Clinics: A New Phenomenon," originally presented at a meeting of the New York Academy of Medicine, November 3, 1971, published in *Bulletin of the New York Academy of Medicine* 49, no. 11 (November 1973), 985–991.

57. Nathanson with Ostling, *Aborting America*, 111–116, 125; Lader, *Abortion II*, 156.

58. Nathanson with Ostling, *Aborting America*, 120.

59. Nathanson with Ostling, *Aborting America*, 121–122; Carmen and Moody, *Abortion Counseling*, 81–82.

60. Carmen and Moody, *Abortion Counseling*, 79; Nathanson with Ostling, *Aborting America*, 134.

61. Carmen and Moody, *Abortion Counseling*, 80.

62. Nathanson, "Deeper into Abortion," 1189–1190.

63. Bernard N. Nathanson, letter to Allan C. Barnes, board president, Center for Reproductive and Sexual Health (Women's Services), May 31, 1972, unlabeled folder, box B, Judson Archive, NYU, stating intention to resign as of September 1, 1972.

64. Nathanson to Moody, August 27, 1974, Health Care folder, box B, Judson Archive, NYU.

65. Moody, *A Voice in the Village*, 334–338; see also Arlene Carmen and Howard Moody, *Working Women: The Subterranean World of Street Prostitution* (New York: Harper & Row, 1985).

66. Bernard N. Nathanson, "Ambulatory Abortion: Experience with 26,000 Cases (July 1, 1970, to August 1, 1971)," *New England Journal of Medicine* 286, no. 8 (1972), 403–407.

67. Christopher Tietze, "Freestanding Abortion Clinics," *New England Journal of Medicine* 286, no. 8 (1972), 432.

68. Hammerle telephone interview.

69. Faye Ginsburg, "Rescuing the Nation: Operation Rescue and the Rise of Anti-Abortion Militance," in Rickie Solinger (ed.), *Abortion Wars: A Half Century of Struggle, 1950–2000* (Berkeley: University of California Press, 1988), 229–230.

70. Dawn Stacey, Crisis Pregnancy Center Watch, "The Pregnancy Center Movement: History of Crisis Pregnancy Centers," Mother Jones, http://www.motherjones.com/files/cpchistory2.pdf (accessed May 24, 2016); Margaret H. Hartshorn, "The History of Pregnancy Help Centers in the United States," Heartbeat International, https://www.heartbeatinternational.org/pdf/History_of_Centers.pdf (accessed May 24, 2016).

71. Hall cited in Lael Scott, "Legal Abortions, Ready or Not," Urban Strategist column, *New York Magazine*, May 25, 1970, 64–71; Mara Gordon, "The Scarcity of Abortion Training in America's Medical Schools," *Atlantic*, June 9, 2015, http://www.theatlantic.com/health/archive/2015/06/learning-abortion-in-medical-school/395075/.

72. Hausknecht, "Free Standing Abortion Clinics."

73. Moody, *A Voice in the Village*, 326; Nathanson with Ostling, *Aborting America*, 111.

74. Moody, *A Voice in the Village*, 326–327.

75. Alden Hathway quoted in Associated Press article, "Arranging Abortions Is Lucrative Business," *Owosso* (MI) *Argus-Press*, March 30, 1971.

76. Gerald A. Messerman, "Abortion Counselling: Shall Women Be Permitted to Know?," in David F. Walbert and J. Douglas Butler (eds.), *Abortion, Society, and the Law* (Cleveland: Press of Case Western Reserve University, 1973), 259.

77. Pat Greenawald, telephone interview by Relf, December 2, 2004.

78. Cynthia Gorney, *Articles of Faith: A Frontline History of the Abortion Wars* (New York: Simon & Schuster, 1998), 124–126; Ione G. W. (Georgie) Gatch, video interview by Relf, May 12, 2011.

79. Gorney, *Articles of Faith*, 204–205; Michael D. Sorkin, "Judy Widdicombe Dies: She Put Women in Charge at Abortion Clinics She Founded," *St. Louis Post-Dispatch*, November 6, 2011.

80. Marvin Lutz, email to the authors, October 24, 2014; "General Operational Guidelines for Free Standing Clinic," for Jacksonville Women's Center for Reproductive Health, Florida folder, box A, Judson Archive, NYU.

81. "Gainesville Women's Health Center," *Radical Women in Gainesville*, University of Florida George A. Smathers Libraries, http://ufdc.ufl.edu/rwg/gwhc (accessed May 3, 2016).

82. National Clergy Consultation Service Newsletter 3, no. 1 (May 1972), folder 21, box 2, Chicago CCS records, UIC.

83. Hammerle telephone interview

84. Carl Bielby, video interview by Relf, February 9, 2010.

85. Hayes F. Fletcher, written recollections sent to Relf, February 2011. We heard of another similar situation from a CCS participant who did not give permission to use our interview.

86. Fletcher, written recollections; Spencer Parsons memo to Chicago CCS, October 11, 1972, Illinois folder, box A, Judson Archive, NYU; [name redacted], letter to Marchietta Ceppos re Sutton Medical Group, October 9, 1972, folder 6, Chicago CCS Records, UIC.

87. Fletcher written recollections.

88. Fletcher written recollections.

89. Sheila Wolfe, "Agencies Combine Abortion Referrals," *Chicago Tribune*, July 7, 1971.

90. Choice, Inc., a nonprofit according to Neil Rosenberg, "Abortion Service to Start Here," *Milwaukee Journal*, November 9, 1971; a for-profit corporation according to Pennie Sue Thurman, "Abortion? Just Call This Number," *Pontiac* (IL) *Daily Leader*, December 9, 1971. Gustin was removed from the Chicago CCS membership list by the time of a February 14, 1973, memo to Chicago CCS re February 27 meeting, folder 5, Chicago CCS Records, UIC.

91. Beito and Beito, *Black Maverick*, 213–214, citing *Chicago Tribune*, March 2 and 3, 1973, and *Jet* 43 (March 22, 1973).

92. Margaret E. (Peggy) Howland, interview by the authors, June 12, 2003, New York.

93. Report to Chicago CCS on February 27, 1973, AIES meeting, folder 5, box 1, Chicago CCS Records, UIC.

94. Moody, *A Voice in the Village*, 324; Gary S. Berger, Centers for Disease Control and Prevention, letter to field officers, October 5, 1971, and letter to Ronald L. Hammerle, then executive director of Planned Parenthood Iowa, both re collecting reports of women hospitalized for complications of abortion, in CDC folder, box B, Judson Archive, NYU.

95. Bernard N. Nathanson, "Ambulatory Abortion: Experience with 26,000 Cases (July 1, 1970, to August 1, 1971)," *New England Journal of Medicine* 286, no. 8 (1972), 403–407.

96. Bernard Nathanson, quoted in Laurie Johnston, "Abortion Clinics Here Face Nationwide Competition and Uncertain Future," *New York Times*, March 19, 1973.

97. Linda Greenhouse, *Becoming Justice Blackmun: Harry Blackmun's Supreme Court Journey* (New York: Times Books, 2005), 90–91.

Chapter 9. *Roe v. Wade* and Beyond

1. Black ministers, such as Martin Luther King Jr., Andrew Young, Fred Shuttlesworth, Wyatt T. Walker, Joseph Lowery, and Jesse Jackson, were national leaders in civil rights, and white ministers such as James Reeb worked in solidarity with them; many white ministers and rabbis were Freedom Riders. Clergy were some of the most vocal peace activists during the Vietnam War—William Sloane Coffin, Abraham Joshua Heschel, Daniel and Philip Berrigan, Spencer Parsons, Finley Schaef, and many others. Some of the same clergy were outspoken advocates for the poor—King and Ralph Abernathy led the Poor People's Campaign, for instance.

2. Howard Moody, "Man's Vengeance on Woman," *Renewal* (February 1967).

3. Rev. Huw S. Anwyl, interview by the authors, February 22, 2006.

4. Howard Moody, interview by the authors, April 25, 2005.

5. Arlene Carmen and Howard Moody, *Abortion Counseling and Social Change, from Illegal Act to Medical Practice: The Story of the Clergy Consultation Service on Abortion* (Valley Forge, PA: Judson Press, 1973), 74.

6. Howard Moody, *A Voice in the Village: A Journey of a Pastor and a People* (N.p.: Xlibris, 2009), 327.

7. Robert N. Karrer, "The National Right to Life Committee: Its Founding, Its History, and the Emergence of the Pro-Life Movement Prior to Roe v. Wade," *Catholic Historical Review* 97, no. 3 (July 2011), 527–557; National Right to Life, "History of National Right to Life," http://www.nrlc.org/about/history/ (accessed October 23, 2015).

8. Suzanne Staggenborg, *The Pro-Choice Movement: Organization and Activism in the Abortion Conflict* (New York: Oxford University Press, New York, 1991), 195.

9. United States Conference of Catholic Bishops, "Pastoral Plan for Prolife Activities: A Campaign in Support of Life," http://www.usccb.org/about/pro-life-activities/pastoral-plan-prolife-activities.cfm (accessed October 23, 2015).

10. Tom Davis, quoted in Caryle Murphy, "Clergy Group to Commemorate History of Support for Abortion's Legalization," *Washington Post*, January 14, 1998.

11. Therese Wilson quoted by Jill Tucker in "Spiritual Battles in Ongoing War over Abortion," *East Bay Times*, July 24, 2005, http://www.eastbaytimes.com/review/ci_2887088.

12. Religious Coalition for Reproductive Choice, "A Proud History as a Voice for Conscience and Justice," http://rcrc.org/homepage/about/history/ (accessed October 23, 2015).

13. Chuck Currie, "Views from a United Church of Christ Minister: Pro-Choice Clergy to Get More Support," May 22, 2007, http://chuckcurrie.blogs.com/chuck_currie/2007/05/prochoice_clerg.html (accessed October 23, 2015).

14. Howard Moody, Closing Address at PPFA Religious Affairs Conference, "Sexism, Religion and Family Planning," November 1973, Planned Parenthood Federation of America Records, Sophia Smith Collection, Smith College, cited in Tom Davis, *Sacred Work: Planned Parenthood and Its Clergy Alliances* (New Brunswick, NJ: Rutgers University Press, 2005), 137.

15. Davis, *Sacred Work*, 139.

16. Davis, *Sacred Work*, 139–140.

17. "Clergy Services, the Poor and Planned Parenthood—A Growing Problem," National Clergy Consultation Service on Abortion Newsletter 3, no. 1 (May 1972), 4–5, box 2, folder 21, Chicago CCS Records, UIC.

18. National Clergy Consultation Service Newsletter 2, no. 1 (July 1971), folder 21, box 2, Chicago CCS records, UIC.

19. Davis, *Sacred Work*, 140.

20. Davis, *Sacred Work*, 144.

21. Davis, *Sacred Work*, 151–152, 160, 179–180, 175, 208–209.

22. Rachel Falls of National Abortion Federation, speaking at fortieth anniversary celebration of the Clergy Consultation on Abortion, Judson Memorial Church, May 19, 2007, New York.

23. See http://www.faithaloud.org/aboutus and http://yourbackline.org (accessed April 13, 2016).

24. See http://www.advocatesforpregnantwomen.org/.

25. Ronald L. Hammerle, telephone interview by the authors, December 18, 2005.

26. Rev. Gregory Dell, interview by the authors, March 2, 2004.

27. Mark Rutledge, telephone interview by Relf, January 5, 2015; Mark Rutledge, "Does Counseling Really Help Abortion Patients?," in Paul Sachdev (ed.), *Perspectives on Abortion* (Metuchen, NJ: Scarecrow Press, 1985), 223–235.

28. Glenna Halvorson-Boyd, interviewed in Kyle Boyd, *Life Matters: The Story of an Illegal Abortionist*, VHS videotape, FilmMakers Library, 2002.

29. Balfour Brickner, interview by the authors, June 12, 2003.

30. Moody interview.

31. Dell interview; "The Rev. Gregory R. Dell," Chicago Gay and Lesbian Hall of Fame website, http://www.glhalloffame.org/index.pl?item=309&todo=view_item (accessed October 24, 2015).

32. Anwyl interview.

33. Elizabeth Kanitz Canfield, telephone interview by Relf, January 8, 2015.

34. E. Spencer Parsons obituary, *Boston Globe*, October 13, 2013.

35. Ronald Hammerle, email to Relf, April 18, 2016.

36. Rev. Finley Schaef, telephone interview by Relf, June 1, 2007.

37. Wolfgang Saxon, "Arlene Carmen, Who Ministered to Society's Castoffs, Dies at 58," *New York Times*, October 14, 1994.

38. Judson Memorial Church, "Howard Moody Obituary," Judson Memorial Church website, http://judson.org/Howard-Moody-Obituary (accessed October 24, 2015); Douglas Martin, "Howard Moody, Who Led a Historic Church, Dies at 91," *New York Times*, September 13, 2012.

39. Susan Brownmiller, *In Our Time: Memoir of a Revolution* (New York: Delta, 1999), 105.

40. Rev. Carl Bielby, video interview by Relf, February 9, 2010.

41. "More Than One-Quarter of the State Abortion Restrictions since *Roe v. Wade* Were Enacted between 2011 and 2015," Guttmacher Institute, infographic, January 13, 2016, https://www.guttmacher.org/infographic/2016/more-one-quarter-1074-state-abortion-restrictions-roe-v-wade-were-enacted-between; Elizabeth Nash, Rachel Benson Gold, Andrea Rowan, Zohra Ansari-Thomas, Olivia Cappello, and Lizamarie Mohammed, "Trends in the States: First Quarter 2016," Guttmacher Institute, April 13, 2016, https://www.guttmacher.org/article/2016/04/trends-states-first-quarter-2016.

42. William Saletan, "The GOP Argument for Defunding Planned Parenthood Is Incoherent," *Slate*, http://www.slate.com/articles/news_and_politics/politics/2015/09/the_gop_s_argument_for_defunding_planned_parenthood_makes_no_sense.html (accessed October 29, 2015).

43. "Liberal Clergy Praise Planned Parenthood 'Doing God's Work,'" Juicy Ecumenism, https://juicyecumenism.com/2015/07/30/liberal-clergy-praise-planned-parenthood-doing-gods-work/ (accessed October 29, 2015).

44. William B. Bradshaw, "Mainline Churches: Past, Present, and Future," HuffPost Religion, October 11, 2013, http://www.huffingtonpost.com/william-b-bradshaw/mainline-churches-past-pr_b_4087407.html.

45. "America's Changing Religious Landscape," Pew Research Center, May 12, 2015, http://www.pewforum.org/2015/05/12/americas-changing-religious-landscape/.

46. Ruth Graham, "Can the Christian Left Be a Real Political Force?," *Slate*, May 15, 2016, http://www.slate.com/articles/life/cover_story/2016/05/how_liberal_christians_can_turn_the_democrats_into_the_party_of_god.html.

Major Works Cited

Alford, Suzanne M. "Is Self-Abortion a Fundamental Right?" *Duke Law Journal* 52, no. 5 (2003), 1011–1129.

Beito, David T., and Linda Royster Beito. *Black Maverick: T.R.M. Howard's Fight for Civil Rights and Economic Power*. Urbana: University of Illinois Press, 2009.

Bonavoglia, Angela, ed. *The Choices We Made: Twenty-five Women and Men Speak Out about Abortion*. New York: Four Walls Eight Windows, 2001.

Brownmiller, Susan. *In Our Time: Memoir of a Revolution*. New York: Delta, 1999.

Calderone, Mary, ed. *Abortion in the United States*. New York: Harper and Brothers, 1958.

Carmen, Arlene, and Howard Moody. *Abortion Counseling and Social Change, from Illegal Act to Medical Practice: The Story of the Clergy Consultation Service on Abortion*. Valley Forge, PA: Judson Press, 1973.

———. *Working Women: The Subterranean World of Street Prostitution*. New York: Harper & Row, 1985.

Chisholm, Shirley. *Unbought and Unbossed*. 40th anniversary edition. Washington, DC: Take Root Media, 2010.

Collier, Carol, and Rachel Haliburton. *Bioethics in Canada: A Philosophical Introduction*. Toronto: Canadian Scholars' Press, 2015.

Davis, Nanette J. *From Crime to Choice: The Transformation of Abortion in America*. Westport, CT: Greenwood Press, 1985.

Davis, Tom. *Sacred Work: Planned Parenthood and Its Clergy Alliances*. New Brunswick, NJ: Rutgers University Press, 2005.

Dickason, Elly, and Jerry G. Dickason, eds. *Remembering Judson House*. New York: Judson Memorial Church, 2000.

Edelstein, Ludwig. "The Hippocratic Oath: Text, Translation, and Interpretation." In Robert M. Veatch (ed.), *Cross-Cultural Perspective in Medical Ethics*. Sudbury, MA: Jones and Bartlett Publishers, 2000.

Fadiman, Dorothy, Beth Seltzer, and Daniel Meyers. *From Danger to Dignity: The Fight for Safe Abortion*. VHS. San Jose, CA: KTEH-TV, 1995.

Friedan, Betty. *The Feminine Mystique*. New York: Norton, 1963.

Garrow, David J. *Liberty and Sexuality: The Right to Privacy and the Making of Roe v. Wade*. Updated edition. Berkeley: University of California Press, 1998.

Gidlow, Liette. "The Michigan Women's Commission and the Struggle against Sex Discrimination in the 1970s." In Paul Finkelman and Martin Hershock (eds.), *The History of Michigan Law*, Law Society and Politics in the Midwest, 238–255. Athens: Ohio University Press, 2006.

Ginsburg, Faye. "Rescuing the Nation: Operation Rescue and the Rise of Anti-Abortion Militance." In Rickie Solinger (ed.), *Abortion Wars: A Half Century of Struggle, 1950–2000*, 227–250. Berkeley: University of California Press, 1998.

Gold-Steinberg, Sharon, and Abigail J. Stewart. "Psychologies of Abortion: Implications of a Changing Context." In Rickie Solinger (ed.), *Abortion Wars: A Half Century of Struggle, 1950–2000*, 356–373. Berkeley: University of California Press, 1998.

Gorney, Cynthia. *Articles of Faith: A Frontline History of the Abortion Wars*. New York: Simon & Schuster, 1998.

Greenhouse, Linda. *Becoming Justice Blackmun: Harry Blackmun's Supreme Court Journey*. New York: Times Books, 2005.

Greenhouse, Linda, and Reva B. Siegel, eds. *Before* Roe v. Wade*: Voices That Shaped the Abortion Debate before the Supreme Court's Ruling*. New York: Kaplan, 2010.

Hall, Robert E., ed. *Abortion in a Changing World: The Proceedings of an International Conference Convened in Hot Springs, Virginia, November 17–20, 1968, by the Association for the Study of Abortion*. New York: Columbia University Press, 1970.

Hammerle, Ronald L. "The Abortion Situation at the End of the Sixties." Dissertation, University of Chicago, Divinity School and Department of Obstetrics and Gynecology, November 15, 1969.

Hasday, Lisa R. "The Hippocratic Oath and Literary Text: A Dialogue between Law and Medicine." *Yale Journal of Health Policy, Law, and Ethics* 2, no. 2 (2002), 1–27.

hooks, bell. *Feminist Theory: From Margin to Center*. Cambridge, MA: South End Press, 1984.

Hordern, Anthony. *Legal Abortion: The English Experience*. Oxford: Pergamon Press, 1971.

Joffe, Carole. *Doctors of Conscience: The Struggle to Provide Abortion before and after Roe v. Wade*. Boston: Beacon Press, 1995.

Kaplan, Laura. *The Story of Jane: The Legendary Underground Feminist Abortion Service*. New York: Pantheon, 1995.

Kesselman, Amy. "Women versus Connecticut: Conducting a Statewide Hearing on Abortion." In Rickie Solinger (ed.), *Abortion Wars: A Half Century of Struggle, 1950–2000*, 42–67. Berkeley: University of California Press, 1998.

Lader, Lawrence. *Abortion*. Indianapolis: Bobbs-Merrill, 1966.

———. *Abortion II: Making the Revolution*. Boston: Beacon Press, 1973.

———. *The Margaret Sanger Story and the Fight for Birth Control*. Garden City, NY: Doubleday, 1955.

Lowe, Janet. *Damn Right! Behind the Scenes with Berkshire Hathaway Billionaire Charlie Munger*. New York: John Wiley & Sons, 2000.

Lowenstein, Roger. *Buffett: The Making of an American Capitalist*. New York: Random House, 1995.

Luker, Kristin. *Abortion and the Politics of Motherhood*. Berkeley: University of California Press, 1984.

Messer, Ellen, and Kathryn E. May. *Back Rooms: Voices from the Illegal Abortion Era*. Buffalo, NY: Prometheus Books, 1994.

Messerman, Gerald A. "Abortion Counselling: Shall Women Be Permitted to Know?" In David F. Walbert and J. Douglas Butler (eds.), *Abortion, Society, and the Law*, 241–274. Cleveland: Press of Case Western Reserve University, 1973.

Moody, Howard. "Man's Vengeance on Woman: Some Reflections on Abortion Laws as Religious Retribution and Legal Punishment of the Feminine Species." *Renewal*, February 1967.

———. *A Voice in the Village: A Journey of a Pastor and a People.* N.p.: Xlibris, 2009.

Nathanson, Bernard N. "Ambulatory Abortion: Experience with 26,000 cases (July 1, 1970, to August 1, 1971)." *New England Journal of Medicine* 286, no. 8 (1972), 403–407.

———. "Deeper into Abortion." *New England Journal of Medicine* 291, no. 22 (1974), 1189–1190. http://www.columbia.edu/cu/augustine/arch/nathanson.html.

———. *The Hand of God: A Journey from Death to Life by the Abortion Doctor Who Changed His Mind.* Washington, DC: Regnery Publishing, 1996.

Nathanson, Bernard N., with Richard N. Ostling. *Aborting America.* New York: Pinnacle Books, 1979.

Nelson, Jennifer. *Women of Color and the Reproductive Rights Movement.* New York: New York University Press, 2003.

Nossiff, Rosemary. *Before Roe: Abortion Policy in the States.* Philadelphia: Temple University Press, 2001.

Reagan, Leslie J. *When Abortion Was a Crime: Women, Medicine, and Law in the United States, 1867–1973.* Berkeley: University of California Press, 1997.

Roemer, Ruth. "Abortion Law Reform and Repeal: Legislative and Judicial Developments." *American Journal of Public Health* 61, no. 3 (March 1971), 500–509.

Ross, Loretta J. "African American Women and Abortion." In Rickie Solinger (ed.), *Abortion Wars: A Half Century of Struggle, 1950–2000*, 161–207. Berkeley: University of California Press, 1998.

Sauer, R. "Attitudes to Abortion in America, 1800–1973." *Population Studies* 28, no. 1 (1974), 53–67.

Schiff, Daniel. *Abortion in Judaism.* Cambridge: Cambridge University Press, 2002.

Silliman, Jael, Marlene Gerber Fried, Loretta Ross, and Elena R. Gutiérrez. *Undivided Rights: Women of Color Organize for Reproductive Justice.* Cambridge, MA: South End Press, 2004.

Solinger, Rickie, ed. *Abortion Wars: A Half Century of Struggle, 1950–2000.* Berkeley: University of California Press, 1998.

———. "Pregnancy and Power before *Roe v. Wade*, 1950–1970." In Rickie Solinger (ed.), *Abortion Wars: A Half Century of Struggle, 1950–2000*, 15–32. Berkeley: University of California Press, 1998.

———. *Wake Up Little Susie.* 2nd ed. New York: Routledge, 2000.

Staggenborg, Suzanne. *The Pro-Choice Movement: Organization and Activism in the Abortion Conflict.* New York: Oxford University Press, 1991.

Sutton, Matthew Avery. *American Apocalypse: A History of Modern Evangelicalism.* Cambridge, MA: Belknap Press of Harvard University Press, 2014.

Thompson, A. Keith. *Religious Confession Privilege and the Common Law: A Historical Analysis.* Leiden: M. Nijhoff, 2011.

Tietze, Christopher. "Freestanding Abortion Clinics." *New England Journal of Medicine* 286, no. 8 (1972), 432.

Tietze, Christopher, and Sarah Lewit. "Legal Abortions: Early Medical Complications: An Interim Report of the Joint Program for the Study of Abortion." *Family Planning Perspectives* 3, no. 4 (October 1971), 6–14.

Ward, Martha C. *Poor Women, Powerful Men: America's Great Experiment in Family Planning.* Boulder, CO: Westview Press, 1986.

Washington, Harriet A. *Medical Apartheid: The Dark History of Medical Experimentation on Black Americans from Colonial Times to the Present.* New York: Harlem Moon, 2006.

Williams, Daniel K. *Defenders of the Unborn: The Pro-Life Movement before* Roe v. Wade. New York: Oxford University Press, 2016.

Wolff, Joshua D. "Ministers of a Higher Law: The Story of the Clergy Consultation Service on Abortion." Undergraduate thesis, Amherst College, April 10, 1998. http://classic.judson.org/MinistersofaHigherLaw.

Interviews Cited

We cited about half of the interviews we conducted. We offer our thanks to all who kindly cooperated with this project, whether they are cited here or not; we learned from each conversation.

Anonymous Protestant minister, female. Interview by the authors, April 26, 2005, New York.

Anonymous Conservative rabbi, male. Telephone interview by Relf, October 18, 2010.

Anwyl, Rev. Huw S. Interview by the authors, February 22, 2006, Laguna Niguel, CA.

Bielby, Rev. Carl E. Video interviews by Relf, February 9, 2010, and March 11, 2010.

Bogage, Rabbi Lewis E. (Buz). Interview by Relf, February 15, 2007, Denver, CO.

Bohnsack, Rev. Benjamin. Telephone interview by Relf, April 7, 2010.

Brickner, Balfour. Interview by the authors, June 12, 2003, New York.

Brown, Rev. Dr. Bernard O. Interview by the authors, March 2, 2004, Chicago, IL.

Canfield, Elizabeth Kanitz (Liz). Telephone interview by Relf, January 8, 2015.

Conner, Rev. Wayne. Interview by Relf, May 30, 2013, Kalamazoo, MI.

Davis, Rev. Tom. Telephone interview by Relf, April 25, 2002; telephone interview by the authors, July 19, 2004.

Dell, Rev. Gregory. Interview by the authors, March 2, 2004, Chicago.

DeRoy, Jewel Carmen. Interview by the authors, February 20, 2006, Los Angeles.

Fewster, Rev. Lowell. Video interview by Relf, December 8, 2014.

Fletcher, Rev. Hayes F. Written recollections sent to Relf, February 2011.

Gatch, Ione G. W. (Georgie). Video interview by Relf, May 12, 2011.

Greenawald, Pat. Telephone interview by Relf, December 2, 2004.

Hammerle, Ronald L. Telephone interview by the authors, December 18, 2005.

Hardgrove, Rev. Orrin T. (Ted). Telephone interview by Relf, July 28, 2010.

Hare, Rev. Robert W. Interview by the authors, April 23, 2005, Croton-on-Hudson, NY.

Herndon, Rev. Dr. J. Emmett. Telephone interview by Relf, October 10, 2014.

Hinand, Rev. Allen J. Telephone interview by Relf, July 16, 2010.

Holderness, Rev. Haywood D. Jr. Telephone interview by Relf, December 20, 2014.

Holmes, Lauretta Talayco (Lauri). Telephone interview by Relf, June 30, 2014.

Howland, Rev. Peggy. Interview by the authors, June 12, 2003, New York.

Jackson, Rev. Richard D. Interview by the authors, December 9, 2002; also present were Lorraine Beebe and Marcia Jackson.

Judd, Rev. Orrin D. Telephone interview by Relf, September 10, 2010.

Lader, Joan Summers. Interview by Relf, February 27, 2009, New York.

Lutz, Rev. Marvin G. Emailed responses to interview questions by Relf, October 24, 2014, and November 3, 2014.

March, Diana. Telephone interview by Relf, February 23, 2004.

McFarlane, Rev. Dr. David. Interview by Relf, July 18, 2003, Sewickley, PA; also present was Emily R. Hanavan.

Moody, Howard. Interview by the authors, April 25, 2005, New York.

Parsons, E. Spencer. Interview by Relf, July 31, 2003, Worcester, MA.

Pierce, Rev. Robert L. Interview by Relf, September 25, 2010, Babylon, NY.

Rutledge, Rev. Dr. Mark. Telephone interview by Relf, January 5, 2015.

Schaef, Rev. Finley. Telephone interview by Relf, June 1, 2007.

Schaper, Rev. Donna Osterhoudt. Interview by Relf, March 1, 2009, New York.

Straut, Rev. Dr. Charles H. (Chick) Jr. Telephone interview by Relf, June 7, 2010.

Ticktin, Rabbi Max. Interview by Relf, March 31, 2006, Washington, DC.

Van Arsdale, Rev. David. Conversation with Relf, January 2002, Kalamazoo, MI.

Wallace, Rev. Dr. Robert B. Telephone interview by Relf, May 14, 2012.

Wightman, Rev. John. Telephone interview by Relf, December 8, 2014.

Zwerin, Rabbi Raymond A. Telephone interview by Relf, February 16, 2007.

Index

Note: *"CCS" refers to the Clergy Consultation Service on Abortion.*